AGING OUT

AGING OUT

AN EXPLORATION OF CAREGIVING, COMMUNITY, AND HOW AMERICANS GROW OLD

LUCY SCHILLER

FLATIRON
BOOKS
NEW YORK

The names and identifying characteristics of some persons described in this book have been changed.

 Printed in the United States of America. For information, address Flatiron Books, 120 Broadway, New York, NY 10271. EU Representative: Macmillan Publishers Ireland Ltd., 1st Floor, The Liffey Trust Centre, 117–126 Sheriff Street Upper, Dublin 1, D01 YC43.

www.flatironbooks.com

Designed by Leah Carlson-Stanisic

The Library of Congress Cataloging-in-Publication Data is available upon request.

ISBN 978-1-250-34452-6 (hardcover)
ISBN 978-1-250-34453-3 (ebook)

First Edition: 2026

10 9 8 7 6 5 4 3 2 1

To S, D, and E

AGING OUT

I

A NEW HOME, LARD SPONCON, A LIST OF FEARS

Many days in Pittsburgh I felt as if I had simply been dropped by some gigantic hand, just as, when I was a child, I used to drop my Sims in different rooms of a house that I had designed for them. I had landed in Pittsburgh not knowing anyone. At the time, I was unsure why I had come there specifically. Now, I see it as a half-desperate plan to simply change the background scenery of my life for the millionth time. "The geographical cure," some people call it—moving. I was always doing it, all the way to Pittsburgh, where I wandered around for a while, wanting to stop time.

Inarguably, time was passing. Sometimes when things that have always existed no longer exist, you are reminded of this: time, yes, obviously, passing. I couldn't believe I was doing it again, I felt, while still totally believing I was doing it again, this wholesale switching-up, alone.

Before Pittsburgh I had been in Central New York, in a little college town, teaching on a fellowship that was meant to span a year. Before that, I was meant to be in Germany on a similar yearlong position, but the pandemic had struck halfway through, and I had landed, after some torturous windings, in a bedroom in a house with my maternal grandmother, Mary Ann, in Denver. It was there that I had begun to become preoccupied, vaguely, with the concept of oldness, and aging, though I would not begin my deep dive into the aging industrial complex until later.

In Central New York, my bedroom window looked out at a perfectly rectangular bit of tree in the distance that lined up neatly against the perfect horizontal line of a telephone cable. I often sat in my bed and adjusted my head slightly to make them line up just right: Still, I can remember the slight click of that right feeling. From there, in the bed, I regarded a map. I settled on Pittsburgh for the fact that it sat six hours away: doable for a person with a bad back and with the ability to basically fit everything they owned into their car. Pittsburgh was replete with universities where I hoped I might be able to pick up work. Also, from the bed I found a small house on the side of a hill to rent for $850 per month, into which I would move sight unseen.

Later that month I drove away from the cozy college town, where the preponderance and fragrance of the swamp cabbages had stunned me, and through the Rust Belt, Buffalo, Erie, then Butler County, Pennsylvania. Then across the West End bridge, a peeling yellow behemoth straddling the Ohio River. Some people call Pittsburgh the "Paris of Appalachia," but to me it felt like San Francisco viewed through warped glasses, so much water and greenery and hill.

The house—my house—in Pittsburgh was less than six hundred square feet but it was nestled into a vertiginous seven-thousand-square-foot lot, a steep slope facing downtown. Because it was built, almost sod-house-style, into the slope, it sat below street level, in a defensive position, hidden from drivers-by. I could see the legs of any person walking by, but not the rest of their bodies. An old stone fireplace, not usable, framed my grandmother's samovar, and I bought a long, pink, dusty couch off Craigslist to grace the living room. A wooden slat kept the lone kitchen counter upright, nearly disallowing entry into the narrow room—you had to squeeze sideways to get past it. Water trickled through the floor under the tub into the basement each time I took a bath. Down there, a previous tenant's shirt hung, untouched, still drying.

Six months earlier, in the beautiful swamp cabbage town from which I moved to Pittsburgh, I had learned and begun to metabolize the fact that my other grandmother, Anita, had died of Covid. I wish now that I had been a different person then, someone more able to understand this news, and make faster sense of it, but I wasn't and couldn't. Confusing me further was the question people always seemed to be asking when I told them what had happened: *How old was she?* It echoed around me, from the supermarket cashier to the mechanic to the far-off friend. In theory there was a correct answer. There was a precise number in the mid-nineties that I still, recalcitrantly, feel no need to state. But the query sounded more like a riddle. And like a riddle, it made no sense and inspired in me an immediate, itchy frustration. Covid of course acted more quickly and with greater deadliness on people who were immunocompromised, older, suffering from other medical conditions—but this was not what they were asking. They were asking something different, both specific and very vague. And the strangeness of that question, to me, dovetailed with the anger I'd already been feeling, something to do with isolation, and how I had started to see myself more clearly as a person hurtling through time. There are certain years where the blue flame of your interior flickers, then strengthens on the wick of you. In Pittsburgh, I began to feel it, the sharpness of my own pains, hubris, and self-removal from the world.

So too did the question of how old she was flicker, then become slightly more clarified. Of course it implied my grandmother's innate vulnerability to the virus. But it also implied an innate meaning to her death: a neat way to make sense of it, to stow it away as maybe less painful, less scary, less incomprehensible. It seemed to me a way of concealing the fear of the virus itself. Because when you think of old people dying, you do not picture them dying by accident, in pain, screaming. *Age* looses them from that vision of death. Old age excuses us from understanding potential pain; regardless of the listed cause of death, old age is both their fundamental killer and their salvation. In our imaginations, anyway, the old generally do not die in agony; oldness supposedly allows a person to slip off the last few things that were keeping them here and greet death as an expected guest.

I still can't totally convey how *wrong* these visions are, at least in the case of my grandmother. She was not, I wanted to say, the "type" of old person to be close to death already, any more than the rest of us are. Then again, in the way of the oldest-old, she *was*—surely she'd be dying in the next five years of her life or so, despite her intellectual and emotional vitality. I am tempted now to theorize that what unnerves us about oldness and death is not death's proximity to the old—death is proximate to all of us—but death's clearer certainty. You hear about teenagers "thinking they're invincible" and finding out otherwise; oldness eventually strips this potential error away. And in the early stages of the pandemic, it was *clear and certain*, the connection between Covid death and oldness—indeed, the virus first bloomed, in the US, inside a nursing home. In the year of Anita's death, 2021, around 825,000 people in the US died, and 75 percent of them were 65 or older. Today, five years after Covid's onset, more than one million people in the United States are gone from the virus. But now there is a difference: Today, I can't tell with any real expediency how many of them were old. The US stopped counting, in September 2023, a few months after the pandemic was declared to be over. (After some digging, I found a CNN article titled "Thousands of Seniors Are Still Dying of Covid-19. Do We Not Care Anymore?" It reported that 900,000 older adults had died of Covid since the pandemic's start, making up around 75 percent of the virus's total fatalities. There is a sense of inevitability living inside this statistic, and I'm still not sure how to get it out.)

In 2025, I no longer really talk about my grandmother's death. I have learned that the results will be disappointing, almost always, unless I go into the *details*, which will then elicit a different kind of response than the one I feel, sometimes, I have been waiting years to hear: *No one deserves to die that way*. Recently, on a walk with a new friend, I mentioned offhandedly that one of my grandmothers had died of Covid. She gasped loudly and said, "*No!*" It was the most honest reaction I've found: straightforward, and with no interest in the mitigating factor of her age. The "no" knifed through what has often felt like a larger mutedness, a mutedness that has repeatedly, weirdly, stunned me, so that I walked around Central New York, and then Pittsburgh, like a fish that had been bashed against a rock.

I was not the only one to feel a confusion around the scale of this loss and the way it was rarely spoken of, let alone spoken of in terms that seemed adequate. This was the case early on in the pandemic, too. The scholar Martha Lincoln writes that "as the national death toll from COVID-19 reached 100,000 in the third week of May 2020, an editorial in the *Los Angeles Times* observed 'little sense of shared grief' and noted a surprising absence of public memorialization despite losses on the order of 'twelve plane crashes a day for months.'" During this time, the scale of death was so large that an individual rarely knew how to address it. The months to come, in which the virus "became politicized"—a kind of vague phrase I started to chafe at—would yield both more fatalities and more people in their close orbit wondering how to categorize what had happened. There is no sense to an accident; neither is there any sense to an individual death inside a mass death event that never receives real recognition. As historian Alicia Puglionesi wrote of the victims, "their names are buried, in the sanitary custom of our country, inside a chart or a county coroner's report. The first year of the pandemic saw public efforts to name and honor the individuals lost, but this generosity quickly ran out . . . Now the absent presence of the dead is a problem only for their closest intimates."

So where does the blazing fact of one painful death inside many hundreds of thousands more, all people who were going to "die anyway," according to the easily perceptible logics of our time—where does that go, for these close intimates? Like any other kind of grief, it doesn't go anywhere, I have learned. It just lives inside you, unable to smooth out to a fainter ripple with time, with conversation. It turns you, maybe, into a slightly different person than you were, and than you thought you would become. As I found out, it forces you to constantly be watching yourself when you'd really rather not. I had lost people before—a friend in a house fire, two other grandparents, various others—but this one did feel different, its boundaries confused by a larger context I couldn't totally understand, and which was changing every day.

In the wake of Anita's death, I moved around in a state of confusion beyond simply what had happened. I was and continue to be someone who turns nearly everything into a piece of writing: a squirrel, an overheard snippet of conversation. I did not, however, tend to do the same of my interior, nor of "trauma"—a category that often felt to me inherently solipsistic and narrowing, as "real" trauma, I thought at that time, was not possible to fit inside a narrative. I recognized, with the endlessly seizing mind of a writer who grew up alongside the blossoming of the internet, what I might "make" of the death, were I different kind of writer: the grandma essay, a form I had identified a long time earlier that appeared with alarming frequency online.

The grandmas of the grandma essay were white, plain, joyous, knowing, giggly, warm. They held very few discernible attributes. They were simply sources of love, and almost endless in their generosity. When they died, their grandchild was called out of summer camp and delivered the news, feeling, it was often implied, the first of their traumas, and possibly the largest. A man I knew, on an admissions committee for an MFA program, once tweeted publicly about all the dead grandmas he was having to wade through. He was eventually asked to remove his tweet by some powers that were, but I had agreed with the sentiment at the time. To me, it has often felt as if grandmothers specifically are flattened in writing—more than parents, more than grandfathers. Maybe a writer doesn't know what to do with these older women when alive, and uses them, and their deaths, for an early exploration of pain. Or maybe all the grandmas simply *were* that good. In any case, I had no interest in writing this way myself, I thought. And yet the question kept coming. The cashier, the mechanic, the friend, the professor, the acquaintance, the lover. *How old was she?*

Those first months in Pittsburgh I became busy with the project of distracting myself. I was not working on a grandma essay. Mountains of freelance writing and editing were keeping me afloat financially and intellectually. I would go outside on breaks. In the strange new Pittsburgh neighborhood where I lived, deer appeared in the doorways of abandoned houses, and old fruit orchards lined the baseball diamond with its testy banner reading "Before you complain, have you ever volunteered yet?" A sewer specialist nearby drove a van emblazoned with the words "Turd Herder" (its side read, with quotes around the phrase, "Your Poop Is My Bread and Butter"). Other vans zipped around everywhere, their sides reading "LIFE." In the dark of the morning I would go stand outside my house with my dog, asking him to pee, and asking the light beyond the horizon not to come up. Each day, as I still do sometimes, despite the knowledge that, as a sign in my office tells me, "Good light makes work lighter," I almost prayed for a divergence from the natural order of things—a divergence from the sun beginning to rise, and a detour from the rest of the world beyond me getting out of bed, the streets filling with cars and the sky with light and me with a sense of oncoming dread. What if it was just dark all day instead, and everyone else kept sleeping, and I could work alone on my things, without the knowledge that hours were vanishing, minutes were clicking, seconds were leaving as quickly as they appeared? I liked the denseness of the night: the way it seemed at 4:30 a.m. like the sun would never appear. Like it would be timeless forever, and like I could be removed from the world again, as in the early days of the pandemic, when time stopped, and I hadn't yet changed in the ways that I would change. But sometimes I felt scarily rooted in the moment in which I stood there, outside my house, and knowing time *was* passing. Without distraction, the result was that I was finally seeing myself. Like the Sims I used to order around on the computer, building windowless rooms around them, I made circles in my tiny world alone, with no one to talk to, and a pile of work, and a low grief that had not metabolized but which hung over every minute. The blue flame inside me felt fed by a kind of gas just barely eked in from the outside world. There were some days I felt I couldn't bear it: the way I seemed scared, in so many ways, of slowly, inarguably joining the future.

• • •

Each day, my dog, Helgi, and I walked about eight miles. We started on Wymore Street, in the heart of Elliott, my neighborhood, and strode past the baseball field with its weird sign, past the city workers' fueling station and dump, where the same old boats sat for months, rained on and sagging. Then we climbed Round Top Street, which punished my legs deliciously, and like many such streets in Pittsburgh, boasted a series of extraordinarily many stairs running parallel to the tilting asphalt, which once, in an icy winter, I saw a moving van slide helplessly down, its driver's mouth making a quaking O. We made a soft landing into Crafton, a different neighborhood whose semi-downtown, boarded up, boasted a lone business, a seemingly empty massage parlor named PINCH ME ("Experience THE PINCH"). Beyond lay a stretch of woods bordering a thicket of huge, old houses whose front lawns we promenaded past, deciding one hill or another to be our midpoint. At its crest we would begin the long arc back home to the tiny house on the side of a now faraway incline. Thanks to its topography, and the presence, everywhere, of water and of bridges, Pittsburgh neighborhoods were fairly distinct from their neighbors, and old-timers would later tell me that there really was no reason to "cross the bridge"—any number of bridges—to go anywhere else. Old stairways of wood or sometimes concrete laced the steeper hills, remnants from the days in which workers found them the quickest way to traverse the city's wild voluptuousness and get to a job at a mill or a plant. Groundhogs sometimes lived underneath the stairways, and people, too, and once I saw, while huffedly raising my head on my climb, a plastic bag so strangely affixed underneath the landing of one of these stairways, that it looked for a second like a shrine.

In the memoir *Bibliophobia*, Sarah Chihaya writes of her "diffuseness"—how, in her "most lost moments, I see myself disintegrating and drifting into everything and everyone else, floating unseen and dispersed." When I read this line, five years after leaving the city, I underlined and starred it, and wrote PITTSBURGH in the margins: This was the feeling I often *wanted* then, because it would mean that I could finally stop living inside my own brain, and my brain and body's adherence to chronological time. This was why I walked farther into the neighborhoods still new to me, and why I began to take on mountains of work that would hopefully allow me to forget that I sat there on a creaking chair until it was dark again. Of course, it is one of the oldest things in the world, at least in some cultures, being afraid of time passing. Taken further, it is one of the oldest things in the world, the fear of emerging as older, and among the ranks of the aged. "Every man desires to live long, but no man wishes to be old," wrote Jonathan Swift. In Western antiquity, writes academic William Ian Miller, old age could be looked at in one of two ways—as a glorious time of virtuosity and wisdom, or as the representation "of everything that is vile about embodied existence." For the humors-focused, centuries ago, old age was "the age of phlegm." Oldness was "about rot, meanness, avarice, cowardice, peevishness, irascibility, moroseness, whining, bad eyes, deafness, dripping noses, hacking coughs, baldness, loss of teeth, reeking breath, loss of libido, sagging flesh, forgetfulness, repetitive garrulity." Opened at random, Simone de Beauvoir's book on older age reminds us of Horace's words toward an old woman: "Antiquity ploughs furrows in your ancient forehead . . . your breasts are as flaccid as the dugs of a mare . . . what a reek enwraps every part of her flabby limbs." Centuries later, in the 1980s, one Illinoisan market researcher likened old age to a "Peoria winter," a term that did, to some degree, make me shudder, having spent my adolescent years not far from Peoria, a city that has always stunned me for its riverine, post-industrial beauty, but where winter hits hard and icy and spare.

From my pink couch in Pittsburgh, I read this hodgepodge of age-fear, the sunlight slanting down through the dark wood windows. I had gone to a few branches of the Carnegie Library—West End, Mt. Washington, Main—to collect the reading. (One day, I combined that errand with a trip to one of the Carnegie museums, where I noted the feedback pinned to a wall by museum visitors, in response to a prompt asking for "your Pittsburgh story." "I don't really have one, I'm 12," wrote one visitor. Another: "I moved here and I will leave hopefully soon.") In my house, the piles of books around me bore the name of the famous industrialist printed on their fleshy stacks of pages, so many years after his life and death here. Reading on this theme felt less about quelling a fear than it did trying to explore it, trying to understand, better, the reality of oldness, which turned out to be a vast, nearly impossible to define category—*how old was she*, that question with both one answer and none that made any sense.

My own fear had little to do with the body. It was something more diffuse. And others' fears around oldness, I read, reflected old age's largeness and variability. One 1974 report I found, administered by the National Council on the Aging, and titled *Myth and Reality of Aging*, asked more than four thousand people to respond to countless questions about their feelings on getting older. The report was not actually much of a report. Rather, it was a dense collection of coding categories such as:

WORST OF BEING 65 OR OLDER
Worst of >65-brain weak
Worst of >65-neglected
Worst of >65-disabled
Worst of >65-wear out
Worst of >65-loneliness
Worst of >65-bordom [*sic*]

And also, I noted, with some degree of wry perturbation:

WHEN AND WHY ARE WOMEN OLD
Women old—menopause
Women old—others dead
Women old—set in ways
Women old—feels old

Distilled like this, to coding categories, a certain clarity shimmered. "Women old—feels old." It was a spare but mysterious, even nonsensical assertion. I kind of liked it. The phrases bumped along in my brain in the following days. *How old was she? Women old—feels old.* Did *I* feel old? Did *my* age line up with what was going on for me, in the way that I had made the tree line up perfectly with the telephone line back in Central New York? These questions obviously didn't have answers, but as time moved forward, they seemed to sharpen.

I parsed the blurry, swimmy data set from a decade and a half before I was born. A good number of people had identified that when a woman was "psychologically old, or she thinks or feels old, or she worries about aging and dying," this was when she was "old." But a larger number of people didn't provide a response to the question. This was because, it turned out, there was some basic confusion, or disagreement, about when people became old to begin with. Forty-one people had said that they thought "the average woman becomes old" before the age of forty, a striking idea in 1974, when the life expectancy at birth for the average woman was around seventy-six years. Then there were some streaks of about three hundred people identifying the advent of oldness to the early, mid, and late sixties. But the largest number of people—nearly one thousand—offered up the following vague, perfect answer: "It depends." Just recently, I read a statistic that more than 20 percent of Americans between the ages of twenty-five and thirty-four considered themselves to be middle-aged. If this was the case, then technically I was not far from the advent of older age, a realization that spun me.

It is true that there is no clear onset to old age. Like liquid mercury, old age wobbles and slides upon viewing. But it has to start somewhere, at least bureaucratically. In the United States, we might say that old age begins at sixty-five—this is when you can begin (if you have not already begun) to use Medicare and collect Social Security. In Australia, the bureaucratic onset of old age, or when you might collect your pension, anyway, is at age sixty-seven, China, sixty-three (for men, fifty-five to fifty-eight for women), Greece, sixty-seven (and many European countries are slowly raising it to this number). Internally, it's murkier. People tend to place old age in the distance—the older you are, the more you think old age is still in front of you, according to a twenty-five-year-long study in Germany. Speaking of that study, one academic: "Some people have such negative views of the elderly that they don't want to be associated with them . . . So if they're 70 years old, they'll say old age begins at 75. And when they get to 75, they'll say old age begins at 80." Like death, "old" bobs on the horizon, a buoy to watch but never pass.

Yet it can also appear suddenly and irrevocably, as in a Cynthia Ozick essay I love, which ends as such: "Your hair is whitening, you are a well of tears, what you meant to do (beauty and justice) you have not done, papa and mama are under the earth, you live in panic and dread, the future shrinks and darkens, stories are only vapor, your inmost craving is for nothing but an old scarred pen, and what, God knows, is that?" Ozick was in her fifties when she wrote that essay. In Pittsburgh, if I was feeling something similar, I had less of a right: I was only in my thirties. It was self-indulgent and embarrassing to claim anything like old age. And yet the last few years, in part thanks to the pandemic, had been such a strange blur that I felt far older, swimming out far beyond the last buoy I remembered. I had the impression of time speeding up underneath me. Many people seemed to feel that the world was hurtling ahead, and that the early days of the pandemic were both very far away and very, very close.

To be more precise, I felt as if my life had done a kind of record-skip from my late twenties to my mid-thirties. I had not yet found a partner or begun to think about children; I did not yet have a "real" career; I was alone in this new place, cobbling things together with no one to really talk about them with. No one besides a few family members knew I was here. A terror surged at night that I would spend the rest of my life this way: without the shell I had prided myself on until now, which, I realized, depended on other people to see it. Alone, I was understanding, a shell served no purpose at all.

My own fears and wanderings slotted in perfectly to what felt like a new surge in a very active current of social worry about aging and oldness. A multibillion-dollar industry focused on combating aging promised advances in Botox treatments specifically meant to target something called "platysma prominence" in the lower face and neck, brain supplements with names like "Maximum Slim Lion's Mane and DMAE," and something called "aesthetic threads," which lift and tighten and contour "bodies and faces." Moving further, I explored, sometimes, the reaches of the internet in which aging was something to be altogether eradicated, and people spoke of living to 100, 520, forever. Being old, someone tweeted, had "little to do with biological age and has everything to do with letting the world grow over [you] like a fairy ring of mushrooms over remnants of a rotted oak stump." A millionaire named Bryan Johnson had famously made it his life's mission to elongate his life's mission, holding summits that entreated us with the phrase "Don't Die" and subjecting his body to his Blueprint method, a minute-by-minute act of data assessment and collection. The idea, familiar to me, of course, was to pause time. Brendan O'Connor later wrote that it was the rich who were obsessed with "so-called life extension technology," but that in time, it would filter down to the rest of us. Then, O'Connor continued, "it should finally become clear that this technology does not offer immortality but a longer working life. That is its primary use case."

I scraped these anecdotes and data off the internet, attempting to make some degree of sense from them, but nothing really coalesced for me about why there surged this focus on older age, and on stopping time, and on maintaining a blankness around the pandemic. Theories abounded, of course, about American youth-centrism, and productivity culture, but they felt to me not quite right. They didn't fully explain the other side of the pendulum: the strange, dehumanizing obsession with older people's supposedly inherent kindness, cuteness, and wisdom. On Instagram, I collected videos by granddadjoe1933, who beckoned nearly a million and a half followers, and whose wide-eyed silliness allowed for seemingly endless sponcon of lard:

Cook an easy dinner in Lard with 91 year old Granddad Joe

Granddad Joe had a full English breakfast all fried in Lard

Cook an easy one pan meal in Lard with 91 year old Granddad Joe

POV you're a ninety year-old granddad and you have designed your own range of merch

I never ever ever imagined I'd be on a photo shoot let alone at age 90 with my own merch range coming out

I didn't know what to think about Granddad Joe. He looked happy, well-fed, and in love with his family, as well as his internet fame. And he was just one of many such older people cropping up in these shoals of the internet, where older couples were stopped on the street to dispense their "how we met" stories, spawning comments that slightly embarrassed me for their earnest infantilization. I preferred the cranky European woman with a pile of silky hair on her head who roared badly along with the Bee Gees and berated her filming son. This, at least, felt interestingly angry and funny: Why was she always singing and yelling?

Breeching nearby was a TikTok account called Retirement House, staffed by Rose, Eugene, Curtis, Bubbe, Mabel, and Larry, all actors. They filmed scripted content from a rented house in Los Angeles, where they told their watchers something about the business of being old. They sold Chili's, KFC, and the music of Instagram-famous violinist Lindsey Sperling, who visited Retirement House to give a concert in the nearly empty room, all the old people–actors dancing around her, caught in the incessant zooming in and out of the camera. They sold Spades Plus, an online betting app anchored by the idea of an old-fashioned card game, and Hill's Science Diet pet food, the kind for senior dogs and cats. They sold GoodRx (Bubbe: "GoodRx has helped me save so much money over the years. It's a joy to treat my friends with the savings! I mean . . . who doesn't love guilt-free spending?"). Though I didn't like to watch for long, it did seem to me that there was a clarity to this kind of sale. Caught and displayed on Instagram, old age seemed to me to be turned into a lucrative and fairly simple performance. Here, it was distinct, clear, separate from youth. Nothing murky about it.

Since 2009, I had been a member of a certain online community specific to my undergraduate college, where reams of alumni posted, every day, and multiple times a day, their secrets, the details of their marriages and jobs, the struggles they were having with their children or lovers, rants, small happinesses, Marxist analyses of global events, rankings of dried bean varieties. It was, during my time in Pittsburgh and at many other times in my life, the steadiest influx of conversation I have ever had. But "i am fully ageist now," one of them wrote, one morning, arguing for "death panels," and against subsidizing the lives of people over the age of ninety. Another wrote, of old people, that they were like toddlers, in the sense that small things brought them joy. While it is hard to say that there was *one* prevailing sentiment toward older people during this time, there was, more largely, intense *sentiment* of all kinds: And it was everywhere. A good deal of public pronouncement in the early days of the pandemic had focused on older people's particular vulnerabilities to the virus, and even a sense of exchange—the old for the young. "No one reached out to me and said, 'As a senior citizen, are you willing to take a chance on your survival in exchange for keeping the America that all America loves for your children and grandchildren?'" said one state official on television. "And if that's the exchange, I'm all in." The phrase "Boomer remover" circulated, brilliantly demonstrating an intergenerational animus that undergirded so much casual conversation online. Often, I felt like I was hearing and seeing things about oldness that other people weren't. It seemed to underpin so much: And this was before age became a defining factor in the 2024 presidential election. I began to drop off from an otherwise deeply helpful podcast I had listened to for years because of how casually they seemed to advocate for the deaths of old people—a kind of fixation on that show, it often seemed to me, and a fairly literal testing out of Antonio Gramsci's famous phrase that "the old is dying and the new cannot be born." The rest of Gramsci's sentence: "in this interregnum a great variety of morbid symptoms appear." Perhaps these morbid symptoms were what I was seeing and hearing on my computer and phone most nights: that focus on oldness that I saw on the billboards advertising Social Security help, and in the book I kept on my coffee table, titled *The Longevity Economy: Unlocking the World's Fastest-Growing, Most Misunderstood Market*, wherein I read about AGNES (Age Gain Now Empathy System), a body suit designed to mimic various limitations of aging, being tried on by various corporate leaders in an attempt to understand the physical limitations of their older consumers. Later, I immediately recognized the same suit on the actor Chris Hemsworth, in the last episode of his show *Limitless*, in which he attempts to confront his fear of aging and death, living in a fabricated "retirement village," playing Ping-Pong ("brutal"), and fixating on a mysterious door meant to symbolize the great beyond. Oldness was so distant from youth, I guess, that you had to painstakingly suit up to understand it.

Pittsburgh was a strangely perfect place to end up if you were interested in thinking about such things. Demographically speaking, it was one of the oldest cities in the country. "Only the retirement destination of Palm Beach, Fla. has a greater concentration of older adults among the largest 40 counties in the U.S.," announced a reporter at *Pittsburgh Quarterly*. This seemed particularly the case in my neighborhood, Elliott, where there were few businesses, per se, besides maybe a doughnut shop with unposted hours, at a treacherous bend in Steuben Street. Elliott could be thought of as a counterstudy to Lawrenceville, across the river from me, with its craft breweries and bowling alley and glassy multibusiness spaces and hip-ish people. In my corner of Elliott, few people walked around, except for maybe the one older man living in a house tucked under one of those Pittsburgh stairways who slowly climbed the steps each day for exercise. "Don't get old," he pantingly joked as I passed him carefully one morning.

Before this place got the name Pittsburgh, it was known, according to *The Decolonial Atlas*, as Jaödeogë, a Seneca word meaning "between two rivers," and Tyaötékë' in the Mingo language. (The Mingo were a diverse group of Indigenous peoples who migrated to the three rivers area in the eighteenth century.) The French built a fort here, called Fort Duquesne, in 1754. After the French burned the fort, the English built a new one in 1758 and called it Fort Pitt. It became known as Pittsburg—no "h"—in 1911, officially. In the eighteenth and nineteenth centuries, Pittsburgh was called the "Gateway to the West." On its rivers, the products of its steady industry of glass and iron and, later, steel, traveled. The spit of land that narrows at the confluence of the Monongahela and the Allegheny Rivers points into the larger Ohio River to the west. Known as Smoky City, Iron City, and infamously, "hell with the lid taken off" for its notorious, sooted skies, Pittsburgh's air was so dense with industrial pollution that I met someone in the twenty-first century still struggling to power-wash the remnants of the twentieth off the outside of his house. Time in Pittsburgh is layered like this, seemingly more so than other places, because it is condensed, concentrated, and cramped.

By the turn of the twentieth century, Pittsburgh had become Steel City, as it was making a vast portion of the country's steel, the material that strung railroads across the land, bridged one part of a city to another, and raised buildings to a higher height than anyone had ever seen before. Certain evidence stacked up: You can click through photos now online whose captions exclaim about the impossibility of seeing the midday sun through the twentieth-century smog. A mountain not far from my house on the hill was littered with signs everywhere warning you not to drink from the water trickling out of the earth. The Pittsburgh potty, a phenomenon specific to this city, as far as I know, was an architectural invention: a starkly gleaming toilet unencumbered by walls but maybe paired with a sink, placed in basements across the city, where steelworkers could quickly wash up before heading upstairs.

After steel production slowed, new industry unfurled in its wake: a huge infrastructure of hospitals, nursing homes, rehab centers, in-home care companies, personal care homes, and, just as notably, insurance companies. The main ones here were Highmark, which dovetailed with the nonprofit Allegheny Health Network (AHN), and University of Pittsburgh Medical Center (UPMC) Health Plan, which dovetailed with the nonprofit UPMC. Both insured care for a gargantuan number of this region's residents; both had a history of not recognizing the other one's coverage. For instance, a UPMC hospital might not treat a patient with Highmark insurance. The struggle was one over market share, but in 2019, attorney general Josh Shapiro, who later became Pennsylvania's governor, reached an agreement with the two companies. "This momentous achievement is the result of 3 entities coming to the table w/ a vivid understanding of the best interest of the people + the region, putting all other differences aside," Shapiro's successor announced online. "Now, patients are no longer caught in the middle - power is returned to the consumer." It was hard not to see a metaphoric echo, in his words, of three rivers meeting: the government, Highmark, and UPMC.

Of course, like many other such companies, UPMC and Highmark had operations outside this region: UPMC had tendrils in China, where it planned to open five hospitals; it also had operated facilities in Ireland since 2006. Highmark and its hospital arm, Allegheny Health Network, were not so far-flung, but AHN operated hospitals outside Pennsylvania. A common complaint in Pittsburgh, in fact, was that both UPMC and AHN were technically local nonprofits, meaning that they did not have to pay taxes, as long as they somehow demonstrated "community benefit." Congressperson Summer Lee, originally from the Pittsburgh borough of North Braddock, argued that UPMC in particular demonstrated "monopoly power"—defining and undergirding the lives of the people in the region, just as the rivers and the hills and the steel bridges did.

It is not random that so many elements of the care economy sprang up in Pittsburgh. Throughout the twentieth century, the city's famous steel mills belched pollutants—sulfur dioxide, ammonium—into the air and water, offering residents illness, alongside jobs. Certain neighborhoods found this paradox more acute than others: Local filmmaker Tony Buba describes the "man-killing jobs" of Braddock's mills, which were often worked by Black men, who along with their families would often find cancer and heart and respiratory problems in their futures. Many other neighborhoods, too, were built by the twinned forces of industry and illness: Homewood, the South Side Flats, Greenfield, Hazelwood, downtown. For a long time, the smog and the city were synonymous. That "hell with the lid taken off" phrase sprang from an *Atlantic Monthly* writer's nineteenth-century excursion to the city, where he saw how the city lay "low, as at the bottom of an excavation, just visible through the mingled smoke and mist, and every object in it is black. Smoke, smoke, smoke—everywhere smoke."

About a century later, a report in *The Pittsburgh Press* characterized that smoke again: "The steam contains a particularly-sticky compound which forms droplets on cars and is hard to get off without taking the finish off," wrote Fred Jones. "Given a mild east wind, smoke from these plants drifts down the valley and blankets under a grayish-yellow haze that produces an acrid taste in the mouth and watering eyes." A few decades after that, the Shell ethane-cracker plant rose like a vertical city in Beaver County, and was fined $10 million for its air-quality violations within the first six months of its operation. On many days, a light wind would blow from one direction or another toward my tiny house, through its open windows, carrying an unmistakable scent of *chemical*, from a plant whose identity I did not know. Some days it smelled like laundry detergent, other days burning plastic. And some days the air simply smelled of warm fall leaves and someone's cooking.

When global competition in steelmaking, alongside the Federal Reserve's 1979 decision to raise interest rates, punctured the livelihoods of the city's steelworkers, an accordion of health crises expanded, along with plant closures and mill layoffs. Historian Gabriel Winant tracks this, alongside how Pittsburgh's mortality rates spiked and alcoholism surged. Same for suicide rates and domestic violence. Pittsburgh residents used their hospitals at extraordinarily high rates, and health care became a gigantic, complicated, and regionally defined industry. By the late 1980s, writes historian Andrew Simpson, Pittsburgh began a healthcare-based rebranding as the "City of Livers" when a star transplant surgeon at the University of Pittsburgh performed then-risky transplantation procedures centered on the often overtaxed organ. His work led *The New York Times* to run an article about the "transplant patients flock[ing]" to Pittsburgh "from around the world." The high-risk, high-visibility procedures ramped up at the same time that Pittsburgh's medical industry was consolidating and shifting, building a landscape in which insurance companies and providers blended, rocketing the city into a new identity. It was now a "medical metropolis," in Simpson's words.

Popping up were new names for the city, now, and new versions of the city itself. "Roboburgh" was one offering, gesturing at the many recent robotics initiatives, including in health care, where robot surgeons often seemed to be spoken of, somewhat unfortunately, as being "cutting edge." Then there was "City of Bridges," of course, though a large one infamously fell down during a visit by President Joe Biden during "Infrastructure Week" (Pittsburgh has more than 400 bridges, about 174 of which were rated in "poor condition" that same year). Other ironies to this newest and affluent layer of Pittsburgh expanded. The old Heinz ketchup bottling plant had become the site of luxury lofts. The best tacos in Pittsburgh, it was said, came from a cantina occupying a spot valued at more than $3 million and run by the AI-boosted language learning app Duolingo. Construction was everywhere.

And amid all the newness, I could not stop seeing the oldness, literal and otherwise. "SOCIAL SECURITY HELP" ran a billboard. "CREMATION? DO WE HAVE A PLACE FOR YOU!" blurted a sign at the vast green cemetery where groundhogs ran amok between the graves. "LIVING IS GETTING EXPENSIVE: FUNERALS DON'T HAVE TO BE," in a local newspaper. At a café I sometimes went to, I would stare at a sticker affixed to a trash can. The sticker featured the Pittsburgh skyline and its new, slightly British-sounding slogan underneath: "A Most Livable City." Before or maybe after they stuck it to the side of the trash can, someone had scrawled an "L" between "A" and "Most."

Here, meaning in Pittsburgh, and also at this time, the future was constantly being invoked. We were either in it or about to be: robots, tech, AI, nut milks. If there was a defining characteristic of that moment, it seemed to be that Pittsburgh was *not* in the present, but poised on the brink of the "future." I thought of writers of the 1974 report on aging, whose anonymous younger respondents I had no way of tracking down and asking about how things had turned out, in their futures, which had become the present suddenly and inexorably. They had been asked their fears of the years to come that were now here, or maybe already gone. I returned to the report:

BRAIN WEAK.
NEGLECTED.
DISABLED.
LONELINESS.
LIVE ALONE.
BORDOM. [*sic*]
NO FUTURE.
FEAR DEATH.
MEDICAL COSTS.
OLD AGE HOME.
OTHER.

I suppose I wanted to know this: What was the future, in the present? What were the realities of older age now, in the moment in which so much seemed to be promised, and changing, and shifting? If we lived in the future now, one of cellular meat and virtual reality headsets, what did the future-future look like? And then, perhaps most importantly, what about fear: What was the relationship between personal fear of oldness and the ways in which oldness was structured in society? For I felt that there was something there, something underexplored, in my mind anyway, between Cynthia Ozick's terrible, sudden, tear-inducing streak of white hair ("you live in panic and dread, the future shrinks and darkens") and my grandmother's unnatural-natural death. Perhaps I was simply hallucinating when I saw oldness everywhere. Perhaps I had my own list of fears, which were forming and calcifying underneath me.

OLD AGE HOMES.
BEING ALONE.
MYSELF.
FINANCES.

BEING UNPRODUCTIVE.
THE UNKNOWN.

I did not realize, then, that not only were these fears outside me, but they also tangled with the realities of older age—and just life—in this country. They each had a history I could move through, in hopes of seeing them better, at the very least, so that when, if I eventually confronted them, I could be, as I liked to always say I was, prepared.

2

"OLD-AGE HOMES," BIG WRINKLES, A DIED-OUT CULT

If I were to start with the first item on the list—old-age homes—I would immediately find myself wrong in my phrasing. Such a thing, by that name, did not technically exist. But before I understood the differences between nursing homes, assisted living, independent living, personal care homes, aging in place, or any of the other splintered options for older people in the United States, I was simply and thoroughly unaware of them. It was from this vagueness around where older people might live that an uninformed fear—of homes, for older people—sprang.

It wasn't like I had never been in such a "place" before. In fact, I had spent a good amount of time in an assisted living facility, visiting my grandmother Mary Ann, who lived there for about a decade. Her "facility," as these places are sometimes offhandedly called, when they are not called "places," was vaguely pleasant, with the slightly stultifying atmosphere of relentless air-conditioning that a mall or a large library can have. I remember a digital screen in the lobby displaying two sales associates high-fiving each other about rooms recently sold. Flanks of older people sat at the sliding door entryway, watching the arrivals and departures. A shared dining room offered baked potatoes, hot dogs, and Caesar salad. A man fell on my grandmother in this dining room, permanently injuring her foot; there, one of her boyfriends told me about a program the facility was working with, which collected the lifetime wishes of assisted living residents across the country, then granted a select few. (A retired physicist's wish—to remain ever ungranted—was to ride in a vehicle that broke the sound barrier.)

My grandmother had first occupied an expansive flat on the first floor of the building. At a certain point it became overwhelmed by cockroaches, and my mom and dad drove up to help move her to a new unit, on the sixth floor. Years later, when Covid began to spread, we watched the building's illness statistics rise, followed by, quickly enough, the death statistics, mostly from the fourth floor—not exactly far from Mary Ann's apartment. I listened to Zoom calls with the building's management, attempting to track what was going on inside: Topics included communication apps that no one on the "outside" could figure out, let alone the people on the inside, as well as the news that HVAC vents were shooting contaminated air out of the building in directions we wanted to ensure wouldn't mean re-inhalation by our loved ones. *Does the virus float?* we wondered, along with other questions that didn't really make sense but felt pressing, vital. None of us knew anything about the virus, nor how long it would remain a threat to our sense of normalcy—our loved ones suddenly locked inside a building, all together, and the rest of us younger people outside. Someone joked, on a Zoom call, about all the residents growing "man buns." At a certain point, not far in, we decided to take Mary Ann out. I would go live with her, we all decided, in a house that Mary Ann bought, or rather, we bought with Mary Ann's money, for her, in a suburban neighborhood of Denver not far from the facility.

She was able to do this because she had the money. I was able to do this because I had recently quit my job teaching overseas, in the month that the pandemic began—my boss had insisted that the virus would be over soon, and that I should return to Germany, or, if I refused to do so, quit for "personal reasons." I resented his unwillingness to bend, even once international flights began to slow. But I did have a personal reason, I suppose: I was close with Mary Ann, who would soon be moving out of her "place" during an extended moment of world panic. She needed help.

Mary Ann was a quiet person whose quietude actually covered a great degree of stubbornness. I had never before had this amount of time with her. She was in her mid-nineties then and, to stay warm even in the summer, she wore a beanie I had given her, everywhere she went. I cooked for her, napped with her, ate with her, walked slowly down the block with her, exercised in front of her while she marveled at my movements, and I worked to outfit her house, to the best of my ability, with the things she needed. On my phone, still, I have inscrutable notes from the summer of 2020, like the following, which I vaguely remember from having to purchase her a new toilet:

american standard, 15.5 from floor to lip

18 to seat

14 wide seat

tank 17.5 widest pt trapezoidal

14.5 high tank

24 in deep from back to front

knobs w cover on that hold seat on from outside to outside
7 inches

bars—5.5 to 6 inches

Mary Ann had not particularly wanted to leave the assisted living facility, but neither had she wanted to enter it in the first place: She liked her earlier house, where she had lived for decades. Before she entered the facility, she hadn't yet needed a gigantic amount of help. I have no idea where I was when she entered it, but in any case, I was not privy to the conversations about why she needed to go there. I understood, vaguely, that she mostly didn't want to. But she did make a life there. She found two consecutive boyfriends—"companions," in her phrasing, or "friends." There was a community. She maintained a steady practice, until it was impossible to maneuver through her arthritis, of making art. Despite this activity, she didn't seem *happy*, exactly—she was never a wildly demonstrative person, but she seemed like a slightly muffled version of herself there. She had friends, but she felt it to be both wonderful and constraining, the way that they all knew each other's business; she didn't have to leave for food but felt bounded by the limited options. She had tranquility, and a beautiful view out over the city's treetops. It was nice, in many ways, but it was also some sort of compromise created by a calculus outside my own understanding.

From my twin bed in her new house, where she slept down the hall, I noticed a calmness overtake me. There was something off-the-trajectory, and nice, about me, unemployed indefinitely, living with my grandmother, whose days, I was discovering, were a mix of routine and rest. She slept in and I walked my dog around her neighborhood, noting its fancier edges and curbside memorials. In the evenings I went out again, sometimes passing a group of women who gathered in circled chairs every Friday night and who once filmed a short video for my grandmother: *Hi, MARY ANN! We love you, MARY ANN!* Under other circumstances I would have found them cloying; here, in this moment, I loved them. Because during the day I was learning how much work went into extending care toward an older person with serious health issues. I have had no other time in my life like this, before or since: And thinking about it in Pittsburgh, I remembered my grandmother sitting there with a light smile on her face, her eyes closed. We both loved it. And during breaks I began to notice the reticence I had toward thinking about her old life, in the facility. I knew almost nothing of it, I realized; I was going from occasional visits to my grandmother to, now, constant contact. The ten years prior had been a blank stretch.

Before landing there, at the facility, my grandmother had had an occasionally painful life, in some ways: a magnetic but dallying husband, a deep artistic sensibility that was not always taken seriously. It is one thing to push your whole life to make it better, more meaningful, more pleasurable, doable: That alone can be hard enough, but to then be asked to spend its end somewhere you never imagined for yourself? Then there was the crawling feeling I had had, and did not want to have, when visiting her old place: the sense of not wanting to stay there for long, when I had always wanted to prolong my visits at her actual house, with its art, and roses, and life.

With a weird avidity, I began, in the mornings, to read her facility's company's 10-K, an official Securities and Exchange Commission document it had to file each year—and noted its language around how "senior living is a private pay business," how most of the residents in these facilities paid for their "stays" via pensions and other fixed-income savings. Sometimes, they sold their homes to land in this one, the document said. My grandmother was lucky to have a large savings account, bolstered by her husband's pension, which she received after he accidentally drowned in the months after he left her for another, and younger, woman. Still, it struck me that she was paying—and she told me once that she had to pay for *everything* there, even a bag of Cracker Jack left outside her door after the dining room closed at the beginning of Covid—to live inside a system of sorts that I had never looked at. Partly, this was because of her interest in privacy. She showed me once a tiny clay head she had made, at age ninety, of a serene-faced person with rings of curling hair. The head was still damp: She kept it so, wrapped lightly in tissue paper inside a dresser drawer. She didn't like to bring him out too often, she said: He would lose his power. More importantly, she corrected herself, he would lose his privacy. My visits to her old facility had been a kind of drawer opening, never for more than a few hours at a time, then closing.

Mary Ann was still alive when I moved to Pittsburgh. After I moved, she was able to find help from aides who stayed 24/7 in her house, and whom she resented for their ever-presence, while thanking them, too, for their help. The aides' schedules my mother arduously managed from afar, driving six hours to the house when needed. It was a weird feeling, to know that Mary Ann was existing somewhere very far from me, not isolated, exactly, but not with family members either. I pictured her almost like a plant growing in a terrarium. She told me more than once she wanted to die. That she was holding on until my first book came out. She would die before that happened, in a bed in her house, underneath a cyanotype that we made together that summer. I don't know where the serene head she made ended up. Maybe he's lying in a landfill somewhere; maybe he's been irrevocably dented after his lifetime in a small, cushy little box; maybe a relative has him, unbeknownst to me.

While bands might perform at the facility, and group trips might be arranged out to the grocery store or maybe the art museum, Mary Ann did not live in a neighborhood, as she had before. There would be no walking, in the mornings, to visit the family of foxes nesting in the grounds of the nearby church. There would be no gardening projects, outside of the small terra-cotta pots beyond her door. An unused mini golf green stretched alongside the facility, a nice idea but rarely touched. A lot of this had to do with her own abilities and interests as she aged, and some of it had to do with the facility's bounded-off-ness. While her situation was by no means dire, there was a clear demarcation between her life before the facility and her life in it. There were no rules, per se, keeping her *inside*, but it was understood that she was supposed to age here, and that upon entry, aging toward death would now begin in earnest. Unexpectedly, then, there was also that weird coda, those months after the facility, a time that no one had expected her to have, and which I had been able to share with her. It was in that coda-time that I saw how much care my grandmother needed.

In the language of eldercare, she needed help with her "ADLs"—her activities of daily life. She needed someone to massage her arthritic feet with arnica cream, to help put on her shoes, to make her food, to do her laundry, to keep the place clean, to go get groceries, to stay on top of the many medications and health needs, to make doctors' appointments and get her to them. And I was just an auxiliary staff member/granddaughter: Other caregivers, experts, many of them (younger) grandmothers themselves, came in to do a great deal of this work. Up close, I understood the depth of her sleep: Old age seemed exhausting. I had not, I was ashamed to feel, really witnessed it at length before. I had assumed that she was getting this level of care inside the walls of the assisted living facility, but I really had no idea if this was the case—and my mother told me that it wasn't, that sometimes medication would get skipped, or a person meant to help Mary Ann down to the dining area would come later than the scheduled time, and the dining room would have closed, or Mary Ann would be too tired. There was no way to really know what happened, unless you were there all the time.

By the time I moved to Pittsburgh, I was not having conversations with Mary Ann anymore. She had moved into a new state of oldness, in which phone conversations were difficult, and entire days sometimes immobilized her with pain. On occasion, she lost entire days to this pain, which mystified the rest of us, but was clearly and undoubtedly real: She would be fully laid out by it, unable to move, trapped in it, and for days afterward might still struggle to form words. Wanting to connect, in my way, I ordered and began to receive assisted living trade magazines to my house in Pittsburgh. One bore a beautiful, colorful slice of cake on the cover—the *Dining Issue*. Inside, ads abounded for robots roving the dining rooms, pulverized frogskin used in wound care, more tiny robots used to "scrub, floss, and rinse experimental teeth," on-demand chaplains schedulable via the MyChap app. Ads asked if your facility might have "irritable boiler syndrome"; campaigns showcased older people dressed in protest gear (the "Grayt Revolution"); and TrueLoo, a smart toilet, promised to collect health information from each "session" (guests to a facility could click a button on the side of the seat "to not collect their session information"). Virtual reality, mentioned over and over again, brought flabbergasting sights and experiences to residents, sitting there strapped into the headsets. The vibe was slick, techy, hotel-y, though I reminded myself that these magazines were not for *residents*. They were for people in the business: owners and operators and industry folk.

In fact, I could not remember Mary Ann dealing with really any of these kinds of things in her facility, but later, on a visit to a personal care home in Pittsburgh for an article I'd write, I did watch one resident marvel at the prehistoric landscape she had been inserted into through such goggles. It reminded her of West Virginia, she said, where she had used to go as a kid. I felt in that moment a queasiness about the escape implied by such a tool, the nearly total release from one's present surroundings. In Pittsburgh,

I read a tweet by Palmer Luckey, who created Oculus's famous VR headsets, the first of their kind, which he sold to Meta. "If someone could do a good job of housing elderly citizens for the price of a Social Security check (~$1500/month), they could massively disrupt the existing nursing home/assisted living industry ($240B/year). Seems doable with existing and imminent tech/autonomy advances," he wrote, mentioning automation, virtual reality, and teleoperators working for $2 per hour in a different country. The gist, as I understood it, was cheaper housing, cheaper labor, an even wider gulf between the people inside and the people outside. Notably, Luckey lumped assisted living and nursing homes together, the idea being, presumably, that they both "housed" "elderly citizens." In reality, they did a lot more, and they did it differently from one another.

It was on Twitter, one night from my bed in Pittsburgh, that I found Big Wrinkles, a Gen Z care worker who tweeted things like "aging is tight," and "more lovey and less institutiony nursing homes plz." There was an "enormous misconception," Big Wrinkles told me over the phone, and that misconception had to do with "the very understanding of what a nursing home is. In the media, people see them as assisted living facilities. Assisted living facilities are *called* nursing homes." When Homer Simpson's dad goes to a nursing home, for instance, Big Wrinkles said, what was actually represented was an assisted living facility. In fact, he said, "Assisted living facilities are what our society likes to think happens at nursing homes. In assisted living, a lot is good. People frequently have their own space, behind a door that often can lock. They have autonomy over their day. They have usually way nicer spaces and a common area. Assisted living looks way less like a hospital, more like a library." These were institutions, Big Wrinkles told me, that people feel relatively good about. Notably, unlike other options that exist, he said, assisted living "seldom accepts Medicare and Medicaid."

While I had known that Mary Ann had paid for her time in the assisted living facility, I had not put this part of the puzzle together: What Big Wrinkles was saying was that assisted living was a very specific option, one that you generally had, as the 10-K had hinted, to pay for yourself. In most cases, assisted living was not subsidized by the government. Medicare didn't pay for it. Medicaid might pay for some of the health services for some residents in assisted living, but not for their room and board. In general, assisted living was an option for a select group of people who could afford its amenities: the Cracker Jacks, the art classes, the social stuff. Yet I wondered about Big Wrinkles's assertion about the blurriness between nursing homes and assisted living, and I began to see examples of their differentiation, structurally. Recently, lobbyists successfully exempted the assisted living industry from legislation meant to better regulate private equity's reaches into eldercare. Certain recent staffing mandates also exempted assisted living facilities, focusing instead on nursing homes. What this all meant was that while both options seemed to house and care for older people (and nursing homes also cared for younger people with disabilities, though the *Olmstead* decision of 1999 pushed against institutionalized settings for people with disabilities, and toward community integration), these services were tiered, and to a great deal along class lines.

Before speaking with Big Wrinkles and beginning to read on, I had thought of my vague fear of these "places" as a thick, cottony, uniform fear, one having to do with being older and "separated" from society. That was certainly part of it. But Big Wrinkles, over the phone, described his own education in such topics, and the fear took on a different tone. In January 2020, Big Wrinkles started experimenting with different psychedelic drugs—an experience that overlapped with his grandmother recovering from heart surgery in a nursing home on the Upper West Side of Manhattan. This was before he had become Big Wrinkles, a rising star in the world of "nursing home culture change," a branch of institutional reform efforts. When visiting his grandmother, Big Wrinkles became subsumed by the feeling that he was "everyone and everything." "Imagine if you're feeling like that in a slaughterhouse," he told me, "identifying with cows. I was identifying with the staff and residents of the New Jewish Home. And what that experience was was loveless, devoid of love, color, humanity. It felt like suffering." Listening, I could not totally understand if he was serious.

Big Wrinkles had then tried to become a Certified Nursing Assistant in New York City; his program, at this time, required applicants to spend a week in a skilled nursing facility. But "they couldn't get us into a floor, because of Covid restrictions," he said. "We were literally unable to help, amidst a shortage." He tried a different tack, getting in contact with a higher-up at a company he called "THE for-profit skilled nursing chain," who funneled him into a three-week certification program in Albuquerque, New Mexico. He started as an activities director in a Covid-positive unit in a nursing and rehab center. "I was wearing a turtleneck," he remembered to me, with a mixture of self-indignation, maybe, and embarrassment. He didn't feel out of place as much as he realized, in that moment, that he was simply unprepared.

One of Big Wrinkles's first tasks was to go into a resident's room—HIV-positive, Covid-positive, and with "one of the" hepatitises—and tell him, in study abroad–level Spanish, that his insurance was no longer going to pay for his stay, and that the resident would have to leave. Big Wrinkles was not fluent enough to understand the man's reaction. Another resident—hospice, Covid-positive, multiple amputations, throwing up green bile—wanted to die. But there was no legal way, Big Wrinkles remembered, to help. "You can't force someone to eat, or take their medicine. He refused." Meanwhile, Big Wrinkles was going through his various training programs, some of them great, some of them less so, including one group led by a man who passed out onions, then asked the trainees to peel them. "Okay," thought Big Wrinkles, "this is gonna be some metaphor about multilayered whatever, or maybe even, like, the units will be really stinky. We all just peeled onions and put them on the windowsill and just started talking about other stuff. Really it was the weirdest thing I've ever done."

When I met him virtually, Big Wrinkles was working as a "concierge" at a high-rise nursing home on the Upper West Side, someone whose job it was to kind of float between residents and staff and administration. It was at the extreme end of the spectrum, he told me—a big, for-profit operation in a big city. Nursing homes weren't always like the one at which he worked, though they tended to have some basic things in common. I asked Big Wrinkles to name some elements of nursing home design that he was familiar with, trying to cross-reference them against the assisted living facility where Mary Ann had spent her mysterious-to-me decade. "Ohhh yeah," he texted me. "Shared bathrooms. Code-locked doors. Hallway design eerily similar to prisons . . . [The] call bell can only be rung once (meaning if you call, the light goes on, but you can't reinforce the call. Meaning once you've called once you have no further means of contacting for help)." He sent me some "Nursing home x Prison floor plans." He continued. "The curtain separating beds is a staple. That pink curtain is a staple! I said staple twice. Why? Bc fuck its such a nasty lil staple." None of these, I noted, had been elements of the assisted living facility where I had occasionally visited my grandmother when I was in town. This makes obvious sense, in retrospect, I can say now, having moved through the long period of ignorance I had about such things. Nursing homes are institutional spaces originally modeled off hospitals, and meant to provide some of their residents with full-time, often custodial care (though some residents might be there on shorter, rehab-focused stays). They are places that people enter often during a longer moment of precarity: being discharged from a hospital, or needing care that is not forthcoming at home, or not having a home at all. A long-term bed in a nursing home is often paid for via Medicaid. Assisted living facilities are something else, something harder to pin down: They are sometimes called "senior living communities," and the vagueness of that phrase gets at the vagueness of what they might look like inside: Parts might be medicalized or locked down (i.e., for residents with dementia), but in general they are oriented toward "independent living." The idea, basically, is that older people opt in to assisted living for a mixture of social benefits and mild-to-moderate help with activities of daily life.

I saw the pink curtain for myself one Saturday morning. I had flown from Pittsburgh to New York in part to see him. Big Wrinkles was younger than I had expected, and tall, with gigantic camo pants made of some sort of silky fabric. He reminded me of my younger sibling, and seemed to operate at a frequency I couldn't totally understand. He spoke exactly like he texted—"I've been a very busy boy"—and I waited for a sense, rising inside me, of annoyance with him, of discomfort with his displays, maybe, of empathy toward people whose situations were very far from his own. But when he brought me into the nursing home where he worked, I noted how conversant he seemed with everyone inside, both staff and residents. "This is my friend Lucy," he told the front desk person, who he hugged, while she snapped my photo for whatever internal record unfurled in my shadow.

We started with the first floor, where a model bed and a model bathroom stood ready for physical therapy and activities of daily life practice. Faux trees with pale cherry blossoms sprouted alongside street signs proclaiming we were close to Central Park, a display that reminded me slightly of Madame Tussaud's. Signs about meditation and wellness enticed. Nary a soul breathed in these rooms, though Big Wrinkles told me they were generally busier on other days of the week. Upstairs, people sat in wheelchairs in the hallway, or lay in beds, seemingly asleep. Some of them, Big Wrinkles explained, had entered with rehab needs—they were there on short-term stays. Then slowly, perhaps, they would begin to live here, moving through the different levels of the building as their needs changed.

Big Wrinkles had developed an evaluation tool for residents, on his own time, that he showed me, and then left me with two residents whom I could ask questions. One was a friend of Big Wrinkles: Big Wrinkles routinely took him out to dinner with his family. He, like Big Wrinkles, he told me, flouted the rules. Wrinkles was one of just a few people in the building he liked—among other reasons, because Wrinkles had once taken a pair of scissors to the device he was supposed to wear around his wrist, which began to beep shrilly if he got in the elevator and tried to head elsewhere in the building. "That was the closest I ever got to getting fired," Big Wrinkles told me, and his friend nodded approvingly. I watched a little mouse sneak out of the wall behind him. He wanted desperately, he told me, to get out of this building, and to live somewhere else. He showed me a family album. His daughter called. A person moaned on the other side of the flimsy pink partition.

I felt a rising fatigue as we moved through the space, a fatigue I sensed covered for something else. I did not know, really, what questions to ask the residents, and felt outside the "holy" equation that Big Wrinkles described to me between "residents and their direct-care partners." He was no fan of the system, and yet here he was inside it, a kind of saboteur. He tweeted, schemed, cut the bracelet, and snuck his friends into the facility in hopes that they'd have a life-changing experience like he had. But he did not want to burn down the system entirely, he told me. He wanted to become, in fact, a nursing home administrator.

By the time we were walking a few blocks down the street to the assisted living facility, where a man Big Wrinkles had known from his short time in rehab now lived, I was feeling strained. Big Wrinkles wanted me to understand the difference between the two places, but I felt myself returning to that feeling, as we walked the streets of the Upper West Side and dallied to get him a Starbucks coffee, that I had had while visiting Mary Ann way back when. Things were taking too long. There was nowhere for my face or body or feelings to exit. People had issues they wanted to tell me about. Big Wrinkles was almost, at times, exhaustingly earnest. It was so much easier not to have to think about all this reality: the mouse, the bracelet, the sense that someone was always on the verge of discovering my presence in the building (Saturdays, Big Wrinkles told me, were the easiest days to sneak his friends in), the man furious that he was still inside the nursing home, the care that people needed, and the way Big Wrinkles made sure, each time, to ask the residents what *they* wanted. In the lobby of the assisted living facility, we had to input our names and contact information into a register of some kind, and we received printed-out name tags proclaiming, boldly, VISITOR.

Big Wrinkles poked the button and we rode the elevator up to his old friend's room. The building was decorated for Christmas, with poinsettias and big, raspy gold ribbons on the railings. Just as Big Wrinkles opened the door to the room—private, quiet—and I saw his friend start turning toward the door, where we stood, I told him I needed to go. And I left, on an endless series of trains back to Bushwick, Brooklyn. My friend's new girlfriend was having a birthday party that night. We would get repeatedly lost trying to get to Red Hook, where she insisted on having her party. Eventually, straining against the palpable frustration in the car as my friend took exactly the wrong exit again, pouring us into, what, the Queens-Midtown Tunnel, someone asked me about how the nursing home visit had been. I started talking about Medicaid, Medicare, Big Wrinkles, the bracelet, the old man, the assisted living facility, but I couldn't turn it into a story interesting enough to hold their attention. The night was very, very cold. In Red Hook, we stood around a small bonfire. I wondered idly about how much it cost to be an artist here. I felt lightly bored and itchy. I was there for only a few days, then back to Pittsburgh, and I couldn't wait to return to my books and writing assignments. There was a spare cruelty to how I treated myself then that felt, I see now, almost like a friend.

Later, I asked Big Wrinkles about the electronic bracelet on his friend's wrist, the one that kept him from leaving his floor. "I'm probably in the minority," he told me, in that "I think we really need to allow for the phenomenological experience of each person to dictate their experience . . . I just think that people . . ." he trailed off, then began again. "This is supposed to be their home, and they should do whatever the fuck they want to do. As long as it's not hurting another person." Big Wrinkles worked with people—nurses and CNAs—who'd been around for decades, who remembered the days of literally tying residents to their beds. "That would just never happen now," Big Wrinkles told me, then paused. "But then," he asked, "what is a restraint? You could get rid of all the restraints, but if someone's not allowed to leave, then every single resident in every single facility is restrained. No one is allowed to leave." The way he spoke of it startled me: It lined up, in a way, with Mary Ann's experience at her assisted living facility. There was an argument to make—and Big Wrinkles was essentially making it—that the bounding-off of older people in general was a restraint in itself. Had my own grandmother been *restrained*, though? Not in any sort of obvious, physical way. But there had been an emotional component to her separation from the rest of us that niggled at me, and always had: the dropping-in we had done, instead of the living-alongside. She needed help we were not prepared to provide for her ourselves, and this was the easiest solution, maybe, for everyone.

In nursing homes of previous eras, "some residents were essentially turned into disabled subjects by nursing home staff . . . physically restrained, sometimes with ropes, in 'geri-chairs,'" or "chemically restrained," in historian James Chappel's words. It was easy to think of those older nursing homes as dated sites of another time, and restraints in the same manner. But today, if you think about restraints in the way that Big Wrinkles did, as an expansive category of tools and strategies that prevent residents from roaming or leaving, often because there are not enough staff to keep track of them, you might see restraints more clearly. A 2019 report in *The New York Times* noted, for instance, that more than twenty percent of nursing home residents were sedated with antipsychotic drugs, and many were given false diagnoses of schizophrenia to facilitate the sedation. Some facilities today routinely restrain, in this way or physically, twenty percent or more of their residents.

The electronic bracelets, shared rooms, flimsy privacy curtains, medicalized settings, restraints—these were not parts of my grandmother's experience in her assisted living facility. And yet I caught my relatives referring to Mary Ann's facility as a "nursing home," an "old folks' home," a "retirement home," all those different phrases blending into the same basic thing, the same basic idea: that here was a fine enough place where old people went to live, once it was their "time." There was a blurriness to how younger people—or maybe some broader "society"—sometimes understood older people's material realities, the options available to them, and the choices they or their families made about housing. Just recently I got an email from a podcast I occasionally listen to, briefing me on a new episode about "how much of our economy is now dependent on putting people away: private prisons, rehab facilities, assisted living, and retreats for the troubled." "Assisted living" blazed out to me. I had become fixated on how my grandmother's kind of "place," which was good, but still not exactly enjoyable for her, was miles apart from what Big Wrinkles showed me in New York, and what most people are able to afford. I wanted to email the podcast host: Assisted living facilities are not in the same category, at all, as, say, a nursing home—or a private prison, I wanted to say. Historically, assisted living is exorbitantly expensive, and generally paid for privately, as that 10-K had said. This means what it sounds like: People pay out of pocket, as my grandmother did, to be there. In 2021, in Pittsburgh, the average cost per month to live in an assisted living facility was around $5,000, almost six times my rent.

Meanwhile, in 2024, more than a million people lived in nursing homes. They are "stigmatized" places, writes researcher Margaret Morganroth Gullette; "it is as if the people and the places merged perceptually, as lepers once became indistinguishable from leprosariums." A great deal of this has to do with class. In the words of Alex Spanko, writing in *Skilled Nursing News*, "The general concept of Medicaid being the primary payer for long-term care . . . [hearkens] back to a time when nursing homes were catch-all facilities for anyone who couldn't live at home anymore. With the rise of assisted living, independent living, memory care, and home health, the relatively healthier (and wealthier) people gradually siphoned off until only the very sickest remained, creating a system where states still pay custodial-care rates for truly complex medical cases." There are good nursing homes, and a great variety within the category: for-profit, not-for-profit, large, small, affiliated with a church, secular, urban, rural. There are also many stories, and have been since nursing homes started, of their flaws and violations.

More largely, it would make sense to be afraid of becoming a "truly complex medical case" whose care needs are delivered by an institution. To be afraid, maybe, of living somewhere without much choice. I had no doubt that fear of disability powered many Americans' fear of ending up in a nursing home, in ways that tangled unpleasantly with their fears around aging, their interest in staying, as we always said now, "productive." And yet there was something else to me that seemed to power the fear beyond all those pieces: something more complex and having to do, I think, with precarity and the sense that the future might be changing very quickly and in ways we could not control. That we might reach a certain age and become, in ways we cannot now anticipate, restrained.

In this country, maybe unsurprisingly, there are many ways to grasp for control, and whole markets built around trying to preserve as many future options as possible. One morning in Pittsburgh, I heard about paying for my funeral ahead of time. It's one way of several to start the process of qualifying for Medicaid, and thereby long-term skilled nursing care: so I heard on the strange elder-law radio program I sometimes listened to as I drove around the city on the weekend. Also, real estate transfers. Carefully structured irrevocable trusts. All these strategies fell in and around the category known as Medicaid spend-downs, wherein a person above the Medicaid income threshold but needing long-term care reduced their assets, kind of, sometimes, not all the way that they became *poor*, just enough that they could cover a stay in a nursing home while remaining in a different class than those who do not have such choices or strategies available to them.

For here was a basic fact thrumming in the heart of whatever strange inquiry I was doing: Medicare, the healthcare program meant to cover older people—old people, whatever we want to call them, the group that will hopefully one day include *us*, if we are not already there—does not cover long-term nursing home care. I did not know this when I started my reading, my interviews, my wanderings. But I was not alone in my basic ignorance. Nearly half of people over sixty-five think that Medicare covers long-term nursing home care.

With such a statistic, you begin to wonder why such confusion abounds.

Perhaps it is the fact that there is no class you take, at any point in your life, alongside everyone else, in which you learn such facts.

Perhaps it is because there are so *many* options, instead of a few, or even more simply, *one*.

There is no one fate that awaits all of us, as we age, besides death. How might Person A take Person B's experience as instructive, when Person A has a stroke at age seventy and Person B has no major health issues to speak of, and Person A doesn't quite qualify for Medicaid but has no real plan or ability to pay for long-term care, and Person B has saved up, with their spouse, a hefty amount of money with which to pay for assisted living?

Perhaps, grateful to have found *something* like a class in such topics, you go to a Learn, Share, Care sponsored by a local elder-law group, as I did one Saturday, the youngest person there, at a now-closed hotel across from a Whole Foods on the wealthy outskirts of Pittsburgh. At the Learn, Share, Care, I sat at a table with three or four women, all of whom were caring for their husbands in various states and stages of dementia. One of them told me she had barely been able to get away from her duties to attend the event. The room was lined with booths: organizations with swag about Alzheimer's and senior discounts. We sat there, and then we left, and the feeling I got was that no one at my table emerged much the wiser.

If you can, you might pay money to work with a lawyer who helps you reorganize, carefully, your assets, so that if you need to go to a nursing home, you can qualify without losing your house, your savings. Or perhaps you have already decided, in fact, that you want to enter an assisted living facility, at a certain age, or your family has decided that you will, and you have the money to do so. Perhaps this feels like a good decision: Your friends are there, or you feel as if you will make friends there, and you no longer have to cook for yourself, if you don't want to, and can pay for access to the dining room.

Perhaps you have never had the option to think about something like assisted living, with its thousands of dollars per month. Perhaps your only choice, per se, is living at home for as long as you can and then entering a nursing home, should you eventually need that level of long-term care. Perhaps you try to get a waiver, which in some cases allows you to be in an assisted living facility with Medicaid's help, or to receive home- or community-based care. Very possibly, in this latter option, you are placed on a waiting list. Perhaps you aren't.

Perhaps your eventuality is something murkier, possibly scarier, and altogether more realistic: You simply don't know yet what will happen. You might look into buying long-term care insurance out of some sense that this will help. But of the minimal numbers of people who have purchased long-term care insurance, many have found that it didn't actually cover what they thought it would: Many insurers exited the market, or tightened up their claims processes, or limited their coverage to people who did not have chronic health conditions, strokes, or psychiatric illnesses. In Washington State, the first-of-its-kind WA CARES fund provided up to about $37,000 in skilled nursing coverage, plus any inflation. This may seem appealing, and it is. But you also learn that the median cost, nationally, of a semiprivate room in a nursing home in 2025 is around $110,000.

At night, perhaps you wonder how to make sense of all these pieces of some larger puzzle whose shape, and picture, you can't see.

The stack of magazines on my coffee table grew larger. Preoccupying me were two simultaneous realities. The first was a phalanx of reports and analyses and stories on the state of nursing homes in this country—one presentation Big Wrinkles sent me went further, referring to the "original sin" of their construction. "Few people dream of living out their golden years in a nursing home. The very idea sparks existential dread in many Americans, conjuring images of grim, institutional dumping grounds where society's frailest and most vulnerable members aren't so much cared for as warehoused," wrote Michelle Cottle in a *New York Times* op-ed. The second was a sense, primarily accessed compulsively via Instagram, that in the wake of the worst of the pandemic, being old, or at minimum, retired, *was* a state to be dreamed of. There was an explicit fascination with one fantasy of oldness: the version involving leisure. On my discount mattress in Pittsburgh, I watched an Instagram video that highlighted an experiential weekend in a stunt early-retirement community thrown together by Taco Bell and called The Cantinas, where you could "feed your inner retiree." There would be "senior-inspired shenanigans," I saw, and you could "embrace your inner old." Vintage thrifting. Board games. Pickleball. Aerobics. Crochet. Even, strangely, a sound bath. "Although retirement is very far away for the attendees, who were mostly folks in their twenties and thirties, that doesn't mean they can't pretend," wrote *Parade* later.

"Live," read a pickleball paddle, "like a retiree." The fake retirees flowed to the gated community in San Diego, then ebbed away, back to their real ages and real lives. Could the bifurcation I felt be located between the "existential dread" of nursing homes and the imagined leisure to be found in assisted living? Sometimes while watching such videos I suddenly remembered that I lay there in a real body, in a real place, in a real time. Usually it was when I managed to look away from the screen, and saw how night yanked the clouds across the moon. Heard the rodents screaming in the greenery. I felt my standard brand of vague disorientation, halfway between Pittsburgh and these internet visions of an oldness I didn't recognize.

I followed this sense of unease to a town called Harmony. The first time, I was there for a horrible, endless date over crepes with a man I would run into again, elsewhere in Pittsburgh, ducking my head as I charged past him to take respite in the bathroom. "Young people think they can change everything," he chuckled about his classmates—he was starting out in a grad program where he was the oldest student, and everyone was harping on, he felt, about social justice and capitalism. They'd grow out of it, he seemed to be saying. I felt my eyes leave our table and focus on the peeling paint behind him, the thick gardens that seemed to front every house. I had been wanting to go there for a long time. I had heard of Harmony before, in grad school, when my professor Inara assigned us a book called *Angel in the Forest* by Marguerite Young. Young chronicled how once there had been "spinsters as numerous as hollyhocks" in this particularly green, lush part of Pennsylvania, tracing the history of the town as a utopian commune. It had been led by George Rapp, a preacher who'd fled Germany with hundreds of followers. "Like eels with eyes enlarged," wrote Young, Rapp's Harmonists "seemed a harmless group intent on suicide." They existed for a full century, across three separate plots of land, amassing a good deal of wealth from making wine, propagating mulberry trees on which to feed the silkworms that spun their silk, breeding sheep, and growing rye. They claimed separation from society, but the Harmonists had also made a series of calculated investments in the outside world: railroads and oil pipelines, and oil itself, all of which made the aging old Harmonists "immensely wealthy communist capitalists." Some would say that they were the most successful communal experiment in American history, though they had built in, basically, an expiration date, thanks to their general practice of celibacy, and the exodus, one year, of most of their younger members. With their communal aging in mind, the Harmonists always had the idea that they would care for one another in older years and disability: all "subscribers" to the society would be supplied with "all the necessaries of life, as lodging, meat, drink, and clothing, etc.," ran the 1805 articles of association.

A century later, at the advent of the twentieth century, the society was on the brink of a different reality. Most of the old people had died. The apocalypse they were waiting for had not come. John Duss, a previous child of the society (it was not *totally* celibate, and anyway, he was adopted in), sat on the board of trustees. He understood the monetary value that so much time and work had created, and "inveigled his way into [the Harmonists'] aging inner circle," writes one historian. He facilitated the sale of one large tract of Harmonist land to the American Bridge Company, formed by J. P. Morgan. By then, only a few Harmonists remained, and they dissolved the society in 1905, splitting the million-dollar cash pool.

I had a tendency to idolize history like this: communes with names like "Harmony," certainly, but also their vision of interpersonal care, their experiments in alchemy, their gardens. Yet today, the way that things seemed to stretch on in Harmony—the preserved wooden houses, the museum at the center of town, the historic placards, the seasonal festivals, the endless bad date at the creperie—began to diminish some of the romance. One afternoon, at a historical festival I attended, a man dressed as a Harmonist showed me for forty minutes how he used replicas of the Harmonists' tools to cut cabbage for sauerkraut. I was pleased to speak with him, and I liked him quite a bit, but remembered too another line by Young: that the Harmonists were perhaps "more interested in their cabbages than they were in eternity." It was easy to romanticize their vision of a communal experience. And their visions of an apocalypse intertwined with their own oldness: I felt a parallel to this moment in time, which seemed focused on a tangle of dread and doom and age.

"These were expensive," a woman muttered as I walked through Harmony on my next visit. She was engrossed in fluffing a plastic, truly evergreen garland she had looped over a bridge's railing. "They're not fluffy enough." I didn't stop to fluff with her, though I considered it briefly. It was eighty degrees and the fifth of November. Winter didn't feel exactly imminent. The insistence on seasonality felt like what it was: odd and familiar together. In the distance, teenagers were festooning the town with Christmas decorations. A portly cardboard Santa, glazed and old-fashioned, stood in the mulched median. I walked slowly through and slightly out of town, down a road paralleling wide Connoquenessing Creek. Then I began to climb a set of wooden stairs to a spot called Rapp's Seat. A warm, weird, pleasant wind began to supplant the noise and the sight, in the distance, of the sun-flashing semitrucks. The wind blew erratically and lustily, buffeting my face, pulling the leaves from the branches all around. Time had stopped here, too.

The next time I was in Harmony, it was because I heard about a strike among workers at a nursing home called the Grove at Harmony, on the edge of town. That morning, I took in the building, which seemed to be a mixture of an old convalescent home and a newer, brick add-on that resembled a motel. It was easy to miss, and did not sit particularly "in" Harmony, just on its edge, down a moderately trafficked little road running alongside Connoquenessing Creek, just down the same road from which I hiked up the hill to Rapp's Seat.

The workers, part of the Service Employees International Union (SEIU), were striking for higher wages and better working conditions. The company they worked for was larger than just the Grove at Harmony; it was called, in the typically and almost beautifully bland way of many nursing home chains, Comprehensive Healthcare. Nearly all women, the strikers formed a big gaggle in the middle of the road; music blasted and lawn chairs sat ready for them once they tired. Cars approached slowly. The group assessed the vehicles. Most often, the drivers honked and slowly drove by approvingly, but some would slowly turn, as if with discomfort, into the parking lot of the Grove. These were temporary workers, and they were treated to jeers.

This nursing home had gotten less press than Brighton Rehabilitation Center, also near Pittsburgh and also owned by Comprehensive Healthcare. At Brighton, Covid had ripped through resident ranks at such a rate that the facility became, at one point, responsible for 90 percent of Covid deaths in Beaver County, according to the county commissioner. After a news report chronicling the facility's years of deficiencies, as well as its lack of separation between Covid-positive and -negative residents, the FBI raided Brighton, where staff and residents seemed trapped on a capsizing ship, everyone getting sick, so many people dying, the result, some argued, of Comprehensive's history more than the virus itself. "Bone-tired, frightened nurses took to Facebook to plead for masks," ran a line in the news report. A woman who watched, through her iPhone, her sister—a patient in Brighton—die of Covid, which she likely picked up from being roomed with Covid-positive patients, noted that "Covid exposed what was happening down there—the lack of staffing, the worn-out staff, the lack of care from the administration."

Standing that morning outside the Grove at Harmony, a woman named Denise Cox seemed to bustle even when she was standing still speaking with me. She had worked at Brighton before becoming a labor organizer with the SEIU, where she focused specifically on care workers in Western Pennsylvania nursing homes. Before Brighton was owned by Comprehensive, it was a county-run facility named Friendship Ridge. For twenty-seven years, Denise had worked in this building, through many jobs, first in the laundry, then in the boiler room, then as a painter and tiler and plasterer. She knew the structure top to bottom, wing to wing, and knew its residents well enough to joke with them: "They'd let anybody stay in this place!" she ribbed two favorite residents, a pair of men who went everywhere together. "Ohhh!" they said back. "They let anybody work here!"

"Anytime you work a place," Denise told me ruminatively later, "it becomes a part of you." When Denise started at Friendship Ridge in 1986, there were waiting lists both to work there and to live there.

It had been a good place, she told me, before Comprehensive bought it in 2014. The halls had buzzed with activity. Quiet and artistic by nature, Denise started to spend the weekends learning to repair Friendship Ridge's wheelchairs, and in fact started to sit in those chairs, just to see how different the world became when she did this—the doorknobs were suddenly at a difficult level to reach, and the whole layout of space seemed new to her. It occurred to her that some basic, unthinking realities for her were not necessarily realities of life for residents. They were often "dependent," she said, on staff to help with basic things like getting their hairbrush down from the top of a bureau, and eating a still-warm meal, and wearing a clean, right-sized diaper. She saw a parallel between the rights of the residents and the rights of the workers. So she decided she wanted to confront the union: She wanted better representation. "If you never had a hemorrhoid," she told the union president, "you're gonna have one now."

Remembering this, she paused. "You gotta speak up for yourself or the world will walk over you." Like this, she became the president of the union's service and maintenance chapter for Friendship Ridge.

In 2014, when Beaver County sold Friendship Ridge to Comprehensive for $37.5 million, the facility went from being nonprofit to explicitly for-profit. Denise fought it all the way, filing right-to-know requests with the county, but the deal was done. According to Denise, Comprehensive cut seventy jobs, including retirement benefits. They added sixty beds, stretching out that all-important ratio any nursing home worker knows: staff to residents. Stretched staffs were a common problem both before and during Covid, at somewhere between 87 percent and 94 percent of nursing homes across the country.

At the Grove at Harmony, as had happened at Brighton, Comprehensive, upon beginning to operate the facility, laid people off. Barb Kozar, a striking Certified Nursing Assistant, had decorated the roadway with a gangly pair of skeletons stuffed into a red wagon—probably not a reference to a "skeleton crew," but certainly a reference to the direness of the situation. Some Comprehensive administrators would later go to trial two separate times. The first was in the fall of 2023 on charges of healthcare fraud, including deceptive recordkeeping when so-called ghost employees were allegedly listed as having worked when they did not, and residents' depression scores were alleged to have been altered. On these charges, the human codefendants would be acquitted, while the facilities themselves—Brighton and Mt. Lebanon Rehab—would be found guilty. The second trial was a federal lawsuit against Comprehensive by the Department of Labor, and focused on back pay. It resulted in a $35.8 million judgment, one of the largest recoveries of lost wages in US history. Comprehensive had "willfully denied" its Western Pennsylvania employees overtime pay, the court found.

There was a specific story I had thought I had known about nursing homes that involved Covid: how it had pushed through their doors and stayed there, roaming between residents and staff, leaving death and injury and exhaustion in its wake. "Why Did COVID Hit Nursing Homes Hardest?" asked the presentation that Big Wrinkles sent me (it was originally created by the Live Oak Project, the nursing home culture change organization he was involved with). "Frailest members of society—Design flaws: shared rooms & bathrooms—Underpaid staff work more than 1 job/17% of C.N.A.s live below the poverty line," the slide explained. But the charges brought to Comprehensive illustrated something deeper than the virus's inhabitation. The failures were not necessarily due to Covid itself but structural, revealing a fragile underlayer susceptible to minor and major threats. For this reason, the Live Oak Project wanted "no new 'nursing homes'" to ever be built again: only new models of care. Covid had provided an angle into understanding these deeper structural issues in many nursing homes that the Live Oak Project, referencing a recent report by the National Academies of Sciences, Engineering, and Medicine, characterized thus: "LTSS [Long-Term Services and Supports] has been functionally broken for decades."

Barb Kozar, a small and fierce woman who told me she would be meeting Joe Biden the following morning with a group of fellow SEIU workers, had worked in nursing homes for twenty-nine years. "We were *so responsible*," she said, about keeping Covid at bay. She remembered seeing the initial outbreak in Seattle on TV, in that nursing home, in February 2020. The Grove at Harmony was on stringent lockdown, the staff testing twice a week. Then one person, a worker told me, tested positive—and all of a sudden, within one day close to Christmas, a bloom of sickness radiated among the residents and staff.

On December 23, 2021, the CDC announced that healthcare workers who had tested positive for Covid but were asymptomatic could continue to work, after seven days of isolation (and this period could be cut down) to combat staffing shortages. The strained staff at the Grove at Harmony were pulling double shifts. "You're sick, sick, sick," a worker told me. "I thought I was going to die. People were getting sicker and sicker." The ill residents, she remembered, were subdued in a way she found eerie. They weren't communicating. They had the flushed faces of the feverish. Her wing was quiet and thick with virus.

The choice, as the worker saw it, was to work sick or not at all. If she didn't work, the sick residents she was responsible for would likely be left alone. There was one night, in fact, when this exact scenario happened: The worker, symptomatic and exhausted, stayed at home to recuperate. "Nobody worked in my hall," she remembered. "They were alone overnight . . . they couldn't go to the bathroom. So I came back the next day." To get to the wing where she worked, she told me, she had to pass through an area where no one was yet sick. She remembered being asked to hold her breath for the forty-five-second walk. Then she unzipped the plastic sheeting and walked into the crush. On each hall, a single nurse and a single aide. They screamed "I need you!" to one another as their residents struggled.

The numbers, and the names, keep changing: Search for Covid deaths for "The Grove at Harmony" in 2025 and you find nothing; it's now called Kadima Rehabilitation and Nursing at Harmony. Since its earlier iteration as the Grove, a hundred residents in total have died of Covid; when I first interviewed the striking staff, that number was at 25, and 115 staff members had gotten the virus. "You take care of these people for years," Barb Kozar said, "and you suddenly can't help them." During that initial outbreak, multiple residents died in a single shift. When Barb had started working in nursing homes, it was as a broke nineteen-year-old with a one-year-old baby. She echoed Denise's portrayal of a different kind of feeling back then, hard work, yes, but a sense of investment in the place. "We never went on strike back then," she told me about her previous work in this building, before it was known as the Grove at Harmony and was still the Evergreen Nursing Center, run by a man who would regularly walk the halls and speak with residents. Now, so many of her fellow workers were not permanent staff but "agency": temporary workers who were paid a high wage but did not receive benefits or paid time off and had no built-in allegiance, really, to one particular facility, as they rotated between several at a time. "Hit it and quit it," Barb summarized wryly.

There had been a gradual transition, Denise told me, toward this kind of cheap labor in nursing homes. Before Comprehensive bought Brighton and the Grove at Harmony, she told me, "We didn't see agency at all, back in those days . . . All of the money was put back in the facility . . . Supplies were better. The quality of supplies. You never had to beg for supplies . . . I don't ever remember any of the CNAs buying supplies for residents, like I hear now." At Harmony, various staff told me they had bought residents a Keurig coffee maker, a bottle of shampoo that wasn't the "all-in-one" kind, and cigarettes from West Virginia, where packs were cheaper. More broadly, Denise listed the things that she'd heard of CNAs buying for residents: boiled eggs, shoes.

A few days later, incidentally, was Labor Day, and I drove

downtown, parked near the August Wilson House, and walked toward the parade. The striking Grove at Harmony staff were there, talking among one another and marching. It struck me how many were older women: Many of them had spent their working lives in nursing homes and knew the story of how that industry had changed better than most anyone else. Four chants about their demands rose up into the air at once, distinct and indistinguishable both. After ten minutes in the crowd, I stopped being able to hear the words, and heard instead a simple sense of force. Feet on the pavement and voices rising. Drums in the background. The thick static of a megaphone careening into another. After seven days of striking, the women at the Grove at Harmony won a new contract with Comprehensive, one that insisted on higher wages, better staffing, and longevity pay.

This felt like an end to the story, one I could take and leave behind me and move on. I had found myself in this story in the first place via my standard operating procedure as a writer, but also as a general rule in my everyday life. I tended toward, I liked to think then, a kind of diffuse sallying through the world, staying open to the coincidence, digression, and movement. It was like walking, this form of life-and-research, and I believed in it fully as a form of truth-finding. There was reality to find in coincidence and randomness, in what the world showed you most easily, as you simply moved through it. The method was, I believed, antinarrative. After all, the world was not narrative. I was—or wanted to be—simply a molecule floating through it, bouncing off obstacles, absorbing into the lives of others. This was how I stayed invisible. It was also how I tended to forget that time was passing.

And so I kept going back, because of something about the word "Harmony" and the fact that I'd read about this place in grad school and the fact that I liked the striking women and learning about the history of nursing homes. That stretched back to, in my readings, the 1970s, when a woman named Mary Adelaide Mendelson toured nursing homes across the country, finding only a single good one. Every time I checked in on the Grove at Harmony, the story had a new chapter, a new angle. In the fall of 2023, Comprehensive tried to sell seven of its nursing homes, including the Grove at Harmony, to another company, Kadima. If the sale, for more than $50 million, didn't go through, the attorneys for Comprehensive argued, the seven nursing homes in question would hemorrhage money and close, leaving their residents and staff stranded. The Department of Labor filed for a temporary restraining order on the sale, arguing that it was a move to protect Comprehensive's assets as the other trial proceeded.

While the trials slowly moved forward, I read the inspection reports. I was learning something very standard about the world of nursing home ownership: that there are layers and layers to it. It's kind of endless. Names change. Ownership shifts. When you dig into this kind of history, it becomes hard to think of these places as static, in the way they tend to be described. And when you read the inspection reports of a nursing home filed with the Department of Health and Human Services, a strange out-of-body thing happens, a knowing that these details happened to particular people, who have been anonymized, and who once lived, or still do, within all the hard-to-parse layers. Rather than such stories beginning to blur, they become, I think, almost more specific, nearer at hand. Names are stripped, of course, of both residents (R) and employees (E). Everyone starts to become part of a larger, detailed mosaic. The fear changes. This is not your future, it is other people's specific presents, or pasts.

I dug backward:

In one room of the Grove at Harmony, in March, R30 falls slowly and painfully to the floor as E3 attempts to hold her from the wrong side of the bed. R30's skin tears, on her left forearm, somehow; when

E2 is notified, R30 is lying on the floor. After R30 is returned to her bed, no incident report is filed with the local state-run field office, despite the fact that E3, who has been a nurse's aide for years, says she provided a statement, in which she described the slow falling of R30, and how R30 actually slowly slid onto E3, who did not tell anyone or get help.

Eight Rs, some with dementia, multiple sclerosis, seizures, malnutrition, depression. Eight residents in total, as reviewed by an inspector in 2023, did not receive the opportunity to share their advance directives—the wishes they had for their own deaths, whether or not they wanted to be resuscitated, or treated in some specific way according to their own wishes and self-determination, should they move suddenly close to death.

Employees E5, E6, and E7, all nurse's aides, did not receive mandated performance evaluations for the year 2022.

In January 2021, R54 entered the Grove at Harmony with major, recurrent depressive disorder. Within a month, R54 was given a diagnosis of schizophrenia and bipolar disorder. In May 2023, R54 was started on a daily dose of 300 milligrams of Abilify, an antipsychotic sedative, and injected intramuscularly.

The Grove at Harmony's sale went through, and the facility settled into its new name. Kadima, in Hebrew, means a few things—"let's go forward," and "ancient." At the time of this writing, the nursing home's rating with the Centers for Medicare and Medicaid Services sits at one star (out of five), and its most recent health inspection lists 25 citations (the national average is 9.5).

Academic Carroll Estes put the historical root of the nursing home "issue" this way, in her landmark 1979 book *The Aging Enterprise*: "From descriptions in reports and congressional hearings, one can only wonder how and why such care is tolerated in a society and by a medical profession that prides itself on excellence of care." The "nursing home crisis," or "old age home crisis," is a long story. It has moved through almshouses and rest homes and then, post-1967, with the passage of Medicare and Medicaid, skilled nursing facilities, which were more medicalized versions of their predecessors, and bound to stricter regulation. I kept encountering it, this narrative, this fear of places that sometimes, in reality, *are* troubled, and yet are sites, too, for a seemingly never-ending push and pull between violations and "we must do something."

Alex Spanko, who had written about the industry and its class lines, among other things, for *Skilled Nursing News*, told me that he was frustrated by this narrative. He saw the problem more largely as one of a "punitive system" that emphasized to people younger than sixty-five that it was their fault if "you're poor. You didn't work hard enough. You were stupid, you didn't get a financial education." Over age sixty-five, he said, these people became, more clearly, the "victims of the for-profit capitalist system." And at that age, "autonomy and personhood" were taken away. It was the "whittling away of the social safety net," Spanko said, that was the "reason we have this bifurcated system. It helps you sell the high-end stuff even more, or regular private pay, [because otherwise] you're going to end up in a nursing home probably. One fact that blows my mind: Two-thirds of people who live in nursing homes are covered under Medicaid. This is long-term custodial care for people who do not have any other options and cannot live on their own anymore." In other words, long-term care in nursing homes was less about *oldness* than about class and disability—Medicare, the health program for older people, did not cover this care; Medicaid did.

Nevertheless, Spanko, speaking in his capacity as a private individual, emphasized that he, like Big Wrinkles, was trying to some extent to work within the system a little bit. "I don't think we're going to see some big nursing home overhaul coming through Congress anytime soon," he mused. And among senior living options, there were many good experiences. Moreover, there was no one preference for how an older person wanted to live. Some people did not *want* to stay at home. Spanko's great-aunt, who was like a grandmother to him, lived alone, in a small house, with multiple sclerosis and both legs amputated. She was lonely, Spanko told me, despite being active in her community. "Home health care didn't work for her. My family tried it. She was miserable." She found a small church-run assisted living facility, where she lived happily until she passed away.

So there are, of course, notable and important exceptions to this, but the majority of older people want to spend their final years in their own homes. This is most often the end they have in mind; whether or not they can pull it off might depend on how easily in-home care can be arranged. Compared to the Harmonists, home-care elders are relatively alone in figuring it out. "It is indisputably true that there is something private about aging," writes James Chappel. A family, chosen or given, can support, but it is not the same, really, as a group of people all going through the process together. This, I think, was at the core of the fear, both my own and the larger societal one. It was less about the "old age home" as a specter, and more about how old age tends to be individualized, and kept as private as Mary Ann's calm clay head.

One day, a man named George Alexander appeared before me. He was a retired tech journalist who typed, throughout the pandemic, word after word into a blog he called *On the Kendal Journey*. Alexander started *Kendal Journey* coincidentally, a few months before the pandemic hit, as a way of connecting residents at Kendal at

Longwood, the continuing care retirement community in Kennett Square, Pennsylvania, where he lived. A continuing care retirement community is a rare beast: not a nursing home, not assisted living, and yet not *not* those things, either. It is a place, like the Harmony Society, where people simply grow old together, once they have decided to enter it, and know that they will have there the support they need as their bodies and minds change. It is also a place, like Harmony and the dream of the Taco Bell Cantinas retirement community, where some degree of wealth generally allows for entry.

An activist who had rallied against Sunoco's Mariner East pipeline, a series of tubes spanning from Ohio to the far eastern edge of Pennsylvania, Alexander came from a Quaker background, and knew as a younger man that he was interested in retiring at Kendal, where his wife's parents spent their final years. The community had Quaker roots, too, and about one-quarter of its residents were Quaker, Alexander told me—"part of the attraction." While Kendal doesn't run like a co-op, exactly (it has a CEO, and a marketing person who was glad I had found their brand, and it was, in fact, a collection of thirteen such places across the country, all operating individually but under the awning of the Kendal Corporation), a sense of resident participation and autonomy, as well as an interest in egalitarianism, seemed to power the place. "A lot of stuff that goes on here is run by the residents when you might expect it would be done by management," Alexander told me. For instance: It was the residents who handled the AV in the auditorium. Residents sat on committees in charge of dining, buildings, and energy. At one point during Covid, the community at Kendal at Longwood figured out it could run for about two and a half years just on its surplus, without charging fees or bringing in any new residents. It was a place, in other words, that was interested in self-sufficiency. It was like Harmony, maybe, minus Rapp, and silkworms, and nineteenth-century millenarianism.

I was interested in Kendal not just because it seemed like a bright spot but because it was one of the reasons that Pennsylvania nursing homes used relatively few restraints: an almost 98 percent reduction in their use since 1996. In the mid-1980s, Kendal had hired a new director of nursing, a woman named Jill Blakeslee, who as a condition of her employment wanted to take on the issue of restraints. Then fairly standard devices, restraints could be everything from hand mitts or wrist ties to "soft ties," also known as lap belts or vests that attach to bed rails or chairs to tip the older person backward and prevent them from standing up.

Beyond the issue of basic dignity, restraints themselves led to injuries, Blakeslee believed, as in a situation colloquially called "the Houdini," when an older person successfully got themselves out of a complex restraint but hurt themselves in the process. Restraints were technologies, really, that kept older people in long-term care settings constrained, often under the rationale that it was for their own safety. They also allowed, of course, the stretched and overworked nursing staff to tend to matters beyond one person's immediate needs.

Joining Blakeslee was Beryl Goldman, pronounced "Burl." Goldman lives five minutes from Kendal at Crosslands now, but when she took the untitled job there—they recruited her without a specific plan in mind—she lived forty minutes away. She knew, before accepting, that she wanted to work at Kendal. A trained nurse and, by then, a nursing home administrator, Goldman had made a name for herself regionally for insisting, basically, on dignity in congregate care settings. She went to Kendal for six months without any specific responsibilities. "In today's world, this would never happen," she told me. "If I wanted to go in my office and close the door and sleep for the day, I probably could have done that." She slowly filtered into Health Services, under Blakeslee. Kendal was tasked with operating a few nearby facilities, a skilled nursing operation and an assisted living one. Suddenly the director of nursing, Goldman made two things her mission: to do away with staff uniforms and to transition the facilities out of using restraints on residents, which Kendal had never done but which was a more common practice at the other facilities.

She had help. With Blakeslee and Goldman working as active figureheads and organizers, Kendal residents and staff organized a movement they called "Untie the Elderly." Goldman and Blakeslee had both worked in numerous senior settings where restraining residents was de rigueur. They knew that the Quaker-ish retirement community might be exactly the right one to publicly stage alternatives. Alexander told me about how, decades ago at one Kendal facility, one resident, a strong, tall, and agitated man who had dementia, repeatedly tried to escape, which worried his wife, the staff, and other residents. He had been effectively subdued at the hospital from which he was being transferred, and his wife insisted that Kendal use the restraints she'd brought with her, but Kendal—in what I would learn was its somewhat typical way—gently refused. The resultant plan they put into action was, in some ways, complex. Writing about it on his blog, George Alexander quoted Goldman's summary:

> A . . . 14-hour, highly-detailed, individualized care plan . . . included coffee in the morning with the administrator or an administrative staff person, riding in the bus while other residents were being transported to doctor appointments, attending scheduled programs with his spouse and friends, working with the maintenance department on the community campus preparing soil, planting bushes and trees, and other basic garden tasks. All departments were involved

> for one or more 30-minute periods of each day. Caring for him was a shared responsibility that built comradery among everyone in the community and gave great support and relief to his concerned wife.

In 1989, when Kendal took the Untie the Elderly movement to the Senate's Special Committee on Aging, Goldman was prepared to speak. So were the stalwarts of the industry that Goldman and company were attempting to disrupt. Reading through the transcripts now makes for bizarre moments of humor. A risk manager, professing to not being a very good public speaker, had spoken with his legal counsel. "We maybe suggested a different title" for the symposium, he said, "from the risk management perspective." That title was Untie the Elderly, Tie Up the Attorneys. Arnold Silverman, of Skil-Care, a manufacturer of "a broad range of patient safety and comfort products," noted he would be concentrating his remarks to three areas: responsibility, input, and operations. "These, by the way, form the very attractive acronym of RIO, which, quite honestly, is where I'd rather be right now," said Silverman. "It sure beats being a restraint manufacturer at an Untie the Elderly symposium."

In just three months, as part of the antirestraint work, Goldman had transitioned a nursing home that Kendal was managing from restraints to no restraints. Later, this facility would become a Kendal property. It was from this experience, and Goldman's track record of rooting out restraints at eight other facilities in the Delaware Valley, that she spoke. "In all of these facilities," she said, "they have not increased staff because restraints have been eliminated, and they have not experienced any increase in cost because of it."

What did happen was that the residents and staff simply moved and lived in different ways than they had before. There were fewer bedsores, more time spent doing activities, less depression, less medication, and, among staff Goldman surveyed, a "tremendous feeling of their own self-worth."

When she spoke with me about Untie the Elderly, Goldman was slightly unnerved—she was doing a presentation to Kendal at Longwood in a few days, about precisely the same thing. George Alexander would be in attendance. So would I, if I could figure out which person to ask for the Zoom info. I got the impression, from George's blog and elsewhere, that Kendal fashioned itself an intentional community in the same way that an expensive liberal arts college did. But talking to Goldman, I found my assumptions of a preciousness or self-righteousness challenged. In her wood-paneled kitchen, she wore a tie-dyed sweatshirt and assessed me wryly. She remembered how she had thought to herself, "I don't like old people," when she had first been offered the chance to start working among them. She clarified. "It was less about them being old, more about the culture" of those places, pre-Kendal, which, she would learn, actually "provided a homelike environment, which everyone said they did everywhere, whether they do or not . . . And they also believed in promoting self-esteem and dignity and self-worth by not using physical restraints."

Brusque and serious about her beliefs—Goldman was Jewish, but considered herself half Quaker—she felt that she fit at Kendal, that it allowed her to move with purpose. Now retired, she was called in more than occasionally to consult on lawsuits about restraints for both the families and the nursing homes, and to work with the Center for Medicare and Medicaid Services when a nursing home sues the government agency upon losing a star in its rating. "Take the money that you [would have given] to all these attorneys," Goldman might advise the nursing home, "and fix your problem."

Of course, she said, people looked askance at Kendal in particular leading the antirestraint charge. No Kendal facility—other than the one it acquired and renamed Barclay Friends, which Goldman turned around in three months—had ever used restraints. It was clearly of a separate stratum than many of the homes it advised. In fact, I had, I remembered, seen an ad for Kendal at Oberlin on rotation in *The New Yorker* for longer than I could remember, alongside the magazine's notices about "the secretly famous cashmere watchcap" and "Sublime . . . luxury barge cruises" through the waterways of Alsace-Lorraine and Burgundy. The whole thing was, in Goldman's summary, "Quakerish," emphasizing social reform, but also underlined by the kind of ease abetted by no small amount of wealth. "'Of course you could do it at Kendal,'" Goldman remembered skeptics saying: "'You're Quaker.' I'm not sure what that meant," she said. Basically some version of "'You're a CCRC [Continuing Care Retirement Community] . . . You have more money, you can do it.'" As a result, Goldman told me, she had been "very careful" to study a mixture of facilities: small, medium, large, owned by the county, for profit, nonprofit, private pay, Medicaid. "The goal was to show," she said, "that regardless of the type of mix or the financial status of the organization, you could get rid of restraints."

But there was a bigger issue at play, Goldman said. It was philosophical more than anything else. "Where we get lost," said Goldman, is in the idea of "taking care of poor old people" at all. "I want to vomit every time," she told me, every time she heard a nursing home say they brought children in to entertain residents. It's as little kids, she said, that we get taught that we have to *care*—in that particular way, that patronizing way—for older people. "I want us to do things *with* children," she said. "I want us to learn together."

Now she was being asked, she said, when she'd be coming to Kendal. As in, when she would start living there herself. A video on the Kendal website illustrated its long, beautiful trails that the residents maintained, cultural programming they decided on, gigantic personal looms that residents could create bright weavings with, shop class, a library, a pond, a sweet location next to Longwood Gardens.

Goldman paused, contemplating the likelihood of her own admission to Kendal. "We'll wait and see," she said. "I think it's the best long-term care organization anywhere." Fundamentally, there were limitations on personal freedom within the walls—however broad and communally agreed-upon—of any institution. Like the dining room being kept locked except for mealtime. For now, Goldman, who had seen the entire landscape of care, wanted to stay in her own house, on her own schedule. "Kendal's not utopia," she said. "It's probably close, but it's not."

I visited. The entire length of the tour—which lasted about thirty minutes, and after which I just sat there, waiting to be kicked out, and never was—I felt overcome by something strange and strong. A deep yearning and a deep shame, that classic combination that usually spells out the exact shape of your loneliness. Everywhere, older people in nice clothing seemed to be happy. They smiled with one another. Some swam in the pool. Some cleared brush on the trails outside. Some received medical care. Some painted in an art studio so stocked with materials, so fragrant with wood, it drew out, slowly, the sense of a memory I did not have. It reminded me of Mary Ann, who sent her kids to a Quaker high school not far away, in Philadelphia, where she also taught art. That was not my memory: I hadn't even seen the school, I had just seen the echo of it on my grandmother's face while she spoke. Past and present seemed, here, to swirl for me, the fleshy hellebores in the mulched beds outside. Something of a past I knew, vaguely, and something of a future I personally and most people I knew would never be able to attain. I had not saved enough money. I had no idea what the future, for me, looked like. This was the thing that kept me moving from place to place, till I landed in Pittsburgh, where it sank in, and became bigger, and less clear. The fear was about aging; it was also a fear about the future; but more than either of these things, it was a fear of how these two things intertwined for me and for everyone. This was the fear that I did not know how to quell. That I could prepare as best I could and still not be able to control where I ended up, and how. Perhaps I would fail.

It is clear that I am not alone in my fear—and that the fear is a blend of classism and stigma and reality. It is concerned with autonomy, with remaining outside the control of people and institutions who tell us what is best. Some people have managed to go a long while without maybe having to negotiate such things. Other people, less so. Still, no one "dreams" about ending up in a nursing home, said that op-ed writer in *The New York Times*. The "places" have become partial proxies for the people they hold. The fear is not just of a building but of becoming someone inside it, a member of a group of people who, in Margaret Morganroth Gullette's words, "are possibly (with the exception of older prisoners, or unhoused older people) the most ostracized, misunderstood, stigmatized, stereotyped, and, alas, easily forgotten."

Denise Cox, the SEIU leader, emailed me years after I first met her. She told me that Brighton, the nursing home where she had first really learned about this part of the eldercare world, and the facility that later sank so disastrously during Covid, was closing. "They are trying to figure out where they are going to place 400 residents," she wrote. A news article announced that piles of trash had been seen inside and outside the facility; the daughter of one Brighton resident who was noncommunicative after a stroke, noted that the trash stacked up to the ceiling. As of this writing, Brighton is open, and was given 70 health citations in the last twelve months (again, the national average is 9.5).

And I touched base, too, with Big Wrinkles. He was a nursing home administrator now, at a small (forty-two-bed) nonprofit nursing home. The nonprofit actually tried to meet the staffing standards, he said: They tried really hard.

Big Wrinkles spoke while ordering ice cream for the residents at an artisanal shop right by the river in the town where he now worked. "If I could do the Cookie Monster in a cone, I'll be a happy boy," he told the person taking his order, then turned back to me, over the phone. He described the feeling of working in nursing homes, right now, as being in a boat with a leak. The rate of water pouring in was really fast, he said: There simply weren't enough people to work the difficult, low-paying jobs, and in any case, some gigantic statistic of older people wanted to age at home, but there weren't enough home health aides either, and *they* were vastly underpaid.

"I was working at a hospitality tech start-up and then my grandma ended up at a nursing home and now I'm a nursing home administrator," Big Wrinkles told me, with a bit of disbelief. "People get really sucked in and have a natural desire to improve that which they experience." Now he was interviewing all the residents of the nursing home and their families: This was a priority in his quest for "patient-centered care," a term he acknowledged everyone liked to throw around. He seemed notably more straightforward, slightly more calm, or maybe depressed (about "the dismantling of public services and our national generosity") than a few years earlier, when I had first met him and he'd stridden across the Upper West Side with me, gesticulating as he talked about culture change. He was now a nursing home administrator who didn't really seem to believe in nursing homes. In fact, Big Wrinkles was developing an alternative that he was calling Grandpods. The idea was that a group of six or eight people, all living in their own homes, would form the basis for a shared home care service. Two home health aides, a wheelchair-accessible vehicle, and shared efficient care in rotating locations: one person's home one day, a museum outing the next. I asked about the feasibility of such an idea: I was wondering about government reimbursement, and the people who might need more care than a museum setting might be able to host. The inability to find a single good solution for the very diverse range of needs people had was, increasingly, what I couldn't figure out. *All* the options for aging distilled into very few, the longer you looked through the lens of finances: There were varieties of assisted living, living at home, and living in a nursing home. They each were entangled with money. It was a fragmented system; no *one* solution existed for Person A and Person B both, and wouldn't, as long as the system proceeded as it is. Some spoke of abolishing nursing homes; in the comments to their op-eds there were always a few people saying some version of "my father had specialized needs and nowhere else to go." Gullette's own argument, in her book *American Eldercide*, about the pandemic's effects in nursing homes, is not that nursing homes need to be eradicated but that a series of structural factors and government decisions, and, maybe most of all, social apathy toward older people contributed to the Covid disaster within their walls. And there would likely always be people—though there didn't have to be—without homes of their own in which to age. "These are the questions I have, too," said Big Wrinkles after a pause. We couldn't talk long: He needed to get the rapidly melting ice cream to the residents. I couldn't totally understand if they were somewhere outside or waiting for him back at the facility. He presented a reverie of sorts instead, a memory of his that I got pulled into as he spoke: Apparently, he told me, they used to go to another ice cream spot, which happened to be right next to a speed trap. "The residents would just watch people get pulled over and get tickets," said Big Wrinkles. "They fucking loved it. There's so much joy in the little unpredictabilities . . . Because it just represents, like, that which is unknown and uncontrolled. That is what we strip right now from people in the name of keeping them safe."

3

FAMILY ON DEMAND, WOODEN TEETH, MEMORIES OF A FARM

Big Wrinkles emphasized how experiencing unpredictabilities could underscore one's autonomy. Before, as a writer and a person, I had courted these kinds of unforecastable moments. But here in Pittsburgh, now that I was mostly completely alone, they sometimes destabilized my long-standing sense of my own resilient solitude, my own desired sense of passive and writerly molecule-ness. Perhaps it was not in my interest to be so alone, despite the comfort or pride I took in it.

One morning in winter, my dog, Helgi, and I were attacked by another dog, loosed from his leash by a heavy-eyed owner. As I tried to get the German shepherd away from my dog's belly, I fell over and over again, as if in a slapstick cartoon, onto the ice-glazed sidewalk, getting up, then falling down once more, so that in the following days, we both needed to recover, my dog with a shaved, soaped, and bitten belly, me with impossibly swollen, blackened knees. Gingerly, and working to avoid being pulled by him onto another ice patch, I trundled up to the neighborhood baseball diamond to gently exercise him there with a ball, and to also exercise my own mind against the creeping sense that my proclivities for solitude were no longer serving me.

Whenever we went to that diamond, I would happenstantially meet people: neighbors I eventually kind of got to know. Steve seeded plants in the depths of winter that would come to bloom and fruit before anyone else's. Corey and I often ran our dogs around together.

It was at the diamond too that I met an older couple—Frank and Kathy. They stood on the other side of the fence and watched from afar as I threw the ball for my dog, who noticed them before I did. Helgi, as he often did, reacted: He would have lunged and sprinted toward them had I not managed to get his leash back on, but he pulled and pulled, wanting to run toward this silent couple and their barking dog. Still, they did not move. I found myself getting annoyed: They could see that they were agitating my dog, and that we were not in fact able to do anything now, for as long as they continued to stand there. "Can you go the fuck away," I said to myself, then wondered if the wind might pull my words into their ears. "Wa!" I heard back. "What . . . you . . . !" Calling words back and forth through the chain-link fence, we held a short and, to me, mysterious conversation. "Lucy," I shouted toward them. "Yeah!" I got an email from Frank the next day. He had perused my website, he said, where he found my contact information. He liked my writing. He and his wife wanted to take me out for Christmas Eve dinner somewhere downtown, where they had a steak-and-shrimp special.

It was a kind offer, though a little full-blown. It was true that most nights I steered through the new-to-me sensation of not being able to bear the weight of my own mind. I thought I was lonely, and that my chickens were coming home to roost. That my tendency to push people away had manifested a reality in which I had no one to count on, or ask for help. Those nights sitting in the comfort of my loneliness were oddly special, I feel now, in retrospect. I remember the late afternoon sun hitting the slightly mud-crusted floorboards near the door, and the wobbling bookshelf from Target holding my lifelong collection of journals. A slightly musty smell, like sheets that have sat for a long time in a closet, hung in the house. I had a growing pride in the place; it was small enough that nothing felt redundant, and every object had its spot. As darkness hit, I lay on the pink couch or on my bed, in the rainbow glow of a cheap oil diffuser tooting its steam into the ether, and I wondered how I got here, and what would be next. Now, looking back, I think I was bored, frustrated by the amount of time I was sitting in my own mind, and somewhat unimaginative about how to fix that problem. To some degree, I was lonely, but really it was something else, something harder to define. All the friends I had ever made rushed through my mind at night like high tide, and when I emerged in the morning, in Pittsburgh, by myself again, it was with the cold spare sweep of a beach in winter, water in the far distance.

I did not want just *anyone* to come and keep me company. And neither, honestly, did I want to go out for dinner with these strangers, from whom I sensed a motive of some kind. I put off responding. Another email came in, this time from Kathy, who had mistakenly included me in a response to Frank's invitation:

> So you need to ask her pronoun too these days. Even if you think you know it.
>
> Lol

It took my breath away: weird, mean-spirited. Jarring, in the sense that I usually forgot what I looked like, and had no idea how other people perceived me. Usually, I didn't feel like a woman, but

I also didn't really think about it. More than anything, the email felt incomprehensible. The messages preceding Kathy's accidental transmission had been friendly. There had been nothing stated about gender, or pronouns, and there had been no stiltedness or offense. I flashed back to them standing on the other side of the chain-link fence, watching impassively as I tried to keep my barking dog close to my side. I had found throughout my life that when you are alone, people want things from you. Ironically, this realization had made me retract further sometimes, become *more* alone, in a way that, again ironically, people tended to pick up on. In Frank's first email, he noted how he and Kathy could serve as a "source of support."

Over the next few months, I avoided them, once even crouching behind a bush. But our neighborhood was small, and my routes through it were deeply grooved. All you had to do was look out your window to see me striding on one of our two or three routes to know where I'd be at 7:30 in the morning, or noon, or 4 p.m. One morning, Frank came up behind me, driving a black van whose sliding door could not close all the way, moving jarringly back and forth with the Pittsburgh topography. It careened back as he pulled up, exposing a car body full of plastic barrels and trash; he leaned out the window and put his hand over his heart as he asked me if he had caused offense. I remember the hurt questioning in his eyes. To me, it looked false in a way, true in another. *Oh my god, no, no*, I assured him, hearing and nearly almost seeing how false *I* was, for one of the longest-standing acts of my life: the pretending to be grateful for human contact, when really I am trying to figure out if I am simply more comfortable alone.

In his book Going Solo, sociologist Eric Klinenberg writes of the "fear of losing one's independence," and how the "fantasies . . . of self-reliance, or the self-made man . . . lead us to ignore the webs of interdependency that give even the most antisocial among us the strength to go it alone." Klinenberg and one of his researchers call it the "tyranny of independence," the way that certain people, living alone, do not admit that they need help: particularly, in Klinenberg's words, the "less healthy elderly singletons." Then there are the shut-ins, whom Klinenberg spent years trying to find, in New York City. Upon speaking with male shut-ins in particular, Klinenberg found they had much in common: "a spouse lost to death or divorce," weak ties to children, "a small or nonexistent friendship network," illness, and, notably, a "repellant personality." In his conversations with shut-in Guy in his Manhattan Chinatown apartment, Klinenberg notes how the older man makes racist proclamations (then clarifies that they're jokes), goes on political rants, and can be "playful, but in a cruel, disdainful way." "Although he says he enjoys having company," writes Klinenberg, Guy "cannot help but drive you away."

My fear was not becoming a shut-in, entirely. I did not envision that fate for myself. But I did envision myself alone as an older person, and when I was feeling particularly detailed, I imagined myself sweeping, for some reason, the wood floor of the Maine cabin where I lived, with a scratchy straw broom. That part of the fantasy—if it was a fantasy—was honestly ridiculous (I had traveled to Maine once, for about two days, on a writing assignment), but the root of it was very real. Aloneness seemed a complicated, correct fate for someone like me, who was difficult. I often couldn't seem to stand the requirements of serious interpersonal work, and wanted, always, to swim a little farther out in a different direction. I had never been afraid of being alone before, and had in fact fetishized this aspect myself, particularly during a four-year period in Iowa where I probably insufferably spoke of living in a "spinster's cottage." But now I was feeling something new: a deepening inkling that I had maybe lived in the wrong way, collecting nice but not particularly deep friendships, and returning always to myself at the end of the day. Things could go wrong, and I would have, I suddenly worried with the feeling of a boulder sinking into my stomach, not really anyone at all.

My great-aunt, on her deathbed, whispered to my grandmother Mary Ann, "I was so mean," and her words ricocheted sometimes inside me. I too could make it to age seventy-five and realize I had made a horrible decision to prioritize my own independence over everything else. What if, so independent, a health issue or something else meant that I could suddenly no longer garden, couldn't drive, couldn't go interview someone, couldn't play music? What if all I could do was what I sometimes felt I was doing now—sitting inside my own brain without respite, becoming more and more annoyed at my own patterns and limitations and idiocies? What if my tyrannical independence, to use Klinenberg's words, which held more than a slight echo of things that various ex-boyfriends had told me, was the wrong strategy with which to build a life? And, finally, how, as a woman (?) who did not like being told what to do, or asked to extend herself and her time and her emotions toward people she did not particularly care about—how would this recalcitrance, sometimes termed by those ex-boyfriends as selfishness, serve me? Perhaps I would end up somewhere I did not plan to end, with no one holding my hand, and no one to even whisper my regrets to. My loneliness, if that's what it was, had to do with the future, I felt, more than the past. I was proud to be proceeding in the way I seemed to be; I was also increasingly terrified of it. And the more I felt like I suddenly wanted company, someone to talk with, the more I didn't really recognize myself. It was just as Garielle Lutz notes in her book *Backwardness*, of the feeling she had wandering solo around Pittsburgh in her sixties: "Suspicions . . . that nobody could count on themselves to be who they really were, that the margins of every error kept getting wider and wider the older you got."

• • •

Many evenings, driving from one side of Pittsburgh to another, on some far-flung errand devised to distract myself, I hollered along to my *Darkness on the Edge of Town* CD, felt mildly euphoric and proud of myself for being analog, parked the car, then settled into another night of figuring out how to be alone in my own brain. I often pondered Frank and Kathy's offer, and what it had hinted about *me*: Solitary woman in need of friends? Ambiguous person open to being dominated by the opaque desires of her neighbors? The hints I had gotten about *them* were of a different sort than the ones I sometimes got from Ancestry.com, about the birth and death certificates of long-lost relatives, more just discomforting details about how they acted and what they might want from me. They wanted, it seemed, connection of a kind I was unwilling to give. But always I wondered if I *should* give it: if this was what was expected of me not just interpersonally but socially.

After all, we were living through an "epidemic," the recent surgeon general Vivek Murthy argued: an epidemic of loneliness. And it was killing people, as epidemics do. To Murthy, loneliness came from "human connection [being] edged out," "racing to be current," and social media. In an article in the *Harvard Business Review*, Murthy argued that "new models of work—such as telecommuting and some on-demand 'gig economy' contracting arrangements—have created flexibility but often reduce the opportunities for in-person interaction and relationships." Work, he said, was "part of the problem. Now it must be part of the solution." I contemplated this: but as a freelance writer I could do little to find in-person community, besides, I guess, pay money I didn't have to go to a coworking space among other millennials on their laptops.

As a void, loneliness asks how it might be filled. Beyond the workplace things, I saw Murthy suggest potlucks, texting someone a note of gratitude, and turning to a free meditation on the Calm app, with which he officially partnered to develop five short exercises. It was in this context that I was delivered an ad that would pull me through the loneliness epidemic, through my own fears around solitude, and through my own confusing inadequacies around human connection. A company named Papa wanted to address, even solve, the loneliness epidemic, and had placed an ad on Facebook. They were hiring what they called "Pals." Pals were workers who went into the homes of "Papas"—older adults often living alone. The company's mission, the website said, was to provide its older adult members, the Papas, with caring, compassionate people, living and breathing antidotes to loneliness who could be hired by the hour. At first, Papa called these people "grandkids on-demand." Originally, the Pals were meant to be college kids working under the noble mission of "the precious compact between the generations," as elder activist Maggie Kuhn once called it. The company wanted "the highest quality individuals" from its pool of student workers, a version of its website from 2017 said. The students would be "carefully selected and vetted . . . We seek students who have a specific health related focuses [*sic*] of study. We feel that students of higher education are best suited to provide care to your elderly loved ones. They have career goals to be in a similar setting and will continually strive for excellence."

By the time the ad found me, in the place, in my tiny house, where all media found me—my bed—Papa's outlook had shifted, and the company no longer selected college-aged "grandkids" specifically. Just anyone of any working age really, to members, who were also literally anyone, from all fifty states, and were sometimes given the option to hire a Pal through their insurance plans. At the time that I first heard of Papa, information was minimal, besides some basics. Firstly, Papa was a unicorn start-up—a private company worth more than $1 billion. The company itself was quite young, birthed in 2017. "I don't want to say that Covid was the reason we grew," said Andrew Parker, Papa's CEO, in a *Forbes* article. But if it was, this wasn't unusual: The Brookings Institution reported that in the first nearly two years of the pandemic, twenty-two large companies all employing frontline workers enriched their shareholders by $1.5 trillion (their workers received less than 2 percent of those gains). I wasn't sure if Papa's workers were frontline, necessarily, but talk of loneliness had seemed to blossom during the pandemic, and it was into this issue that the company leaned.

"I just think that anyone that didn't believe in loneliness, or isolation definitely does now because all of us have experienced it," Parker continued. In the past few years, it had seemed to me sometimes that Covid began to stand for "loneliness," particularly for people who had been spared the experience of losing a loved one: Maybe loneliness was the injury everyone could agree on, an injury made more acute by the context, but also something that everyone surely already understood, to some degree. Indeed: "No one's going to debate whether loneliness is an issue," said Parker in a 2022 interview with one of his funders, the venture capital firm Initialized. "I call loneliness the only universal disease. Almost everyone's felt it in some capacity, so it's an interesting problem to solve." "Cure loneliness," the company's website said. "Taking Action Against Loneliness," read the headline of one blank page. Loneliness was a kernel burning brightly inside the lives and minds of older adults living alone, we were to understand.

(Later, Parker would write me that "the traditional healthcare system is designed to treat illness, but it largely overlooks the social determinants of health—factors like loneliness, access to transportation, and food insecurity—that disproportionately drive health outcomes." Papa had reduced loneliness among many of its members, he wrote. "In a randomized, controlled study of chronically ill members, 69% reported a significant reduction in loneliness after using Papa's services, while 39% reported no longer being lonely at all . . . From the beginning, our mission has been to create a new kind of care, built on human connection, in service of our vision of a world where no one has to go it alone. That hasn't changed. It has expanded. Papa Pals, drawn from the same communities as the members they serve, provide personalized support where and when it's needed most, from a ride to a doctor's appointment to a listening ear at home.")

The only thing was, older adults were actually far less lonely than, for instance, Gen Z. A 2018 survey by Cigna, which would lay the groundwork for so much loneliness epidemic writing and reporting and thinking, announced that, generationally, the loneliness rankings, from high to low, went like this: Gen Z, millennials, Gen X, boomers, Greatest Generation. I was struck by the implication, which I began to see everywhere, that older people were inherently lonely despite stark evidence to the contrary. "Loneliness . . . is a grim fact of life for the old," writes Paul Bloom in *The New Yorker*, arguing that AI solutions to loneliness are potentially dangerous for the young but "humane" for the "elderly or the cognitively impaired."

But the survey in which the loneliness epidemic was rooted revealed that it was young people who were loneliest! And youngish people, like me! So why, I wondered, the insistence that it was *old* people who lay in their beds alone each night, staring at the wall, who went weeks without speaking to a soul, who wandered the streets of their neighborhood forlorn, whose visages could be easily assessed for a pitiful sadness, who tried and failed to get close to people and then maybe eventually stopped, who were alone on Christmas? (On Christmas Eve I went out, across the city to a street tucked up behind Millvale, and bought a dozen oysters and a knife, and slurped them with a briny, spiny sort of solitude the next day.)

Then again, even the assertion that Gen Z is the loneliest group, bobbing in the unbearably still waters of an ocean of loneliness, is more complicated than it seems. According to scholar Claude S. Fischer, such worries about an epidemic of loneliness have long preoccupied Americans. In 2012 he chronicled a rash of literature asserting it was already upon us (just like it had been upon us, he noted, in the middle of the twentieth century, the early twentieth century, "and so on, ever back in time . . . Americans have either been getting lonelier since time immemorial or worrying about it since then"). And the 2018 Cigna loneliness survey results, Fischer noted, rested on how you interpreted the word "sometimes." Glancing at the survey, I saw his point: Respondents had occasionally answered "always" to queries of how often they felt that "no one really knows you well," that they feel "alone," that they "lack companionship," and that "there is no one you can turn to." But *by far* the larger response category to these questions was "sometimes." In other words: I sometimes feel lonely. I sometimes feel bad. In reports of the results, the "sometimes" responses were lumped together with the "always" responses. The effect, in Fischer's words, was a "scary estimate" of American loneliness. "Resulting newspaper headlines would have evoked different reactions if they had read 'About half of Americans are rarely if ever lonely; almost all the rest are sometimes lonely'"—an imaginary headline that the real survey data supported.

In any case, before the Cigna survey came out, loneliness was not something that Papa *could* solve. This was not because of loneliness's intractability in the American psyche as much as it was about the bureaucratic systems in place. In 2017, Papa was stuck at a smaller scale, because of what was considered "sick." Its website:

> Since individuals who require non-medical home care are not sick in the traditional sense, traditional health insurance programs such as Medicare and Medicaid do not provide coverage for their needs. Medicare does not pay for non-medical home care, meal delivery, housecleaning services or any other personal care needs. Because Papa offers strictly non-medical services at this time, we do not qualify for these government reimbursements.

What was sick in the "traditional sense" would change, in 2019, when the Centers for Medicaid and Medicare altered their reimbursement structure to more fully address social determinants of health. The CHRONIC Care Act, passed in 2018, allowed a broader spread of services, including telemedicine, to be covered by insurance companies working through Medicare Advantage, the privatized arm of Medicare. "You know times are changing when a health plan starts paying for dog food, as Anthem and its affiliated health plans will do in some markets this year," announced the Commonwealth Fund in 2020. Now, unlike before, through Papa and similar enterprises, insurance companies could be reimbursed by the federal government for addressing nonmedical things: a development falling under the "social determinants of health" idea, that general understanding that finding and understanding the many complex needs of a person beyond their medical ones could be important to their general health and well-being. And so companies like Papa, shifted by these redrawn lines and the bloom of collective loneliness during the pandemic, suddenly became a necessary service, a central rather than peripheral form of care.

• • •

There are many beautiful qualities to Pittsburgh that I miss, now, as if the city were a person. In retrospect, the richness of Pittsburgh astounds me: the city's bounce between softness (fall) and hardness (winter), the long stretches of rain and the way that the moisture, as well as feet of river-deposited soil, help almost any plant grow. Then there are the ways that entire neighborhoods are visible as you're approaching them in the car, so that the city looks to be a collage of styles and history and color. There is a closeness between the history here and the surfaces of the city: plaques commemorating old marketplaces and vanished air-conditioning companies, strikes, and closed-up mines.

I felt this closeness acutely on my way to the Papa recruiting session I had seen advertised on Facebook. The session was held in a place called the Waterfront, a gargantuan stretch of strip mall spanning three municipalities fronting the Monongahela River. Here, rumor on the internet had it, sat one of the best-performing Dave and Buster's locations in the country, and a vast restaurant called Storming Crab where you could order gator meat. You had to work to get to this long, thick fingernail of land. It was empty-feeling, a non-neighborhood, a strip mall with a river view and seemingly devoid of cars until you nearly got stampeded by them all rushing around a corner in slow motion. But little strangenesses nested here: Once, I saw a wild turkey crossing the road in front of the Giant Eagle grocery store, and later, I would meet an old man, David, who described, in a watery kind of way, a life lived right here, before it was "here," in a house overrun by crabgrass.

The past was very present here: The Waterfront is punctuated visually by a set of twelve mammoth smokestacks, so big and so alone that the eye is tempted to skip over them to make them make sense. These smokestacks mark this land as belonging, once, to the Carnegie Steel Company. The stretch of land was once the site of the

Homestead Steel Works, and of the famous Homestead Strike of 1892, where Andrew Carnegie and Henry Clay Frick tried to break the back of the union. They locked out workers from the steel mill during contract negotiations. The workers withdrew. The company sent in a few flotillas of Pinkertons, for whom a crowd of workers and their families waited in the darkness—and shots were fired, people killed, the workers winning, kind of, the Wikipedia page endlessly updated today to neutralize the language.

I walked into the hotel conference room where the Papa information session would take place. I was a writer, I told the group of men, Papa company representatives. "When are we ordering lunch?" one kept saying, barely looking up from his computer. A kind man asked me some questions, took my picture, and gave me a shirt. "Family on Demand," it read, in the cutely chunky font of all the many companies that call themselves, first and foremost, platforms.

There was something poignant and obviously ironic to my solitude, that day, as the lone potential worker. This was gig work, work that kept workers removed from one another, as Murthy had pointed at in the *Harvard Business Review*, signaling that this was, in fact, a cause to what he called the loneliness epidemic. In the hotel conference room, I could have met my fellow potential-Pals, I suppose, but even that would have been, very likely, the only time I might have absorbed their company. Later, sitting alone on my bed, I turned to the Papa Facebook page, which held absurdities in the comments dangling off the company's posts and customer reviews—reviews that were very often written, it seemed, by both its workers and its clients.

This was a fascinating, though unverifiable, place to wander. One comment, in particular, snagged me: a woman who wrote that she had been contacted by the company at around 5 a.m., and called back "trying to find out how my name got put on the list after reading review stating that people have had someone show up from this company when they did not sign up for it." On a later day, she wrote, she then received a message at 5:08 a.m. announcing that she had an appointment with a Pal. "I am not in need of a caregiver," she wrote, asking to be put on a Do Not Call list.

Yet she would not have received, exactly, a caregiver, had someone shown up at her door. "Your visits will NOT involve anything such as administering medication or hands-on contact with a member. No previous health care training is required," read a line on the company's website—in other words, this was nonmedical work. In fact, continued the website, a Pal's work might consist of engaging in great conversations, helping a Papa send an email, driving a Papa to the grocery store, or light cleaning. The work was meant to supplement traditional caregiving, and to quench a tide of loneliness racing across the land. Many reviews online mentioned housecleaning. Photos abounded: smiling while playing chess games, doing yoga, grocery shopping. "No one," said the website, "can do it alone."

One of my neighbors, who I met at what I had begun to refer to, in my head, as the "dog diamond," learned what I was focused on, though I generally found it hard to explain. "Um, like, loneliness and old people," I would say when pressed. "Aw," some people would respond. "Yeah, that's grim." The neighbor told me she worked in geriatrics, and had a friend, a social worker, who I should talk to. This was how I began to speak with H over the phone. Each time I spoke with her I felt a rush of energy. It was something about her voice—raspy and warm, and she took a few seconds to think about what I was saying before responding. "One thousand percent," she'd affirm, "one thousand percent," and I'd try to figure out if she had a slight

New York accent, or if it was just an old Pittsburgh one. "If you ever want to meet in person," I said, but she demurred the first time—she had lung trouble, and was extra careful about avoiding Covid. The next time, she didn't give any kind of reason, other than it was clear to both of us how difficult it was for her to find any free time.

H worked specifically with older adults to find and secure them housing, to coordinate with their care teams, and to generally understand the qualities of their lives—their needs, the way their needs were and were not being met, how she and her connections might be able to help. She could run through the list of senior care options in Pittsburgh, spit facts about their bed numbers, their histories, and their attributes. Occasionally, she got very serious. The county-run nursing homes here, she said, had made magnificent changes. "I have no compunction," she said, about referring someone there. "Other nursing homes," H said, "it will break your heart. This is no bullshit." She put it to me this way: "I have nothing positive to say about the majority of the nursing homes. Unless you can pay. You are taking your life in your hands if you are going in as a low-income individual." Such people, she told me, "are between a rock and a hard place. Do I stay home and have inconsistent caregivers come in, or do I have inconsistent or poor care in a nursing home?" She spoke frequently, to me and to others, about her "hesitation about even referring people to long-term care."

If older adults did stay in their homes, H described how difficult it was to construct a comprehensive landscape of caregiving, one often plagued by inconsistency, low wages, and the sudden disappearances of caregivers. I asked her about Papa. Yes, she said, she was familiar. She had had one or two clients use the service. One of the Pals, she remembered, was really wonderful. She was really great at what she did. "But when she left," H remembered, "it was really difficult for the client because she did not understand the role that Papa had played in her care. She thought that this person was long-term." After the Pal's abrupt departure, H called Papa herself, because she (H) was "undone." There were a few things, she said, that she had an issue with. "One was my understanding that the insurance company provides the patients' information to Papa. I felt as though that was . . . a boundary issue," H told me.

In 2019, a program called Direct Contracting arose, later to be retooled and renamed ACO REACH. ACO REACH came under fire from certain corners of the medical and political world for allegedly upcoding patients, that is, defining them as sick in ways that they might not really have been, or, rather, collecting more data on them to imply sickness where none needed to be pointed out. Then, the insurance company and contractor would bill the federal government, through Medicare, for these medical issues. Direct Contracting also was criticized for signing up patients for health services without their knowledge. Richard Gilfillan and Don Berwick, writing in *Health Affairs*, titled this the "Medicare Gold Rush." The Direct Contracting Model, they wrote, was a "vehicle for privatizing Medicare's projected 2028 $1.6 trillion spend." Progressives in the House of Representatives wrote, similarly critically, that ACO REACH sanctioned "third-party middlemen to manage care without seniors' full understanding or prior consent, and often through for-profit businesses with incentives to restrict care."

One ACO REACH affiliate, Pearl Health ("democratizing access to value in healthcare"), mentioned several companies, including Papa, in a philosophical 2022 musing about Pearl Health's future, and the future of Medicare.

> The healthcare system will increasingly wire engagements to be opt-out vs. opt-in . . . Organizations like Lyft, Uber, Capsule, and

> others will increasingly integrate with medical providers to minimize fail points along an individual's care journey. Other programs will seek to expand the reliability and complexity of home-based care, allowing services to come to patients, an inversion of the typical paradigm. Addressing mental and behavioral health drivers like loneliness and social isolation will increasingly be considered a core component of effective primary and preventative care. Organizations like Papa will increasingly move from novel to mainstream as a way of prolonging longevity and preventing chronic conditions.

I asked Papa, which was not a member of ACO REACH, about how they contacted their prospective clients. Valentina Pecoraro, director of operations at Papa, told me over email that "when a health plan or employer partners with Papa, they share an eligibility file that lists members who qualify for the service . . . Papa only receives this information in compliance with strict data privacy and security standards, and solely for the purpose of delivering the benefit." Then Papa member specialists contact these members over the phone to "inform them of their eligibility, share more information on our services, assess their needs to ensure we can cater to them, and if the member is interested, enroll them in Papa and schedule their first visit."

In other words, in one vision of the future care came to *you*, and if you didn't want it, you *opted out*. I was reminded of a quote from a book I was reading at the time, Leonora Carrington's *The Hearing Trumpet*, wherein the narrator is moved, against her wishes, into a nursing home. "I am never lonely," that narrator says. "Or rather, I never suffer from loneliness. I suffer much from the idea that my loneliness might be taken away from me by a lot of mercilessly well-meaning people."

The rebuttal to any worries about an opt-out system of prearranged services, delivered automatically via insurance company, is easy to imagine. How could it be *bad* to receive conversation, and possibly some help around the house, from a stranger who simply arrives at your door? If such things were delivered without you having to arrange it, wasn't that extra wonderful? The questions were weird, poignant ones. I almost didn't trust myself to answer, knowing my own tendencies toward isolation, which were chosen and not accidental. I was not someone who treated all interaction as inherently good, or every conversation like the right-sized plug for my particularly fritzy outlet. I could err far on the side of self-removal, and then, indulgently, call myself lonely. Generally, I kept myself untethered to others, and I found it easiest—not just easiest, but *important*—to sit alone in a room at night, on a couch or a bed, a candle blooming near me and music on the speaker. Much can come from solitude, or it did for me, I felt. I believed I understood Carrington's character deeply: You could be alone and this did not have to be a problem. You could be *lonely* and this did not have to be a problem other people needed to solve. In fact, maybe loneliness was like anger, in our contemporary moment, the slogan ringing in my head: *If you're not angry, you're not paying attention*. If you weren't lonely in one way or another, I felt, you were probably, conversely and horribly ironically, insulated from the very lonely world around you. But given the fact that older people—if we were to use that Cigna survey, or any number of others—were *less* lonely than young people, were we to understand that their "loneliness" was something different, something about a more material isolation that we understood them to have? That maybe, I suspected, we felt guilty about? I thought of Big Wrinkles sneaking his friend out of the nursing home he hated, and of my grandmother Mary Ann's own emotional landscape: not lonely, exactly, and surrounded by people, but rarely emotionally fulfilled. I thought too of a personal care home I visited in Pittsburgh, which had an intergenerational program that the residents loved, though I could recall suddenly the voice of a younger woman there, and the cut-ins of the older residents:

> YOUNGER WOMAN: *Since working with older adults, I absolutely love you guys. Older adults are my best friends. I think you guys are so nice. You understand me!*
>
> OLDER WOMAN [LAUGHING]: *What's to understand?*
>
> YOUNGER WOMAN: *I feel like . . . some people in my generation have a very different attitude, a very different vision of how life should be. And, I don't know . . .*
>
> OLDER WOMAN: *Are they spoiled?*
>
> YOUNGER WOMAN [PAUSING]: *Some are. Yeah, yes.*
>
> OLDER MAN: *Well, they don't know what happens in places like this because they're not here.*
>
> [CACOPHONY: *That's good! They can wait till they get old! Places like this, they've changed over the years, too! After Covid, they brought it in [unintelligible] and then left!*]

Whenever I listened to this interview, the first of many in the personal care home where I'd gone to report a story about oldness in the news media, I found myself smiling: Large sections of the recording were completely, frenetically unusable because residents were talking over one another, often getting into spats that cooled as quickly as they'd begun. There was so much life to the conversations we'd had. They had not totally trusted me. Much of the time I'd sat there sweating, trying to get a word in edgewise. It was less an interview than a freewheeling conversation I was simply listening in on. And the younger woman who sat in on that first session quickly faded away on the recording. I had the sense that while the older residents enjoyed her, and while she felt understood by them, they understood one another in a way that she didn't have full access to. I was particularly struck by the moment when the older woman laughed at the younger one's confession of feeling understood: *What's to understand?*

When she spoke to me about loneliness among older people, H further complicated the picture. She told me how "loneliness can be a part of aging . . . It's a natural part of aging." Think about it, she told me. "Things change. Your friends die." Old age, that massacre. "My mother was in a study club for fifty years. She'd always say, 'I don't want to be the last one alive.' And she was." H laughed grimly. But what older adults dealt with more specifically than loneliness, she told me, was a lack of "resonance." "The people who they have been closest to, their siblings, their friends, when someone dies . . . there are so few people who we have that resonance with. When they're gone . . . We not only feel sad about them being gone. There was part of us that was met, known, and seen. That part has been eclipsed. I often think that that's what happens." Funnily, maybe, when H said this, I realized for the first time that the people I most "resonated" with were all going to die before me, barring some accident. My mother and father, namely, both of whom met, knew, and saw me, in H's words, better than anyone else. The future "eclipse" of which H spoke was different than whatever loneliness I felt now. It was something specific to older age, to losing certain person after certain person.

Many think of the nuclear family, of course, as having some higher possibility for the resonance H described. I had been lucky in that regard, and I saw, suddenly, how the eclipse would come for me, should my parents die before I did. Grief, distending. "Hints" about them delivered to me far in the future. The dissolution, as it is phrased, of the nuclear family has often been cited as a major reason that many older people live alone now, and, by extension, feel loneliness—even though a great number of older people do not want to live with their children, and feel loneliness at a lesser rate than certain younger generations. But many of us did not grow up in families in which we were allowed to be our full selves. Moving further, Mandy Len Catron writes how the nuclear family has actually encouraged loneliness, and how marriage as an institution turns us away from other social ties, citing a study that found that "being single increases the social connections of both women and men . . . single individuals have greater involvement with the broader community." When I read this, I wondered why I often glossed over loneliness in my own tendencies toward solitude. I had thought myself to be a nearly invisible molecule, but I was, in fact, meeting people, and having fun sometimes. I was painting myself with loneliness—why? It lent a kind of sheen to me, I felt, and covered more complicated feelings and realities. Like: I hadn't yet figured myself out, and felt torn between the vision of myself sweeping the floor in Maine and a different one, in which I was surrounded by children and grandchildren and laughing. Like: I was uncomfortable with my own feelings of vulnerability, and with being perceived. Like: I was just a kind of afraid person a lot of the time.

But loneliness was real, of course, and as the Cigna survey illustrated, many people had, at one time or another, felt it—maybe just not *all the time*. Stephen Katz, a Canadian academic focusing on gerontology who I began corresponding with, called loneliness "a kind of black hole, a master concept used to explain or disguise all kinds of other problems for older adults." Pointing to the work of Faye Bound Alberti, Katz wrote elsewhere that the black hole contained nostalgia, homesickness, anger, or mourning, feelings that "change and migrate across bodies, biographies, temporalities, and material environments." There was a long history, Katz wrote, of seeing loneliness as "sedimented into the aging process"—an inevitable part of being old. Like anyone else, an older person might live alone—and perhaps they did so as an active response to a difficult family situation, or to an experience of harm. Other times, living alone was not an active choice so much as the received experience of "spatial isolation and inequality." To Katz, both loneliness and this form of social isolation had roots in "decades of neoliberal austerity and government attacks on health and welfare provisions that weakened the protections for older vulnerable populations." Loneliness had itself been made an individual problem. I was struck in particular by something Katz theorized to me: "The answer to loneliness has been more social engagement . . . but that means that what we call social engagement is also being configured by loneliness." If social engagement was delivered as a "cure" to loneliness, in other words, what of the other kinds of interactions and experiences that just happen without being intended as a *cure*? If social engagement was delivered as a remedy to a specific ailment, then it was to be understood, at some point, as finite, and not all around us—just as loneliness was now a precise and potentially fixable problem, and old age the same, to the longevity community. Perhaps "commodification" is the easiest word to reach for here.

"Be a Friend to the Elderly, Get Paid," ran a 2020 *New York Times* headline about Papa. Around this time, Papa was incubating at Y-Combinator, the famous start-up accelerator that has taken fledgling companies like Airbnb and Instacart and propagated them with a steady shower of money and the bright light of exposure, until they grew to the point that they were real, operating not just in a Silicon Valley bubble but in the world outside it. One of the initial focuses of the company was Medicare Advantage, which would provide Papa for free to many older adults. "We acquire customers by the hundreds of thousands through health plans," read the title of one of Papa's pitch decks in 2020. Papa picked up partnerships with ten new insurance plans and funding from investors. Of course, Medicare Advantage plans are primarily for older people, not for members of Gen Z, the "loneliest" group of all.

And it was individuals, and individualism, that Medicare Advantage underscored. More than half of Medicare-eligible people were on Advantage plans, which had a well-reported pattern of denying care while simultaneously charging the government more than standard Medicare pays. Unlike Medicare, a government program, Medicare Advantage caters to the same market but emphasizes consumer choice: If you have particular needs and desires, here is a marketplace of Medicare Advantage plans that you get to *choose* from, instead of being lumped into stolid old one-size-fits-all Medicare. But the marketing for these plans, notes an article in *The American Prospect*, "nearly always fails to mention how hard it is to return to traditional Medicare once you are in Medicare Advantage, and that the MA plans have closed provider networks and require prior authorization for medical procedures. Instead, the marketing emphasizes the fringe benefits offered by Medicare Advantage plans like gym memberships." Or dog food. Or Papa.

Because of the legislative changes to Medicare Advantage plans just before the pandemic—the redefining of "sickness," the focus on "social determinants"—Papa's focus, the loneliness of old people, could now be solved, or at the very least, markedly improved, through government reimbursement. This was a big new world, and not just for Papa. "Medicare has traditionally steered clear of funding nonmedical services and instead leaned on state Medicaid programs," the Commonwealth Fund recollected. The difference is important: While Medicaid is reserved for many of the poorest of society—or for older people who intentionally "spend down" in order to qualify for it—Medicare is for those over sixty-five, and/or those with disabilities. And Medicare Advantage is, trickily, the privatized version of Medicare, often sold to seniors who want to augment the places where Medicare falls short, or enjoy extras that the more straightforward government program doesn't pay for.

Medicare.gov operates a 24/7 chat line designed to help anyone with questions about coverage. I had, potentially, thirty years before my own Medicare coverage, if the program still exists by the time I age into it. But I remained curious. I instigated a chat to ensure I understood how the program functioned, and what it was for. Sharon was first: A Medicare representative who spoke in long, formal sentences very likely preprogrammed for her, she ended our chat as soon as she had answered my question about how to pay for dental care when I got old ("You can enroll in a Medicare Advantage plan or find private dental insurance"). She was brisk, a little too efficient. I wondered if perhaps she was not human at all.

Q was next, an agent who asked me questions back in a way that felt helpful, kind. "You're wanting to know some of the cons of joining an advantage plan?" Q asked, and then noted that they couldn't give an "opinion," but could give me some things to consider. They began a litany: Would the services I need be covered? What would my out-of-pocket costs total? What were the star ratings of the plan? And then: "The most important one to consider for me is, is my doctor in this plans network?" Q noted that on a Medicare Advantage plan, "you have to use the plans network doctors," and "almost all referrals to specialists will have to be approved."

I thanked Q, and resisted asking them for information I knew they were not allowed to give. Like: Where do you live? Like: How do you feel about this job? Like: Who are you, really? How do you know so much about Medicare Advantage? Are you real? You have to be, right? This was before ChatGPT. Q had made an error I noticed: They had omitted an apostrophe in "plans"—and I wondered if this meant that somewhere on the other side of my questions was a person.

A poet once told me about his idea for a series of poems that were all going for that sensation you sometimes get while reading Wikipedia: little rub-throughs of humanness, little threads of voice, little blurry zones that feel less objectively encyclopedic and somehow, intangibly, formed by a human brain. He was interested in how we could sense that humanness through the text. How the technology behind Wikipedia, its crowd-sourcery, could lead to these moments of slippage, whereas the *Encyclopedia Britannica*, for instance, contained none. Why, he wondered, are we often surprised to encounter each other in the digital landscapes we haunt alone?

Loneliness is easy to see, or think you see, in part because it is easier to see that more people are living alone, and more older people are living separate from their families than ever. Historian Steven Ruggles describes how families once gathered around agricultural labor, with 75 percent of older people living in multigenerational families in 1800. A long slippage began, moving through industrialization and Victorianism, the world wars and the Cold War, postwar wealth and the rising current of feminism, and economic collapse. In the 1960s, according to researcher Ethel Shanas, between 80 and 90 percent of old people with children lived less than an hour away from one of their children, and 40 percent saw their children almost every day. In 1962, only 20 percent of old people professed to feeling lonely "sometimes." Nevertheless, writes David Hackett Fischer, there was a separation of daily routine between older people and their younger families at this time. Andrew Parker, of Papa, made his own argument on a *Today* show segment, about the nuclear family being "not as together" as they once had been.

During my research into Papa, I met a man named John through the comments of a Facebook page for the company. By the time we met in person, at a Dunkin' Donuts on the north side of the city, I had abandoned the idea of attempting to work for them. But I had kept reading about loneliness, and Medicare Advantage, and still knew nearly no one in Pittsburgh. For some reason, I had thought John would be older, somehow, but he was probably ten years older than me, at most, with clean, possibly even pressed clothing. He preferred a starchy pomade to his hair, and owned, with his wife, a house in a subdivision about twenty minutes from my rental. He had started with Papa after a short stint with a ubiquitous lawncare company. The lawncare company hadn't given him boots to wear for when he'd eventually be spraying chemicals onto the desiccated grass, so John quit nearly immediately.

The nucleus of John's nuclear family had once operated from James Square, a nursing home in Syracuse that his uncle owned. His mother worked in the activities department, his father as a maintenance man. "Nepotism, nepotism," he joked to me in the Dunkin' Donuts. "No, it wasn't anything like that. It's just, like, let's take care of our family." As a four-year-old, remembered John, he spent a lot of time in James Square, "helping my mother play bingo with the patients, helping serve them food, and snacks, and filling up the chip bowls, and walking them back to their rooms . . . And then there were days where I'd be hanging out with my cousin and my uncle would say, 'You guys, want to come to the nursing home?' . . . He would be in this big executive office and we would get bored and we would just go running around there. It was like our playground." He made friends with residents, could still remember them to this day. It was easy to extrapolate from these stories that John liked working with older people. Once, he sent me a drawing he'd done as a kid, of himself with several of his older friends.

John told me that Papa started out paying him $15 an hour. It was good money, said John, particularly because most of the visits had bonuses attached to them. The lowest bonus, he remembered, might be $30. Some might be $75. "So, you know, you'd go somewhere for three hours, at fifteen dollars an hour, that's forty-five dollars plus a seventy-five-dollar bonus." The work was varied: Sometimes it was light cleaning, other times it was heavy-duty lawn work (technically not allowed), sometimes trips to the grocery store, sometimes not much at all, sometimes conversation. Often, he said, there was no way to avoid touching a Papa, which was also not allowed. Often, the Papas he worked with would express frustration about their Pals: They might have been expecting a Pal who never showed up, or would ask to not be given a certain Pal who gave them a bad feeling, but that same Pal would sometimes be scheduled again.

Most of the work was transportation: "Doctors, grocery, bank," he told me. A close second was housecleaning. There was one lady, he remembered, who "couldn't get used to the idea of me doing things for her." They'd just sit at her kitchen table drinking coffee and smoking cigarettes. The only time John didn't do something a Papa requested was at a house he visited often—"so dirty," he told me, that when cleaning it, as the client asked, "it felt like I was barely putting a dent in it . . . two-hour visits once or twice a week wasn't cutting it." The Papa told John that he was an anomaly: that most of her Pals would show up once and never again. She had had bedbugs in the past, she told John, and worried that she had them again, asking him to lift her mattress to investigate. He declined.

"Honestly," he said, "I grew up in a similar environment of dirtiness and disarray for periods of time. Then out of nowhere, I'd wake up on a Saturday and the house was spotless." His mother had never gone to sleep. When he was an adult, John suspected that his mother had been abusing her prescription drugs—amphetamines, in his opinion today. By the time he was ten or so, though, the cleaning of the house rested completely on him. In the background of his childhood, she had developed a long, secret alcoholism, about which she would feel permanently guilty and tell him so, even when, as an adult, he wanted to move on.

Slowly, John began to mention to me his friend N, formerly a Papa client, the one who he smoked cigarettes with. "My adopted grandmother," he called her once to me. "It's part of my mental health, visiting her. It's mutually beneficial." She lived alone in a building, though her neighbors, a couple of younger men, popped their heads in the first few times John visited. "They're making sure she's okay," he said. She had family nearby, too. Even when he did not have a gig with her, he'd sometimes call her or go visit. Certain Saturdays, and Christmas Eve. Her birthday. N was not a hugger; she was someone who came across, he warned me, as gruff at best. He liked this about her. "Those motherfuckers," he texted her when he learned that she would no longer be able to use Papa—her free allotted hours per year had run out, and her insurance was dropping the service. All their visits together suddenly vanished. They were no longer tied by a company or a transaction.

John had his own theories about the way the service operated. After a little while, John remembered, the bonuses began to decrease significantly—the ones that he suspected, he told me, sweetened the deal for Pals who didn't want to go into particular neighborhoods but he felt fine visiting. Usually, John (who was white) told me, these neighborhoods were poorer ones with higher populations of Black residents—McKeesport, Hazelwood, McKee's Rocks. The bonuses went down to $15 or $10. "And then the bonuses went away. And then the clients went away." Suddenly, said John, "You weren't being requested by the people who you had previously formed relationships with as Preferred Pals." ("Preferred Pals" was a Papa-specific term for those workers who jibed well with particular clients, who were sometimes able to request them to come back, as N did with John—first on the books, then, after she ran out of hours, in the space of real life, both of them operating with no financial undercurrent to their friendship.) Now, those clients, John told me, were "essentially told, 'well, too bad.'"

Papa told me that:

> like many marketplace businesses, we occasionally use bonuses to make sure visits are reliably filled. Because Papa is largely offered as an annual benefit through health plans and employers, our geographic footprint naturally shifts each year. That means demand can vary by location depending when and where new members become eligible and enroll. In some cases, such as entering a new market or responding to a temporary spike in demand, we may offer bonuses to encourage Papa Pals to take visits in those areas. These incentives are determined by an internal process and are not tied to neighborhood demographics . . . Over time, as demand in a given area stabilizes, bonuses may change or phase out. To date, Papa has supported nearly 3 million visits across more than 7,300 cities. We continue to use bonuses strategically when needed to ensure reliable service for members.

One woman, seventy-three, in the Quad Cities, hired a Pal who was a "cleaning machine," mopping the floors better than anyone else she'd ever found. "My guy lives thirty-eight miles away," she told me, "but the app shows that he lives zero miles away," meaning he had to ongoingly figure out mileage reimbursement for every visit. She loved how he "worked circles" around the female Pals she'd sometimes been paired with, getting deep into the corners of the house, and finishing fifteen minutes early, then asking what else he could do. The housework focus appeared elsewhere, in online testimonies from Papas and Pals both, emphasizing how much cleaning was expected or accomplished. Another woman, fifty-eight, was a Pal. All four of her grandparents died of Alzheimer's. She scheduled herself for lots of visits, all of which seemed to disappear—then, finally, a good one, forty-one minutes from her house. "I drive there all excited to get this job started," she told me. It was rural, no cell phone signal. She heard "*Deliverance* music" running through her head. Old cars stacked one on top of another. "You can't really knock on a cowgate, but I tried," she said. No one answered. She went home and was not reimbursed, she told me, for the 45¢ per mile that she traveled, nor the $13 per hour. (A Papa representative, Valentina Pecoraro, told me that "We take feedback seriously" and have "built processes so that when concerns are raised—whether about scheduling, payment, or visit logistics—they are reviewed and resolved in a timely manner." These processes include direct communication tools and a support ticket system, as well as reimbursement protocols.) I interviewed the women over the phone, tried to assess if there was that sense, as you sometimes get, of connection, which, the longer you go, you realize is rare. I had found, as a writer, that you can force connection where there might not be an inherent one—a resonance of the kind H described. There are tricks to it: empathy, namely, and not blinking too much, and active listening. But the more honed my strategies had become as a writer for establishing these kinds of near-resonances, the more I started to wonder if I was cheapening the very idea of connection. The best resonances came almost randomly, I had found, without pushing or trying: They *did*, in fact, almost show up at my door unannounced. I felt it with H, with my parents (though that was different), with certain friends I knew for short periods of time, who I'd long ago left behind, in some other place.

I went with John to visit N, his favorite ex-Papa, and now simply his friend. He told me about a different Pal he'd heard about, through three other Papas with whom he'd worked: He'd told N about this guy, "That's how crazy it was . . . He was real heavy, really big, and the lady told me he pulled up in front of this house, and he was just sitting there for the first half hour of the visit, sitting in his car. He finally gets out, and he's just one of these people that talk, talk, talk, talk, talks. And he's like waiting to speak instead of listening to what the other person has to say," John recounted. One of the Papas "couldn't even get a word in, to where it felt like it's been two or three hours. He hasn't done anything, but she didn't care. [She felt like] *it's time for you to leave*." John shuddered. I liked how he was becoming more voluble. He'd invited me over one night for a Super Bowl watch party at his house, with his entire family, who were really all his wife's relatives. The only non–family member there, I felt initially awkward. What was I to John? And then I heard him say "my friend" while introducing me, and the evening relaxed. Rihanna took the stage at halftime. A wedding album came out. Now, weeks later, it was the far edge of winter, one of those in Pittsburgh with the big grimy boulders of snow on the side of the road that weep water on unexpectedly warm days, their shapes slowly whittling down to nubs, then nothing. Inside N's apartment, Papa and Pal both lit up, right away, and embarked upon a chain-smoking session that lasted the entire visit. For days afterward, my coat smelled of their mingled breaths there in the small room, and would again each time I visited with John over the next few months.

N was seventy-seven, and she held her cigarettes, long and slim, out on her knee as she crouched over, speaking intently. She had a mold problem in her bathroom and a bad landlord. She had short hair and didn't wear a bra. She was tough, as John indicated: definitely not a hugger, and I watched myself retreat quickly from the ways in which we are meant to show care—*Wow! Amazing! Oh my god!* the TV blared; a fat, impossibly slick-furred cat named Snuggles wended its way around our legs. Snuggles had replaced a previous one who N kept framed photos of by the TV, alongside a piece of fur that I originally took to be feline. (It was not.)

N grew up in Braddock Hills, the daughter of a father who worked at a rubber plant in New Jersey. "He was what he called a *lover*," she said of her father. "Someone threw him off a fishing boat in New Orleans." "Is that . . . how he died?" I heard myself say, later, on the tape. She regarded me like I was an idiot. Yes, of course it was how he died. Just as her uncle, who worked for the railroad, was killed by a cowcatcher. N had grown up under the care of a few different people, but mostly, her stories illustrated a particular self-sufficiency, amplified, now, by her age. She kept a vegetable garden as a kid, and every Easter got a new animal: little ducks, then two chickens, one of which killed the other. She wanted to be a vet, till she began to realize how much schooling and cost was involved: "I might as well be a brain surgeon," she said to herself. In the garden, perhaps due to the soil quality, everything came up in miniature: mini carrots, mini cucumbers, mini watermelons, all of which she severed from their stems or pulled out of the soil, washed, and then sprinkled with salt, eating them right there, right then.

The life she led between childhood and older age was long, tumultuous, and full of death. I asked N about something I'd read about her online, upon googling: that she'd once done a hunger strike, when she worked as a janitor, for better pay. She looked at me, hard.

And she said it was false. But it was there, right there, pulsing on my monitor, and I liked her for it, the way she maintained her privacy. As N spoke, little details emerged about the various losses that stack up, for some people, over time: children and siblings, body parts that decide, after enough thankless work and chemical exposure, to break down. A bad, violent ex-husband living on the other side of town, embroiled, if he was still alive at all, in drugs. John sat there quietly, as he often did. And then the two of them would connect their eyes and laugh, and I felt a little dizzy at it suddenly, the way the invisible world can work to make the shapes of our need clear to us, then blurry. I was watching their resonance, which I hadn't expected to find. I wasn't jealous of it. It just made me happy, the way someone's lit candle, viewed through a window on a snowy day, can make you happy as you pass by. If someone were to have given me a loneliness survey that day, I would have said I "sometimes"—or maybe "rarely"—felt lonely. Mostly, I would have been confused about how to even quantify it.

"I don't want to go to the doctor anyway," N said while we spoke about her emphysema, which involved, she said, air bubbles that messed with the pressure she needed to summon to inhale. She was on her fifth medication for it. The doctor had prescribed her, or tried to, an oxygen machine, which simply became a "cute little piece of furniture" in its nonuse for a year. She'd put in the cannula while going out to shovel snow, then take it out, come in, and light a cigarette. The doctor had also tried to persuade N to go to some kind of respiratory therapy: "I don't need to learn how to *breathe*," she said. In general, "If it breaks, I'll let you know. It ain't bothering me." The doctors, she said, tended to diagnose things willy-nilly: "You can tell them one thing and they'll go off on a whole other track." Meanwhile, "they don't even have a cure for the common cold." Doctors today, for N, were a far cry from her old family doctor, Dr. Primas, who used to come to her family's house in Braddock Hills. "You can't find a doctor like that anymore," said N.

N remembered getting a call from Papa out of the blue. She answered, and they mentioned the name of her insurance company. "They led me to believe it was their program," she remembered—that is, that this new service was straight from the insurance company. N was on a D-SNP, a particular kind of special needs plan, falling under the Medicare Advantage umbrella, for people who are "dual-eligible" for both Medicaid and Medicare. She would be getting sixty hours of Papa for the year, she learned, which translated to "a little more than an hour a week," John interjected, quickly doing the math.

Before John, N had started with a different Pal: a woman she remembered having wooden teeth. John caught my eye and laughed, raising his eyebrows. "Yes, wooden teeth," N insisted, nearly laughing. She asked the Pal to run the vacuum, and to put Gorilla tape on some of the cabinets where the wood was peeling off the frame. But the woman didn't do anything, N said. In fact, her strangeness unnerved N. The wooden-toothed Pal said her phone was dead, and that she needed to get a charger. Then, she left for the better part of an hour—the same hour she was meant to be there talking and helping. N looked at the Pal's handiwork: nothing. N had written her own name in the dust atop one of the counters, as she sometimes liked to do. It was still there. So was the "cat shit," N remembered, in the litter box she'd asked the Pal to help with. It wasn't that N couldn't do this herself, she emphasized, but more that there was truly nothing, really, for the Pal to do, unless she wanted to just hang out and talk, which was not the Pal's strong suit. Not everyone, the implication seemed to be, can be a friend.

Though she was scheduled to return, the original Pal didn't show up. And the next time, John did. That was their first meeting. The two went to Lowe's, where the power went out, all the computer systems slowly rebooting. N and John—seventy-something, forty-something—stood there in the dark. It felt comfortable. "You make sure you find me in the goddamn app," N told John later, so they could keep spending time together. It was not out of a sense of need. "I don't *need* company," N told me. "That's why I got a cat." "I mean, you got people coming in here, visiting all the time," agreed John. N continued. "I'm not really a people person. Because most of the people I talk to . . ." she paused. "I'm a smart person. I don't like to talk to dumb people. And I have a lot of nonintelligent friends." She and John liked to talk politics. They were on the same "brain wave." And now she told me about the difference, as she put it, between two separate things. I thought she was going to say "loneliness" and "isolation," that constant contrast people like to make when talking about this stuff. No, said N. "There's a big difference between being lonely and being lone*some*."

When you're "lonely," you're really not, said N, leaning forward to light another cigarette. Her place was clean, with a warm feeling. It was Christmastime. A relative had dropped off pig intestines for her to clean in her sink. (He could do it himself next time, N declared.) When you're lone*some*, said N, it's not necessarily a choice. You're by yourself in an existential way. But in her case, N said, we're *not* lonely. It's *our choice. It's because we want to be. We had kids. This is our time. That's our choice*. I didn't totally understand her distinction, though the internet told me later that there was a slight difference between "lonely" and "lonesome"—the latter was a deeper, profound, philosophical case of the feeling, while the former, the internet said somewhat chipperly, just meant you desired some companionship. But I noticed N's use of pronouns: "I" cleaved, or multiplied, however you wanted to look at it, into "we." She was speaking not just about herself but about other older people. Sometimes, the two friends smoked weed, laughing in the small apartment where they had found themselves together, thanks to this strange service, paid for indirectly by the government, that had somehow assigned them to each other, then insisted they were friends.

One day, John texted me: An exposé about Papa had come out in *Bloomberg Businessweek*. "Assault Allegations Plague a $1.4 Billion Home Eldercare Startup," ran the title. A Papa alleged rape, at knifepoint, by a Pal. Another Pal was reported to have been locked in a room by a Papa insistent on taking her temperature. The article pointed at Papa's practice, at the time, of not anonymizing phone numbers between Papas and Pals; that is, once connected, even if the relationship did not feel positive, each had the other's real contact information—just as N and John had made use of. Papa's background check mechanism, unspecified, had not caught people with disturbing incidents on their records. Instead, the platform simply connected the person needing work with the person needing something else.

Years later, Jane Yu, Papa's head of trust and safety, told me that "Papa takes the responsibility of sending Papa Pals into members' homes extremely seriously, and we hold our community to the highest standards in the industry." She said that there was now a selective hiring and retaining process that involves a multilayered series of background checks that reviews "more than 3,300 government sources at the municipal, county, state, and federal levels, and are supplemented by manual reviews for an added layer of security." She emphasized the importance of "constant vigilance," with the first Transparency Report "to be released by a caregiving platform."

Was it loneliness that plagued us, and by "us" I am gesturing at N's "we"—her, John, me, and the rest of us—looking at, in one way or another, older age? Was it not a moldy bathroom, or a life of death and toxicity? Isolation, in the broadest sense? A gap seemed to stretch, in my admittedly limited foray into Papa's world, between what it was meant to solve—loneliness—and what people actually did: cleaning, running errands, going to Lowe's during a power outage, chain-smoking while people filed in and out of the house. "I suspect that there is yet an additional reason, too, for the power of the loneliness meme today," writes Claude Fischer. "It sidesteps class and material conditions. Loneliness is an emotional pain that, while more common among the poor, the infirm, and the angst-ridden teens, has been felt by every modern American at some time. Making *this* common experience a focus of our public concern avoids confronting harsh, worldly, and politically volatile inequities in our society." I emailed Fischer to ask: Why the loneliness epidemic *now*? He sent me a few hypotheses. The first: "It's real." The second: It was like any other "social problem meme" in American history, and would fade in time. The third: "It's a middle- and upper-class social problem," easier for readers of, say, *The Atlantic* to care about than deeper, uglier issues like rural nutrition. The fourth: It dovetailed with the belief—and I snagged on these words—that modern life entailed a loss of community.

I wondered what it meant if someone like N proclaims they are not lonely, and that they were then assigned such a feeling, from the outside, based on their age, insurance coverage, and solitude. What it could mean, too, that they might benefit from it, but not in the way that the insurance company or the start-up intended. I loved thinking about N and John spending entire smoke-filled days together in her living room, off the clock. There was a subversion here to the way they were supposed to be, supposed to benefit from each other, according to the loneliness logics of our time, which informed us that older people living alone had a black hole the rest of us could fill (and get paid to do so). Perhaps they *were* lonely, like anyone else, or perhaps it was more complicated.

Clearly, while this was nonmedical work, it was also close neighbors to caregiving work, and, in fact, it sat under the heading of "companion care," a service that Medicare did not reimburse but Medicare Advantage often did. In other words: If you went the private route in your Medicare coverage, you could now get your house cleaned, your errands run, your transportation provided. If you went the traditional route, good old Medicare without the perks, you couldn't. Medicare was changing. It was privatizing. Loneliness was too, spreading to envelop us all in its cold arms. I hypothesized to myself that older people were sites of the future, in which we would all be assessed as having black holes in our hearts to fill with finite solutions. You would have to opt out of loneliness, particularly, perhaps, if you lived alone. How did one *opt out of loneliness?* Did you download an app for that? Did you work within the system, or did you step outside it? I felt crazed, sometimes, trying to trace it to myself: It could be nice to have a companion in the house. It would be nicest to get to ensure that this person was who you wanted, that they were safe. It would be nice to not be assigned one thanks to an insurance company's understanding of your innate loneliness. It would be great if the person was paid a good wage, and the expectations for their work were clear. It would be amazing if the gauze that was loneliness was pulled back, and the wounds underneath were dressed. Stephen Katz, the gerontology scholar, suggested to me that asking somebody if they were ever lonely was "practically meaningless." What surveyors should ask instead, he said, is "What is your definition of loneliness?" He listed some elements, it seemed, of his: buildings for older people "blurred" from public sight, neighborhoods without intergenerational livability, lack of public transportation, childish sing-alongs. I wasn't sure what my own version of loneliness would entail.

I arrived to Caroline via phone at first. We had been connected through her insurance company, which I did not work for, but for which I found myself, in a strange twist of things, volunteering. It was the same insurance company to which I paid money each month for my own coverage, and whose name I saw winking on various walls across Pittsburgh. Like many companies, Papa included, the insurance company wanted to help the plight of older people living alone across the city, but unlike Papa, their service did not pay Pals to befriend the elderly. The idea here was charity. Friendly phone calls, I learned. But then, of course, I flailed at the idea: How to make a friendly phone call to a stranger without knowing the other person first, and to do it without a sense of either sanctimony or scamminess. I mean, really: How do you enter the life of a stranger and announce you are there to help them?

If someone were to do this to me, I would have been taken aback by their presumption. There would have been a long silence as I figured out what to say. Maybe: "What do you want from me?" Maybe: "Ooookaaaayyyy?" Maybe, and most likely, a demure and polite answer I would hate myself for while hearing it come out of my mouth: "Oh, okay, hi, yeah, how are you?"

Perhaps, as ever, I was overthinking. I sat on my front porch and noticed that my heart seemed to be beating a bit faster as I geared up for the first call to Caroline, who I had been told by a company rep was a sweet lady. I liked to sit on the porch and watch the goldfinches flit down to perch on the strong, bendy strands of grass. There was something really moving to me about spying them there, those hardy little birds holding on easily as the grass moved in the wind, and something notable, too, about how they chose to perch on something so seemingly lightweight. Before I could think much more, I dialed, and then I started to flail, and said something like "I'm with the insurance company."

But that wasn't right, and I clarified. "I'm here," I said, even though I was across the city, "to chat." Chat about what? I had no idea.

Neither did Caroline seem to know. "Oh," she said. "The insurance company."

"Yes," I said, "I mean, kind of," and then began the conversation: the weather, my neighborhood. Food. Who was this person I was speaking with as I stared at the goldfinch swaying, unafraid of me only feet away? I sensed that asking her questions about her life would be too much, too soon—but to continue speaking only of myself was starting to feel insulting. I sounded, I thought, like I had a motive. She seemed, on the other end, to not particularly enjoy this. She was in her mid-nineties.

In my experience, the mutual recognition of condescension quickly snuffs any potential life out of a conversation. I petered out. So did she. The goldfinch finally flew away and the grass swayed emptily. "Can you take me to get some bacon," she asked me, after which I paused, unsure—what *were* the rules? *Could* I drive her? I hadn't met a single person from this program, had sped through the training video while making bread pudding—*of course*, I said, and she gave me her address and told me to call her half an hour before my arrival on a Saturday.

Caroline had various systems for getting in and out of the house, of which I only saw, initially, the entrance. I noted its old-fashioned silhouette, and how a garden of sorts wrapped around, with bushes, she showed me, from Home Depot. She used a cane, and suffered from breathing problems that kept her inside her house for a great deal of the year—when it was hot, when it was cold. It was only when it was relatively temperate and mild that she found respiratory ease.

We drove to the market for the bacon, her guiding me there, showing me where to turn. She lived in a historically Black neighborhood, and she showed me—"Slow down," she said—the alleys, the church where a child was being memorialized, the nursing homes where she had worked for much of her life as a nurse, and then the market. I mentioned a well-known writer who has written a great deal about this neighborhood: *Oh, yes*, she knew him. We parked; walked slowly inside; she held my arm for extra balance but said, repeatedly, that she was an independent person. Despite this, she said, her family was trying to put her in a nursing home. Later, she'd point at a carton of Mike and Ikes in the Dollar General and tell me that some staff in one of the nursing homes where she used to work would give those to patients instead of their prescribed medication. Like so many people here, she was a veteran of the industry, and her stories casually wove in health care—her own received health care, and that which she dispensed to others.

With Caroline I didn't want to press. This was partly because I saw, especially as we grew closer, how others spoke to her, an older Black woman—particularly white people, of whom I was one. We walked into the market, arm in arm, and immediately I understood that Caroline was not, as is usually said of older people, invisible. She was the opposite. People looked at her, made room for her, or in many cases, purposefully did not. Children liked her, and she called them all sweetheart. The man selling her radishes and turnips quietly donated his weekly bacon to her when it was revealed that there was not enough left for her order. People my age flitted their eyes away from her. One woman, waiting for her debit card to be run, stood resolutely in place, in Caroline's way, as Caroline steadfastly moved along the side of the vegetable display, holding on to the platform's wooden edge with one hand, on the hunt for something specific. "If you could just *wait*," the young white woman said, with an itchy, angry anxiety to Caroline, who was slowly oncoming. Caroline did not visibly register her words, just kept moving slowly toward her, holding the vegetable display's edge. Finally, the woman moved, with a palpable, petulant resentment, looking for my eyes to catch. I glazed them over. And Caroline moved through. The woman returned to the debit card machine as if it were a magnet and she a flinty, helpless piece of metal.

Then there was the white woman, ten seconds into our arrival at the market, who saw Caroline and honed in like a drone. "How do you cook your collard greens?" she asked her, and I stiffened, but Caroline paused and then said something about how she did it, and the woman nodded, beaming, raising her voice in both directions—loud and high—and told my companion how she *must* do it, with ham hocks, *right*, and vinegar, and garlic, and Caroline just nodded as we started to walk away. "That is an ELDER," the woman, now behind us, announced to a pair of college boys selling microgreens. "I just LOVE her."

"A little . . . condescending," I muttered to Caroline, who said nothing.

"You can't plant those yet," Caroline told me after I pointed out some healthy basil seedlings. "They'll just die."

"Oh yeah, you garden, right?" I asked her.

"I grew up on a farm," she said.

The next weekend: Home Depot for bedbug spray for a friend of hers, she told me, and a walk down the garden aisles. "So the farm," I asked her. "Outside of Pittsburgh?"

"No," she said. Outside the city in Georgia where she was born. It was four hundred acres. Her grandparents'. There were snakes everywhere: Once, she was standing on the head of one without realizing it. Her brother—one of her fourteen siblings—said, "Run when I tell you to run." He held the end of the snake's tail in his hand. Told her to run and she did. He cracked it like a whip to break its neck, if you can say that a snake has a neck.

The next weekend: an hour moving through the aisles of the Dollar General, where we ran into the bus driver who was meant to be doing some of her gardening. She never showed up, and Caroline called, instead, an impatient white man I had met earlier that morning, who was holding a Weedwacker. I could tell that Caroline didn't like him. "He whacked my plants," she told me later, in the car, "and he quoted me a flat fee but keeps asking me for more money." In fact, before we left on the errands, the man asked Caroline straight out for the money she owed him. "I have to go to the store," she said, getting into my car. "When will you be back?" he asked, and she calculated. "Three," she said, and he said, "Well, I have to leave at twelve," to which she then shut the door of my car and told me to drive us away fast.

For a few months, then, I saw Caroline nearly every weekend. We began to casually say "I love you" at the end of the visits. I did love her, but there was something else that undergirded our relationship, the way that I could have been anyone, coming to her. The insurance company that had originally delivered me to her door didn't care. I was simply a volunteer, working under the auspices of "charity." I could have been anyone "beneficent," as she too could have been anyone "needy." There was, perhaps, a resonance, but there was also something more complicated. I tried, in various ways, to temper the merciless "well meaning" that Leonora Carrington had described. I was more than a passive molecule bouncing against her life, but I was unsure what to do with that fact, and how to metabolize it. Honestly, the best thing to have done, probably, would have been to stop thinking about it, like John didn't really think about why he visited N, beyond some sense of mutual enjoyment. But it struck me that, without the insurance company, Caroline and I never would have met each other; without Papa, John and N never would have met each other. Within the kinds of structures I'd always feared, and removed myself from, there was room, always, for subversion. Fischer's final hypothesis, about the power of the "loneliness meme" slotting into a deep American belief that modern life entailed a loss of community, preoccupied me. I did feel that modern life entailed a loss of community, but I also increasingly felt that it was more complicated, and insisting upon the loss of community made the idea of community itself one of those finite "solutions."

One day Caroline had me kneel in her house while she encased her hands in mine and prayed over my tendency, I was startled to learn, to be too trusting of strangers. Just an hour earlier, after leaving Dollar General, a youngish white man approached us as we got close to my car. He had his hand in his pocket. She just ducked her head and got in the passenger seat. I'd closed her door and walked around to the other side. But he was standing there, and I had to brush past him, and as I brushed past him, he leaned toward me and insisted I Venmo him money. I felt myself flail, just as I had flailed at first on the phone with Caroline. I flashed back to the email from the weird people at the baseball diamond who wanted the surf and turf dinner with me on Christmas Eve, and something else I couldn't discern. And once I was back in the car, the doors locked, and the man pressing against the driver's-side window, piercing his eyes at me, Caroline got mad. "You never know what other people want," she said. I was filled with a familiar rushing of self-hatred and despair. "You have to keep your head down," she said. "You can't trust people."

We drove back. Hers was an old house, nearly full with things and papers and photos. The insurance company had brought us together but it had faded to nearly nothing in the background by now, like John smoking weed with N. I was never supposed to cross this boundary: to see the actual parts of her life that she might have described briefly, if at all, over the phone. Still, the phone was how we arranged our visits. And there were many months when I heard nothing from her, and she didn't pick up when I called.

I have been thinking recently about what it was that turned, that changed, to show me myself then. It was not loneliness, but it did feel like a black hole. The black hole held grief. More than that, though, it held a long, shuddering realization of regret. "I've never felt like I *knew* you," I remembered my grandmother Anita telling me. I pressed down this memory almost nightly, but it would haunt me, I sensed, for the rest of my life. I *had* kept myself separate from the world, because of fear of getting pulled in and then not knowing what to do.

Okay, so call it "loneliness," I thought some days, but the word didn't totally feel *right* for the thing I was feeling. Maybe it wasn't. "Loneliness is grief, distended," writes Jill Lepore in an essay surveying the recent rash of literature on loneliness (much of which I had read, and found frustrating). Grief: I felt a ping of that when sitting at my desk, angling my body away from the bright, slanting-in sun, and getting one of those awful emails from Ancestry.com: "Lucy, we have a hint about your grandmother," as if—and maybe it *was* the case—a website trawling for obituaries and birth certificates and passport renewals and border crossings and newspaper articles could mete out clues to us members of the contemporary moment about our own most intimate gone relationships. Sometimes, I got "hints" from Ancestry about the living, too: my mother, my father, far away. But these didn't make me feel *lonely* as much as weirded out. And also as if, increasingly, digital powers I couldn't totally see were attempting to shape my understanding of intimacy.

More than anything, clearly, I was cranky, not as noxiously as shut-in Guy, but not that far from him either. I knew I did not enjoy many aspects of the "modern world." I enjoyed putting quotation marks around things I felt skeptical of, distancing myself from them with a pointed and delicious sarcasm. I made mental lists sometimes of the things I detested, which signaled to me a terrible oncoming future: the "hints" from Ancestry.com; the location data plucked from my wanderings; smartphone technology and social media; all of the ways things seemed to change without our permission, and were foisted upon us as simply the new chapter in "reality." And then a neighbor would leave a bag of green beans he'd grown himself on a chair outside my front door, and from my porch I'd look up to wave at him and he'd wave back from his yard up the hill, garbled words floating for a second between us in the air of Wymore Street.

Caroline told me of a life spent in the hospitals and nursing homes of Pittsburgh, and a life spent—a hard life, too—fighting for her own rights, her own ability to ride a bus through town without being knocked around by the driver. Her own distance from her past, a childhood spent picking cotton for her father. One day she escaped and started a journey that would eventually land her in Pittsburgh.

Why I was supposed to think of her as intrinsically lonely, I didn't know, but I could guess it had to do with the fact that she lived alone, and was poor. I did know she deserved more than she had: She deserved to be spending time with anyone she wanted to spend time with, and money enough for whatever she wanted to eat. Caroline spoke to me there in her house. Rarely did I ask questions.

None of it, really, was fact-checkable. And then I caught myself: Why would I want to? So I barely asked questions. I was relieved, I found, to not have to think about a black hole inside *me* anymore: We seemed to be inside it together, two molecules bouncing around.

"*Don't let nobody* put you in the gutter," Caroline whispered to me fiercely one day. She was holding my hands. We sat in her house. "You're my friend. I was down, down! I was hurting," she said, describing the time when I had arrived to her. I did not want to ask why. Later, I would describe the conversation to an old and distant friend, a writer, who had previously told me about days she spent facing the wall in bed, pinned there by anxiety and shame, hatred at taking stories out of people and putting them on paper for others to read under her own name. "Conduit" was the word my friend used. "It is giving yourself over to someone else," she said. "You're breaking the barrier between yourself and the other person but you're also upholding it, showing it, even, so that they can see it more clearly." Or maybe those are my words. I sat for three hours, and Caroline told me about herself, in an unbroken flow, simply shared it with me as a gesture, with permission to share it in this book. She told me about a rock that she'd been carrying around, from her childhood in Georgia. She kept her rock in the refrigerator. It had been in her possession now for ninety years. "When my kids used to come in bleeding," Caroline told me, "you take that cold rock, you put it in a bucket, it goes down in the well, and sits under the cold water. You put it on somewhere that's bleeding, it stops the blood, because it freezes it." When I think of her now, I don't think of her alone in her house. I think of the rock in the back of her fridge, solid and cold and stalwart, held onto with dignity for almost a century.

The more I learned and thought about loneliness, and my own fear of regretting my tendencies toward solitude, the more I returned to a quote from Stephen Katz. "Fragility, dependency, and impairment," he said, these were conditions "probable for all of us throughout the life course, rather than . . . expected medical outcomes of ageing decline." Moreover, he wrote, "If all lives are to be recognized as worthwhile, then the precariousness within them must also be recognized and supported, rather than exploited and excluded." My fear, I saw now, had little to do with becoming regretful about my own choices toward solitude and independence. I did fear some version of final weeks, alone in a room, the bottom dropped out. But I also feared that loneliness was, in fact, becoming a billable entity for everyone, and that both loneliness and the deeper structural conditions it pointed toward were cheapened by this fact. I feared that my loneliness, or whatever it was, that black hole, would be probed and explored by endlessly well-meaning people whom, in one way or another, I needed but could not choose. I feared not being able to figure it out for myself: a "dependency," I guess, of the kind that Katz mentioned, but made extra-individualized. I worried that loneliness was made private, at the expense of the things that undergirded it: black holes of health care, poverty, housing.

One day, in West View, I watched my pal John get a haircut. He didn't like the police, he had told me, but he went to a salon near his home that offered military and police personnel a hefty discount. There was free beer there, he told me. It was 2:30. I had just come from dropping cherries off for P. I sat on a leatherette booth next to the free-beer fridge and watched the stylist shave a sixteenth of an inch of hair off John's head, the haircut I was only now noticing for the first time. It was buzzed close all around the sides and then left long on top, long and slightly asymmetrical, and swooping. And it was nearly pure white. How had I not taken in this detail before? I wondered, and the reason, I supposed, was that I couldn't totally categorize him. He was immensely normal and immensely strange to me. He made tacos with gloves on, and chain-smoked inside for fun with an old cranky woman he'd met via an app. He had two geriatric dachshunds in a house in a subdivision far from my neighborhood. If pressed, I wouldn't be able to say what we were: if we were friends, if we were collaborators, if we simply hung out from time to time. I stared at the back of his head, and then his face, reflected in the mirror before me, before realizing the stylist was watching me watch him, also in the mirror. I smiled. She smiled. John smiled. I smiled. The loop, the mirror, the moment expanding. Afterward, on the sidewalk, we said a temporary goodbye. "I don't have many people I consider close friends," John told me, "so thank you." And then we walked to our cars.

4

FEAR OF MYSELF, DEATH, ANOTHER LUCY

In Pittsburgh, my evenings were both tranquil and strange. I kept the wood floors of the little rental house gleaming, repeatedly sweeping and oiling the boards. I staged elaborate meals for which I had to cross the city for ingredients, putting things together on the old stove, which plugged in via orange extension cord. Sometimes I would open the door to the balcony to watch the rain come in over the city. One day I started a garden on the side of the hill, spending hours out there each day, filling it with poppies and plants I didn't have the names for. I piled on the work. More than anything I wanted to simply disappear into the clouds of the city, its wet dirt built up from things long ago decayed on the river bottom.

I'm going to just write it out as plainly as possible, just the facts. My grandmother Anita contracted Covid from a home health aide who had likely taken off her mask. She was fine, though Covid-positive, for two weeks, moving around her house while the rest of us, from afar, worried about how she might do without the help that could no longer come inside. She had no assistance, now, with preparing food, or bathing, or going to the bathroom, or getting around the house, and she had developed, in recent years, a debilitating tremor, a half blindness, a stooped-over posture, and a series of needs that required regular support. She had long resisted going to a "home." Now, alone in her own, with the virus sitting inside her, she began to fall, including once while attempting to get food a friend had set outside her door. There, on her threshold, she managed, probably by calling out, to attract help from a group of teenage passersby. They retrieved her cell phone, then left her there. And then one day amid this endless chain of hazy-yet-emergency moments, she was in the hospital, and then within days we all understood that she was dying. Time stopped, as the cliché goes, but it also warped, blooming and rearranging as faintly but surely as a drop of milk in a glass of water. It would continue to warp after her death, when I broke up with my boyfriend, slowly packed up my house, threw many things away, and drove alone down to Pittsburgh, where I had barely ever been and was sure to be alone for a very long time.

But the facts, while facts, were also immediately blurry. In the gap between my grandmother's death by Covid and "normal" death, I became unsure of how to think of what had happened. I could not tell if her death had been natural or unnatural. This was the murky question I was preoccupied by. If I could answer that question, I felt, I could figure out how to grieve, or maybe more precisely, how to file away this piece of personal history. It would become sharper, and I would know what objective heading to use. "I didn't know how to hold a grief so vast," writes Meg Bernhard of her own grandfather's Covid death, and the way it sat inside a much larger landscape of loss.

At the center of the murkiness sat something that seemed like a paradox: My grandmother Anita had been old, and had died in a different way than we had "expected" her to die. You don't really think of your grandparent dying of anything *other* than old age, or at least I hadn't. Like a warm pool, death by old age seemed to glimmer in the distance, waiting for all of us, ideally, to one day wade in. I thought of a boyfriend's mom telling me about her grandmother's death: *She had a massive heart attack while sitting on the couch with her grandkids, and just kind of slumped over. It was the perfect end. She had a hard life.* But as this story anecdotally illustrates, dying of old age isn't what actually happens, even in these "perfect" circumstances. Medically speaking, no one dies of old age. They die of the things that might happen more *frequently* during old age: heart attacks, "frailty," cancer, strokes, pneumonia. In fact, a year after my grandmother's death, "old age" was removed from the International Classification of Diseases (ICD, managed by the World Health Organization) as a cause of death, in part because of what has been called "Covid ageism"—the experience of many older people during the pandemic—as well as, according to authors in *The Lancet*, more general violations of older people's human rights. As of 2022, you no longer die of "old age," according to the ICD, you die of "ageing associated decline in intrinsic capacity." Very official.

This development was not without its detractors. Some in the longevity community fought against the stripping of "old age" from the ICD, arguing for the "pathologization" of biological aging. If something is pathologized, it can then be treated, prevented, and more generally understood as an objective problem. The longevity people seemed to be arguing that aging was *not necessarily* natural: new technologies were being developed to treat biological aging, they wrote; "decline" was not an "inevitability." They wanted a return to the "death by old age" classification, from which we had only recently diverged as a society. I spent hours combing through their arguments, attempting to understand, among other things, telomere length. Somehow, this moment in time seemed to present two different versions of old age: In one, it was a problem to fix; in the other, it was the *natural* reason for so many virus deaths. The two pieces of thought seemed to work well together. Nowhere in this thinking, it seemed to me, was the maybe naive sentiment I used to hear everywhere, helplessly partial but also hopeful: *Everyone will one day grow old.*

In general, although I understood my grandmother to be "vulnerable," it remains intrinsically hard for me to process that she had died in any way "naturally." Years later, when my other grandmother, Mary Ann, died in her own bed, at home, nearly 101, I felt the dissimilarity acutely: Mary Ann's days, for years, had been increasingly devoted to sleep. Her death felt like a waited-for eventuality, an enactment of that tangled ICD code ("ageing associated decline in intrinsic capacity"). For years, her death seemed always around the corner. Anita, meanwhile, had gone from her previous, fairly standard self—embattled by physical ailments, but acutely aware and intellectually vital—to knowing, suddenly, that she would die within a few days or a week. It was a shock. In fact, it was a bigger shock than I had room for in my mind, at the time or for years afterward. What made it more shocking, and hard to understand, was that of course Covid had not existed as a manner by which loved ones died, in our imaginations or in reality, until a few months earlier. This was a new category of fact, and neither personal essays nor journalism seemed sufficient to understand it: its particularities, its scale, its personal impact, its social impact, its place in time. The entire thing was a shock inside which we all—those of us who survived—lived, either mourning or not. The horror of that time is hard to return to: not emotionally, I mean, more that it is extremely hard to summon back to the page. The scale of loss was so immense, and the deaths themselves often violent and alone. They were couched in the language of innate vulnerability, preexisting conditions, inevitability, and sometimes age.

"People do die," said a banker, quoted in *Vanity Fair*, talking about personal responsibility. "That is kind of what happens." A fact. One commentator asserted that "if someone who is 81 dies of Covid-19, that is not the same thing as somebody who is 30 dying of Covid-19." A fact?

Disaster felt close at hand. Sometimes I wanted to laugh at the types of things that occurred in what felt, increasingly, like a thinness to my everyday life in Pittsburgh. The things were ridiculous. The day my dog killed a groundhog in the backyard in a horrific battle, I wiped the blood from his trembling coat, grabbed a shovel and put a mask on to dispose of the groundhog's body, and apologized to the neighbors, who had seen the whole thing and were themselves traumatized (they had statues of groundhogs in their front yard and were devoted to the species). We exchanged numbers. It was the first time we had ever spoken, and it would be the last. I scroll past them sometimes in my phone now—*Dave and Nick*—next to the others I collected from those years, their real names foreshortened to mixtures of place and circumstance (meeting via the exertions of my dog, Helgi) and sometimes total mystery. *Sarah Dog Woman Pittsburgh, Carissa Helgi, Buck Helgi, Barbara Helgi, Chris Helgi, Nurses Station, 99.*

While generally keeping myself to myself, I also felt pulled out into the world in a new way, which was ironic, I guess, given the fact that we were all supposed to be isolating. But there were other people—*many* other people—whose relatives had died like mine, with variations on the experimental drugs, the antibodies, the ventilator, the overstuffed medical wards and morgues, the solitude, the terror of never having experienced anything like this before. Many of them were trying to find one another. Within days of my grandmother's death, in Central New York, I sat down and found several in an online support group meant to connect us, which I had stumbled upon by googling "Covid" "death" "group." They were all young people trying to make some sense of it. A young woman had lost her fiancé, whose cancer had just gone into remission before he caught the virus. A med student's mother, who became sick after her husband, the group member's father, whose job it was to purchase PPE for his hospital staff, brought the virus home. A young man's multiple—as in, five or six—grandparents and step-grandparents died within a few weeks of one another. The stories had some elemental things in common: The deaths had happened suddenly; and with a horrible, dawning realization of what was about to happen, there was nothing any of the mourners could do but watch from outside the hospital. The mourners felt suddenly and strangely isolated from the world and did not generally feel equipped with the right language for what had happened. We met once a week under the guidance of our leader, who had not suffered such a loss, and toward whom I felt a mixture of gratitude and unfair annoyance: She was one of those overtly *kind* people, I felt, who knew the right mannerisms and contemporary lingo for loss. She allowed silence to stretch, closing her eyes while she nodded and *hmm*ed and used words like "feedback."

I searched for a mirror. Sometimes, another griever in the group, another woman named Lucy, seemed to catch my eyes and connect through the computer screen. Her father had just died, she said. But her presence quickly became intermittent, and then she stopped coming.

Later, I would read an essay caricaturing a certain political group: It promised a look "inside" "white grievance churches," and featured a drawing in its header of a crowd of mostly older white people raising their arms to say "amen." Many of them sat in wheelchairs or used oxygen. Instead of being a reported piece, as I had assumed, the essay was an exercise in imagination, and the writer seemed focused in particular on imagining oldness among people who, in her words, "would rather pass the plate for ICE than for insulin." "Half the congregation can't actually stand up without a walker," she wrote. "Look at Cathy waddling down the aisle with her ankles spilling over white orthopedic sneakers like rising dough. She shifts her weight off her bunions and praises Jesus while her oxygen tank hisses in tow . . . Every 'Amen' is punctuated by a phlegmy cough that says COPD is the way, the truth, and the light . . . One woman is laid out under the holy ghost. The varicose veins in her legs look like Google Maps traffic jams." Part of the point of the piece, as I understood it, was to emphasize how these imagined people were themselves ailing, how the people "cheering for cruelty" were the ones "most wrecked by it." I understood the writer's point, but I felt both disturbed and unsurprised by the portrait, here, of oldness and disability. In the years following my grandmother's death, I had become convinced that oldness had entered a new realm of metaphor. It had not just become, among many, cultural shorthand for death; it had become, among this same many, cultural shorthand for the death of a sense of possibility for this country. I heard, sometimes, the ease with which "boomer" was deployed as a pejorative, and while I wouldn't say it was *offensive*, exactly—though many might—I felt it to be careless. My grandmother was not a boomer in any sense—

generationally or culturally/politically, in the way that the word is used. She was a radical, and had been from youth through old age.

She could talk for hours. She knew what books were coming out when, and on what topic. A reference librarian, she gathered facts like this, in a way I sometimes note myself doing, just not as elegantly as she did. She regularly read the basketball scores, the baseball scores, the *New York Times* Style section, the entire *Wall Street Journal*, the *London Review of Books*, *Library Journal*, and, to my eternal chagrin, the publication *Nutrition Action*, long a semi-ironically purchased and perused periodical for three generations of us—my grandmother, my father, and me—that advised us to, among other things, "sidestep contaminants (like endocrine disruptors and mercury)." We hated *Nutrition Action*; we lived by *Nutrition Action*, just as we abided by the aspects of ourselves that we knew were ridiculously particular. Some of these ways of being were, in a certain light, quite good. She had a habit of sending newspaper clippings to people she knew, on subjects that she knew they were interested in. At her memorial, in fact, a physical therapist she'd briefly worked with ten years earlier told us that Anita had learned he was interested in birding and sent him clipping after clipping of articles about birds and birding-related books. I myself received many clippings from her, full of facts about photography, documentary, documentary photography, purple (the color), the color spectrum in the natural world, plants, flowers, botany, landscape, literature, Scandinavian literature, Scandinavia, fancy Scandinavian restaurants, cooking, baking, the right direction in which to stir cake batter, and far more. I'm sure that I could, if I had all the clippings in front of me, organize them along a large fraction of the Dewey Decimal System. But they would end somewhere, in some year I can't immediately name. A tremor overtook her hand, and she began, I assume, to be unable to cut or tear them out of the paper. It's also possible that she simply slowed on sending me clippings for a different reason: I was hard to get to know (she had said as much). I mostly kept myself and my interests separate from her, I didn't have many interests I talked about, I moved so relentlessly that she couldn't keep track of my address, I had a habit of digging my toe into the ground while she spoke to me on the phone, endlessly, sullen in a way that she could not totally place in her energetic understanding of things and people and relationships.

I also saw, when I looked at my grandmother, a difficult and alternative model for myself. She was vulnerable and fierce in a way that I admired. If I could tweak some fundamental piece of my approach, I felt, I could be like her: a sharper mind, a more straightforward writer, an activist who did not quail when the moment to speak arose. I longed to have been forged in a different time, like she was, made by happenstance and politics into a red-hot poker, somehow both glowingly kind and sharply correct about everything. I absorbed her tales of old New York, long-gone radicals, the rubble of immediately postwar Berlin, the raucous parties she and my grandfather held. I marveled at how she could love beautiful clothing while also asking people how they lived with themselves, working, as they did, in whatever blasted and inhumane structure they'd decided after a while not to interrogate. She said the things that I felt but mainly kept to myself, wondering about them in private.

For me, much of life, in fact, was lived in private, from when I was a child onward. Sarah Chihaya writes of her way, throughout her life, of "abdicating selfhood, dispersing myself willfully into a kind of mist that spread thinly across the landscape of my life, almost invisible to anyone . . . almost invisible to myself." Similarly, I had worked to float from place to place, steering clear of attachments, and moved along when any might snag me. In Pittsburgh one night, a story came to me. After her engagement party, Anita would be boarding a ship to Europe, where she'd go meet up with my grandfather. For some reason lost to me, she had to make a choice. What would she bring with her on the long ship journey—the lovely large bottle of fancy liqueur she could nurse in private, or the delicious but obviously perishable cake she'd have no choice but to share with others, just to get through it? "She brought the *cake*," my mother, who was telling the story, said, laughing. "Can you believe it?" The honest, ridiculous, open choice punctured me, and I could hear my grandmother's laughter, an endless bell.

I did try to write about what had happened. I just remembered this recently, as a newsletter that published an essay I wrote about Anita decided to run the essay again. The editor, republishing it, noted that it was one of his "favorite" things they ever published. That was a strange word to use, I thought, considering the subject and the way he had cut it down from meandering assessment of her death to short but emotional wallop. He had turned my effort from asymptotic almost-there to a fully there thing that I didn't really feel came, exactly, from me, whoever "me" was. I got many messages about this essay after it was published. "It cuts to the bone," someone said. An Irish reader tweeted that he cried as he read the essay at his desk. I felt moved by these reports from far away.

Recently, and reluctantly, I forced myself to click on the essay. I saw, among many other things, that I had written about a comment sitting underneath her obituary, which a friend had tweeted. A stranger had written, beneath my grandmother's face, captured among roses, "94 years old. Another life shortened by Covid. Are you people insane?"

I often felt frustrated by how individualized the event of the death seemed to have made me. I did not want to be in my own mind as much as I was, and even my molecular wanderings seemed inherently bounded by my own subjectivity at the end of the day. It was hard for me to stay dissolved, though I wanted to. I missed that ability. I kept trying to do it, and I kept coming back to what had happened, to how it was making me interpret this landscape of oldness. More ridiculous events seemed to be pulling me through and out of myself, like thread reattaching a button. I drove through a disastrous car wash unthinkingly, the machine snagging on the carrier atop my car and nearly pulling the entire roof off as I sat there amid the blinking lights. In that moment, I thought, insanely, that I would drown. On another occasion, I whisked my hand out of the garbage disposal a half second before my other hand flipped the switch to turn it on. Strange, that impulse to remember that life continues, pulling you along and forward—the linearity of it, which during certain moments can get disrupted or forgotten. When I forced myself to remember anew that my grandmother had died of Covid, of all things, I felt a bright and brief shock. This was not how she was *supposed* to die, I realized each time, attempting to hold myself there, in a moment that faded in front of me. But the fact was that she had. Sometimes I felt as if I had decided to be alone in this moment in order to best attempt to clarify reality. As a fact, what was oldness as a thing separate from death? What was Covid as a thing separate from oldness? What was I as a person, if I were to hold my own molecule-self under bright light, and really look?

• • •

And yes, the thing about her telling me she had never known me. She didn't say this sadly. She said it with an accusatory tone, I remembered often at night in Pittsburgh, in the bed I shared with my dog. And I knew it was true: I hadn't really *allowed* her to know me. The words, while painful, had also felt like a relief. She had delivered the recrimination I had been waiting to hear for much of my life, as I floated along, watching others.

In the essay, I wrote that "society" had dismissed her as "one old person among many who had ceased to be useful, attractive, productive, interesting, independent." While it did feel this way, I, personally, had actually seen her as all these things, despite the fact that I had never allowed her to get fully close to me. It was because of the fullness of my grandmother—her dignity and her intense personhood—that I was afraid, for a great deal of my life, of the vision that she presented to me: an older person who was very like me, and who I didn't know what to do with. Regarding her, I saw two things, two pieces of a self that I could not seem to merge: I saw her oldness as a thing that made life difficult for her and I saw her utter, unshakable personhood.

We had many traits in common. We were suspicious of certain types of people, and we did not take NSAIDs like Tylenol or Advil casually, under the vague but sure sense that to take minor pain relievers was to lessen their power, or our power. We had similar bodily ailments, in particular what is likely a version of Raynaud's disease specific to our large feet. Many of these shared things—the foot thing, for instance, and, for instance again, a constant knee-jerk resistance to incursion into our private lives—were not happenstance, of course. They were genetic or otherwise generationally deposited as a family trait. But she was often sunny where I was gloomy, oriented toward connection where I pulled away, said what she thought (even when it was dangerous) when I stayed mum. An older person for the entire time that I knew her—I never knew her to have anything other than soft, totally white hair, like a Q-tip loosed from its tight roll—she seemed to me always wildly energetic and surrounded by friends. Sensing my retreat, she pushed toward me. I retreated further.

Let me attempt to probe more deeply, and say it more cleanly, to the best extent I can. I still love and did love my grandmother, and, simultaneously, who she was scared me. Or maybe fear is the wrong emotion: I see it now as a version of loneliness. She made me feel lonely, in a way, because she illuminated to me how it was possible to be different than I was, but still basically the same person. I wanted to be the way that she was. To use all the things we had in common to be less internal. But for most of my life I haven't known how to be, and understood that to be *her* way—vulnerable, laughing with her mouth thrown wide—was to risk hurt.

For most of her working life, my grandmother followed her own interest in what was private and what was public. A reference librarian, she published articles about the wage gap between female and male librarians, and advocated for stronger protections around public access to government information. She believed deeply in the idea of the library as a democratic institution, where facts, and information, could be accessed by everyone. When I consider her and her work, I often think of a phrase I found of hers, in reference to the wage gap in librarianship: *If you know something*, she had written, *you can do something about it*. I knew, in 2020, as I watched, that these deaths were becoming passive and private, not active and public. It seemed to me that it moved, very quickly in fact, from "Covid killed her" to, in the minds of others, "she died of old age." I couldn't figure out where this came from. And of course, many things are spoken of in passive voice. As if they are more rain barrels collecting rain, less clouds releasing fat droplets. More empty land segmented by barbed wire, less men stringing fence line out along a boundary. More blue package waiting cutely on the doorstep, less delivery person racing to deposit it. More person lying dead, less person doing the shooting. More trees bending crazily, less invisible wind pushing around the canopy.

I didn't realize it, I guess, is what I'm saying: that wandering around talking to people, and attempting to understand the shape of contemporary oldness, was an attempt to become more active, and to understand the fact of myself, which was changing. For a long time, I couldn't find the right container for these investigations, and couldn't understand how they fit together. The assisted living trade magazines and the man huffing "don't get old" as I passed him on the stairway near my house, the relentless solitude that forced me to see myself and the endless readings about loneliness. The elder-law radio show that seemed to find me as I drove, when I tired of my *Darkness on the Edge of Town* CD. All the content on Instagram showing visions of oldness, commodified, marketable. All the longevity stuff everywhere. These were visions of a static kind of oldness, one that was separate from me, whoever "me"—quotation marks again—was. It wasn't that I was immersing myself in oldness, "immersion" being a word that suggests, again, inherent distance. It was that oldness, and "me," and her, all these things were actually all around us, all the time, and I was actively attempting to arrange them into a factual narrative that made some degree of sense.

Five years later, I would begin to understand that I lived with, and had been living with for a long time, a severe strain—if that is the right word—of OCD. So much of the world seemed to have OCD, self-diagnosed or otherwise, that I didn't know how seriously to take this, either. I found some structural reassurance in the fact that my own official test had stretched for days—sometimes you could breeze through them in forty-five minutes, my therapist said—and that it had made sudden meaning of some of my younger behaviors, including my reluctance to ever share how I was feeling. It turns out, laughably, that an interest in privacy, and staying quiet about internal feelings, are hallmarks of this condition. Maybe it was not a lack of bravery that I had, or an internal passivity, but something else, a mixture of genetics and circumstance.

Not knowing about the OCD framework yet, in Pittsburgh I started saying things to myself and to distant friends like "I want to turn my brain off." "I wish there was a button on my brain that I could push and turn my brain off." "I want to disappear." "I can't stand being awake." At night I lay in bed seized by a twisting panic. I became extraordinarily confused by what, in the truth of Covid death, was a privately known fact (these deaths were avoidable) and what was a publicly understood one (they were ascribed to vulnerabilities). Only later did I begin to disconnect my life from the OCD, in the way I was beginning to disconnect this Covid death from the simple fact of old age. But I could not disconnect myself from the world, nor, eventually—thankfully—would I want to.

Helgi and I discovered a new favorite route: down the damp steps of Wymore, past the leaf-covered roof of the house squatting nearly underneath, with the barking brown dog, and down sloping Elbon Street, a right at the "no dumping" sign, continuing down a hill that had as many empty lots as houses, everything covered in or surrounded by a mixture of wood chips and split wood and dead branches and vines. Continue on through what was basically a hilled forest, no one in it, emptying out near a huge old stone church—West End United Methodist Church—built in the late nineteenth century. A billboard for help with debt cancellation bearing the heads of three lawyers in football helmets. Then up an achingly steep set of stairs, passing houses on either side that seemed to have been built long ago in these woods without any thinking about, or need for, driveways. Past a bone-shaped wooden sign in someone's front lawn warning ominously of, I took it, a dog named Chopper. Past the old mansions with thick-stemmed sunflowers. Back toward the house. I spoke to Caroline, to N, to older people where I found them. I called Rachel Ann Bovier, the older woman who had a strange billboard I kept seeing around Pittsburgh, proclaiming herself the "poetess" of the city (we played phone tag for a while and then gave up). I interviewed a Vietnam vet turned spice company executive who had fallen in love with his gym companion, who died suddenly, and the man told me he felt like he was watching a movie of his life as it unfolded. It wasn't *loneliness*, he said. It was something else. I walked in the weird park near my house, where I never met a single person, but where the rock structures and muraled bathrooms hinted at a busier, communal past. I oiled the floors of the rental house, and oiled them again. I sprayed newspapers with Windex and scrubbed the window glass, just as I had done as a teenager, in my first job at a florist's. I saw myself through glass, from the outside: lone person walking dog around neighborhood for hours. When I retrace my steps now, I'm amazed at how far I would go sometimes, and how I even found these networks to begin with.

One day, I did think of the other Lucy. This is what we'd called each other, briefly, in the grief group, when we said things like "Yeah, no, what the other Lucy said resonated with me." Lucy Little was her full name. At the time, I had begun not to believe in old age.

I mean, I believed in it, of course. Time passes, skin falls. Death, despite what its disrupters say, finds you—whether at thirty-four or one hundred. But I began to see old age, I guess, as a construction: something that kept me scared of myself, the same way I had stayed slightly afraid and distant with Anita. There was no way to know if, had we been the same age, or had I not encased her in so much worry and strangeness, we would have been able to throw our heads back together and laugh, open-mouthed. Sometimes, maybe often, I wanted to simply take the oldness out of the equation: Someone I loved had died in a way that she shouldn't have. To emphasize her oldness seemed to cheapen it: turn it into a story, when really it didn't have to be.

Lucy had begged her father not to go to the store during that first year of the virus. He wouldn't listen, so she packed her car full of her things and drove to New York to take care of him. She ended up staying for months. "During that time, I was trying to explain why he shouldn't be the one to go out," she told me. "I was constantly saying, 'If you go to the hospital because you get sick and they look at your chart and how old you are, and compare it to someone who is thirty or forty or fifty, you are not going to be the one who they prioritize.'"

Lucy had a thoughtful, almost birdlike bearing—slightly shrewd and open simultaneously. She had thick, dark curly hair and a tattoo that spanned her two wrists, reading "the world is" and "still beautiful." She and her father did not necessarily always have a terrific relationship. He was a "hard guy," she said, an alcoholic, and somewhat abusive. But when she'd drive places, she'd call him. When he did finally enter the hospital, he was extremely anxious. "Because he was older," Lucy said, "he was plied with psychotic drugs and it made him lose himself." When he started pulling out his oxygen, he was moved to the ICU. "Part of why I think he wasn't able to fight and his system shut down was because he was really confused and overwhelmed," she said. "We couldn't be in the hospital to help him advocate. He had no clue what day it was, what time it was. If he'd had someone who could wheel him to a window, talk to him, read to him, engage him, there is a part of me that believes he would have made it."

She remembered almost nothing of the grief group. In fact, she remembered little from those weeks after the death. She felt a deep disorientation, and journaled in an attempt to stay on top of it. Entire swaths of her memory were gone in the aftermath of the death, spreading backward all the way to childhood and stretching forward again to the semester in which she lost her dad—her last semester of graduate school, from which she almost dropped out. Then there was a time when her memory almost seemed to be sparking, short-circuiting, in a different way: She saw her dad everywhere, on the street, in older men who had some small physical commonality with him. Once, she had a memory so vivid she could smell him, and she began to sob.

She had been afraid: afraid to play her violin, to move forward. The only thing she could do, and this itself was difficult, was improvise. To move through graduate school's last semester, and also to continue along as the person she thought she was, she forced herself not to plan out a piece of music but to be carried by whatever might happen. I don't know how to describe what happened inside me as Lucy spoke. I just kept thinking "the other Lucy," "the other Lucy," but whether that was myself or Lucy Little was unclear.

For a long time, I was afraid of my new self, the self I was becoming in Pittsburgh, and what she meant. She—my actual other Lucy—

was a divergence from the person I thought I might one day become. The joy and the horror of having to live with yourself forever: It reminded me of that line from *Annie Hall* about a meal being terrible, and being served in such small portions. I was bored of feeling this way, and angry that I felt I had never found for myself another larger, better, kinder, braver option. I see it better now, the way the boundaries I have been holding since I was a kid simultaneously formed me, maintained me, and slowly threatened me—the me, that is, who increasingly wanted to connect with other people. And in this way, I suppose, via this breakage with my old self, I became more like my grandmother. In the years to come I would see her more and more in my posture, my shoulders, my nose, my hair, my mannerisms. The longer life extended, the more I remembered myself to be not a solid fact, but changeable.

One day, a moving truck appeared and deposited a pinkish glowing lamp, and a table Anita had saved for me made out of rosewood, once belonging to her mother, my great-grandmother. She had already planned for this one-way transaction, just as she had placed a key under a flowerpot for me, in case I ever needed entry into her house. I cut the Bubble Wrap off the lamp, carefully, set it on the rosewood table, plugged in its ancient cord, and turned it on. I saw the glow, which had glowed for my grandmother and for her mother. I felt my heart tear wide across its surface, beginning, for the first time maybe ever, to kind of bleed out. This was the first part of my life that continued after hers.

5

A CATEGORY, A SCAM MAP, INSURANCE

"Women old—feels old." Of course not. But also, maybe. Why not? The phrase seemed to emphasize one's subjectivity, one's individual truth, something that, as an essayist, I was taught is both "real" and limited. For my part, I knew I was youngish, but I often caught myself somewhat unthinkingly fighting off certain signs of time. Correcting posture, and exercising my core, in compensation for the "degenerative changes in the spine" that a CT scan revealed as the cause of the pain I had in Pittsburgh, which had me sleeping on my back with my knees raised some nights, and won me a prescription for opiates that I never took. Boring! I was bored of all of it.

There was only one uniting factor, one truth, that I could think of that encompassed older people, in all their diversity: membership (or invitations thereof) in AARP, a gigantic organization that offered discounts, solidarity, advocacy, and information, among much else. The category of oldness as represented by AARP intrigued me, because regarding older people politically, a basic tension seemed to exist between two stereotypes: the powerful and selfish boomers and the older, vulnerable people who were sometimes recipients of pity or loneliness assignation. I would imagine that many of us knew older people who did not fit easily in either of these categories. But AARP seemed to cross all divisions, and collapse such categories. I was interested in this: what truly bonded members together, and what that meant.

AARP was founded in a fury, in 1958, after California principal Ethel Andrus faced mandatory retirement. Activated by the plight of retired teachers more broadly—she famously met one living in a chicken coop—Andrus had created in 1947 the National Retired Teachers Association (NRTA), AARP's predecessor, which focused on keeping the retirees occupied and then, eventually, housed in a place called Grey Gables, in tranquil Ojai. The idea was similar to a continuing care retirement community: Residents paid a lump sum to enter Grey Gables (between $5,000 and $7,500) and then paid a monthly fee for care, room, and board for the rest of their lives.

What was needed next, Andrus felt, was health insurance for her group of retirees, who no longer had insurance because they no longer had work. But older people were not particularly appealing prospects to insurance companies: Because the cost of insurance is based on understandings of risk; and because old people are, generally speaking, going to die sooner than younger people, they are not a good risk. Andrus's applications for group insurance were denied by thirty-one companies. Still operating the NRTA, in 1955, Andrus met Leonard Davis, an insurance broker from Poughkeepsie, New York, who "realized that a scarce commodity sold to a captive audience would produce a profit," as the *South Florida Sun Sentinel* noted many years later. Business and membership both boomed with the inclusion of insurance into the NRTA's offerings: "Retired teachers got their insurance, Davis made a profit and the NRTA received a commission on every policy sold."

The expanding organization, to which retirees of all stripes—

not just teachers—flocked, was renamed the American Association of Retired Persons. This was before the passage of Medicare or Medicaid; and AARP, through its partnership with Davis's new insurance company, Colonial Penn, sold insurance to a bloc of people who would otherwise often find it difficult to buy. It started its own magazine, called *Modern Maturity*, in the first issue of which Andrus offered reader-members an "invitation to security" through the insurance plan. I found the cover of that first issue online: a radiant photograph of cottonwood trees in autumn, all burnished gold, between summer's vitality and winter's doom. *Modern Maturity* would extend from the late fifties all the way to 2003, when it was renamed *AARP The Magazine*. It remains the magazine with the largest circulation in the world, though Frederick R. Lynch, in his book *One Nation Under AARP*, relates that the magazine was at the time of his writing actually multiple magazines, "quietly segmented" by age group: "fifties, sixties, and seventies or above."

The cultural understanding of AARP is that it is actually *not* segmented: that it enwraps all of us in its arms, at one point or another, and this is how we know we have crossed the shimmering barrier between youth and age. It may come for us before we, ourselves, have thought to identify as "older." "Membership in AARP has been cultural shorthand for old age, and no matter how many photos they show you of kicky grey-haired ladies holding an iPad in one hand and making a *yesssss* fist with the other, it is a reminder of one's mortality. But you also get discounts at hotels and stuff, so I joined," wrote Dave Holmes in *Esquire*. As with other organizations, AARP awarded members discounts in great, flashing schools swimming toward them with every passing year. They were for car rentals, Ancestry.com memberships, food and drink from Joe's Crab Shack and Auntie Anne's, online savings accounts with certain banks, up to two-thirds off the cost of a subscription to Norton antivirus software, and extra time in which to check out from Motel 6. Then there were other perks: a free hearing test over the phone, free games, free book chapters about brain health and love and yoga, free plays, free events and classes at a virtual community center, free online movie screenings, the free Interview an Advisor tool to prepare for meeting a financial advisor, free money tools, and free scam-prevention tips.

It was this latter theme—scammery—that pulsed in my mind. It pulled at me, because I saw it everywhere in real life, and it dovetailed with the question I was mulling over, about what was *real* when it came to older age. Scamming seemed to be *the* topic of the extended moment. My phone rang constantly; I googled the numbers but didn't pick up. Texts like "Are you up for a quick check-in, at your convenience?" filtered in. Culturally, with scams, the targets seemed to be older people in particular. There was the Netflix film *I Care a Lot*, where Rosamund Pike played a conservator-fraudster targeting elderly potential wards. The miraculous blood tests of Silicon Valley. The former cast member of *The Real Housewives of Salt Lake City*, Jen Shah, who (at the time of this writing) is serving time for targeting older Americans in a telemarketing scam. "Older adults may be ideal targets for 'hunters,' as many of them live alone following the death of a spouse, and the resulting isolation may make them more willing to communicate with strangers, including motivated perpetrators who can satisfy their social needs," wrote the authors of one study on why older adults were disproportionately targeted by various types of fraud. Yet there were different types of scammery—some fell under the category of "financial abuse" and were perpetrated by trusted figures; others came from strangers. On the scam-tracking map on the AARP website, I used the zoom-in tool to move from North America to the eastern United States to Pennsylvania to Pittsburgh. Red dots bloomed there like poppies:

older people being scammed all around me, I saw. The map listed elders' self-reported scams:

> North Carolina Dept of Vehicles Final Notice of outstanding ticket. Please pay immediately before enforcement to avoid license suspension. (Reply Y and re-open this message to click the link, or copy yo your browser.)

> I recieved an email saying they were renewing my virus softwear the amount was 201.99 I called the number to cancel,they had me get on Google Chrome download a site to get into my computer. They said I had to fill out a cancelation form,but it wouldnt come up so she said I needed to talk to her manager.so he got on the phone & asked me a bunch of questions again saying I needed to fill out form.then asked me to sign into my banking so they could refund the money .Nope,wouldnt do & he became persistant & I said no not doing that.I said I was calling the geek squad & he insisted he was the geek squad.

> He called about medical alert systems. I said LEAVE ME ALONE.

Within these reports, there was little analysis: just a mosaic of collected self-reportage, which vaguely reminded me of the reports collected by Daniel Defoe in *The Storm*, his account of a massive storm that hit London in November 1703. There can be great shame in the individual experience of a scam: because there is a blurriness between the scammer and the savior, and you have erroneously trusted that the knock to your door was from the latter. And in that moment, you were exposed as trusting, gullible, and vulnerable, instead of gimlet-eyed and hard-edged. Poking around, I saw on the scam map that a common hoax seemed to involve Geek Squad: hundreds of reported instances of scammers pretending to offer technical assistance for computers and other electronics. It was the tension between aware and being accidentally gullible that suddenly unnerved me as I stared at the map. I could see myself, as I was now, age thirty-whatever, easily falling for any number of these schemes. I certainly had before, accidentally succumbing to a phishing swindle that kept me signed up to a maritime law newsletter for literally years. You could try your best to stay alert and intelligent, but still, you could be fooled. Geek Squad was meant to help, to solve problems; it was unnerving to think that so many scams were conducted under the auspices of care.

Perhaps this was the thing I was scared of: that no one person could remain invulnerable. We all stand inside sweeping systems of fraud, bending like palm trees in a hurricane, just trying to stay upright in the wind. If you were to break, it wasn't necessarily your fault, but maybe there was *something* you could have done to be better fortified. Or maybe not. As Hannah Zeavin wrote in *Harper's*, gullibility and scams both "serve as a neat foil for capital. [Scams] are framed by financial institutions and governments as ugly, extraordinary moments of economic activity, speciously cordoned off as a bug rather than a feature." In other words, we thought it was our fault when we inevitably got fooled, because it was easier, and encouraged, to focus on the painful little red dots, and not the map itself.

It was terrifying and heartbreaking, reading through these self-reports from my pink couch. But it must also be said that a major feature of getting old involves losing money—and not even via scam. According to the National Council on Aging, 80 percent of people over sixty-five, as of 2024, were either financially struggling or at risk of that. "Living independently in the community without some assistance is out of reach for most older adults," the report said. It is reasonable to be afraid of the financial side of aging, I saw, particularly if you come from any kind of experience with precarity. Unless one had generational wealth, they needed to be extraordinarily canny and perspicacious, the message went, to make it to older age in our moment with any real financial buffer. One report on scams I read announced that "to the extent that people reach old age mentally sharp, physically fit, and financially secure, the problems of individual and societal aging fall away." In other words, the extent to which such a thing was possible seemed slim.

The old AARP that Andrus envisioned—room and board and health care for its members, and a heated swimming pool, and shuffleboard—was designed to ease retirees from the border of old age into its depths without too much trouble. Staring at the photos of the old Grey Gables, I saw older people lounging together, swimming, laughing, and eating under the Ojai sun. In many ways, the contemporary AARP continues in the same tradition that Andrus envisioned. It is concerned, absolutely and fundamentally, with welfare: The AARP Foundation helps older people apply for property tax relief and simplifies the task of applying for SNAP benefits. They work with Legal Counsel for the Elderly to connect older people to lawyers, and they sponsor something called OATS (Older Adults Technology Services), which gathers groups together virtually to discuss books, play games, stretch, etc. AARP Foundation Litigation has regularly drawn upon the landmark *Olmstead* decision to argue the cases of older people with disabilities who want to live not in nursing homes but in the community—as most older people, including Caroline and N and both of my grandmothers, do and did. And then there is AARP Policy, Research, and Thought Leadership, a heavy-duty, serious enterprise that studies aging, anxiety and depression, desires around living at home versus living in more institutional settings, age discrimination, attitudes toward technology, loneliness, emergency savings, age-friendly communities (Pittsburgh is one), voter engagement, and far more. There is the entire scam-oriented arm of AARP, a big and burly one, offering document shredding and the scam-tracking map, the fraud resource center, Watchdog Alerts, and data on scamming. There is the Advocacy division of AARP, which pursues, in lobbying and elsewhere, issues relating to caregivers and older people; its website notes that the organization believes that Medicare should "be strengthened and improved so both current and future generations can count on having access to high-quality, affordable coverage."

I signed up for some of AARP's newsletters: *The Ethel* ("Do This 2 to 3 Times a Week to Stop Growing Weaker"), *The Girlfriend* ("Revealed! Our Top 10 Favorite Undergarments"). AARP fascinated me: It represented an ever-changing group that younger people could expect to join, and yet the reason it existed in the first place was because older people had been carved out from the rest of society, as if with a chisel, by health insurance. What preoccupied me was the idea of a typology that was both clear and blurry: not just AARP, but older people as a group more broadly, so internally diverse and with such porous boundaries. Also, with a tumultuous history of both power and vulnerability.

Indeed: After Medicare was passed in 1965, older people were transformed into powerful "uber-citizens," writes scholar Mark Schlesinger, people with an interest in protecting the health care that had been set aside for them in far-earlier efforts to pass more radical proposals for universal health care. Older people became understood, culturally and politically, as "advantaged" compared with preceding generations: No other group had this kind of health care, nor the associated ability to strategically leverage their voting and lobbying power. In this sense, though, their power depended on a larger precarity. Medicare had some things it did not cover: It did not cover long-term care, nor did it cover outpatient, self-administered prescription drugs, among other things. When, in my birth year of 1988, Congress passed the Medicare Catastrophic Coverage Act (MCCA), which was meant to limit out-of-pocket expenses for seriously ill Medicare beneficiaries and expand prescription drug coverage, AARP helped in crafting the amendments, promising, writes Schlesinger, that their members would "rally around the legislation." Of course they would: It would expand their benefits further. The legislation, writes scholar Debra Street, "held the promise of protection from financial ruin in the event of an acute catastrophic illness or an accident requiring prolonged hospitalization."

But counter to AARP's expectations, the amendment was surprisingly controversial. A flurry of opposition arose, organized, in part, by the National Committee to Preserve Social Security and Medicare, which began a direct-mail campaign to its nearly five million members, emphasizing that the new legislation depended on a high tax levied upon its senior beneficiaries. This warning that the amendment would raise taxes was partially true: The MCCA would have depended upon the top 5 percent of upper-income older people paying an additional $800 tax, and it would have raised premiums for everybody. But "many middle-income elderly believed that they, too, would be responsible for the full $800 surtax," writes Street, and fury mounted to the point that fifty older adults surrounded a congressman's car in protest, beating on it with their signs. "I don't think they understand what's going on. That's too bad," the legislator said after escaping from his car, which picked him up at a gas station down the street. The extra tax and confusion over who would pay it made the entire MCCA look and feel like a scam to those it would have benefited most.

In some ways, it could be argued that it was a scam. The MCCA was supposed to be paid for not by future Medicare beneficiaries as a long-term investment toward growing old but by older people themselves. It was not an extension of the social contract, but almost a contraction within it. Notably, Maggie Kuhn, the founder of the radical Gray Panthers, who sometimes defined themselves in opposition to AARP (the Gray Panthers were intergenerational and far to the left; AARP was neither), opposed the MCCA altogether from the beginning, emphasizing that it did not provide any real structural reform. She went further, even arguing that *Medicare itself* was too limited. Kuhn testified before the Senate Committee on Finance, in fact, saying that "her organization could only support legislation that provided a national health insurance program for citizens of all ages." As a result, in any case, of older people's split on this issue, fueled by class interests, AARP lost its status and credibility as a "peak interest group" and as a cohesive body that stood for a clear, unified set of older people's interests. I felt struck by this little chord of dissonance in the history: how a seemingly obvious piece of legislation might be opposed, simultaneously, by people who recognized that Medicare's larger structure didn't go *far enough*, and by wealthy others who felt its tax burden went too far. Perhaps this pointed, I thought, to the fundamental difficulty of organizing anyone around the identity of old age. It was not that old age itself was a scam, exactly—it was real—but that it meant different things to its constituents, who wielded it in different ways. Older age became entangled, because it had been forced to do so, with a larger American precarity. Once you joined older age and sat somewhere in the interior of its vast map, it was up to you to protect any power you'd amassed.

While it supports the existence of Medicare, AARP has also itself always brokered insurance. Via a partnership with UnitedHealth, AARP has received "royalties" on every UnitedHealth insurance plan sold to its members, insurance plans that were either Medicare Advantage or Medigap plans—that is, built to fill the holes in traditional Medicare. In other words, there was a tension between the existence of the public program and the ways in which the holes in the public program allowed for private options to take root. One lawsuit, filed against AARP in 1995 by a retired doctor named Joseph Schiff, poked at this tension. "The crux of the complaint by Dr. Schiff and other AARP members is that, while the AARP has pretended to be a non-profit organization with the purported objective of helping its elderly membership, the reality is that the AARP is using its members to generate millions of dollars in profits," wrote Schiff's lawyer, continuing:

> In plain words, Dr. Schiff claims that the AARP injured him and millions of other members by taking their money under false pretenses. He contends that the AARP engaged in a massive deception about what it really is and what it does with the money it gets from members. Specifically, the AARP misled members and prospective members into believing that it is a non-profit membership organization whose purpose is to serve the interests of persons 50 years old or older. In reality, the AARP has become an enormous profit-center which generates unrelated business income to fund lavish salaries for its officers and directors, and for the benefit of the affiliated entities which it owns or controls.

Schiff lost. Another lawsuit, in the early 2020s, pitted two men, Jeremy Nichols and Leon Wilde, as part of a class action lawsuit against the nonprofit, alleging that while "AARP has long been regarded as a protector and advocate of the nation's senior community," it was also a "defacto" insurance agent for UnitedHealthcare, the insurance company with which AARP had a business relationship, earning a nearly 5 percent "royalty" on each Medicare supplemental insurance plan sold to AARP members. The class action lawsuit argued that the men, as well as the larger group of people they represented—older and disabled members of AARP—had been paying extra money for this supplementary insurance because, in part, it was "AARP-branded." The royalties from such insurance sales contributed, the lawsuit said, to more than half of AARP's revenue. In fact, the lawsuit said, the insurance royalty revenue was more than three times the group's membership revenue.

It was funny, I thought to myself, how I could not tell for some time if the Jeremy Nichols I found online, the president of a bird rescue center in Sonoma County, was the Jeremy Nichols I was looking for. The man I found also seemed to be an expert on cemeteries, and, if he was the *same* Jeremy Nichols as the bird-oriented Jeremy Nichols, spent much of his time documenting his area's known and lesser-remembered resting places, noting in a local news profile of him that "everybody dies, except maybe you and me. We keep telling ourselves that until it's too late." I emailed him, unsure what I would find: the right Jeremy or the wrong Jeremy.

"I have an empty hummingbird feeder, shame on me!" he exclaimed early in our conversation. It was the right Jeremy. But when I asked him about the lawsuit against AARP, which doesn't seem to have gone anywhere, Jeremy told me he didn't remember much. "The firm of attorneys was looking for AARP members/clients to be token plaintiffs in the suit. I suspect they trolled until they dredged up a few people. I had to fill out some paperwork and after some months got a check for $1,500 or something like that. I didn't have to appear in court," he recalled. In his first email to me, Jeremy told me that he had always "wondered at the lack of a guidebook, 'How to Be a Human Being,' that we should be given when we're born, but we're not. For example, as we get older, simple cuts and bruises take longer to heal. Did you know that? I did not. It's true—I googled it (everything is on the Internet and it's all true, 'especially the lies,' to quote Garak the Cardassian of *Star Trek: Deep Space Nine*). But no doctor has ever warned me of that, or anything else, in advance. That should all be in the book!" So should information about insurance, he said, which he had learned about as he aged. Now, in fact, he loved his insurance. "The AARP/UHC secondary insurance is expensive but fortunately we can afford it," he told me. "The nice thing is that, between Medicare and UHC, all the doctor and hospital bills are paid. We pay nothing except for some portion of the drugs my wife takes, and again, we can afford it. I can certainly understand the anxiety of people faced with a choice of paying the doctor OR the insurance OR food OR rent." As we spoke, he rustled through his monthly bills and reported to me exactly how much he and his wife paid together: the standard $185 to Medicare, multiplied by two, the supplementary UnitedHealthcare Medigap plan through AARP, which individually cost $283.04, and then a supplementary drug plan. Altogether, the couple spent $1,055, plus some cents, for their per-month insurance coverage.

Jeremy understood that there was a series of holes in regular Medicare that encouraged him to buy private supplementary insurance. He understood that this private supplementary insurance had been sold to him by AARP via an arrangement that a lawyer, referencing Jeremy's name, had literally argued about in court. And yet he also felt happy with his situation: the fact that between the primary insurance and the AARP-boosted secondary one, most of his health care was covered. "It's worked out well for us," he said. Formerly an engineer in Silicon Valley, Jeremy had always planned to retire at fifty, and did, the combination of circumstance, extreme saving, and in general what sounded to me like a very frugal approach to living. In their planning, he and his wife had counted on *not* receiving Social Security, assuming it very well might be gone by the time they retired. Social Security was still around, and it was their only source of income now, while they sewed their own shirts and bemoaned the rare occasions that they had to call a handyman out to fix the well at the house they planned to continue growing old in. I delicately asked Jeremy if he had long-term-care insurance, or what their plan was, exactly, for the next few decades. "We do not," he replied, then paused. "It's very expensive." Their plan, he told me, was to hire a live-in caregiver, "unless we are vegetables and can't stay home, in which case, please shoot me."

Jeremy had a Medigap plan, not a Medicare Advantage one, and the difference was important, though I found it incredibly hard to understand for literal months while I pored over forums on the internet. It might have been easier to simply talk to someone and ask, but I couldn't figure out who that person would be. After much reading, I gathered that while Medigap plans add on to traditional Medicare, they often have higher premiums than Medicare Advantage. On a Medigap plan, you can go to any doctor who takes traditional Medicare. Medicare Advantage plans, on the other hand, require you to stay in-network, and sometimes these networks are limited. Medicare Advantage plans are also renowned for a very particular combination of usually low premiums and high "freebies." The reason that these supplemental benefits, as they are sometimes called, exist, had to do with Medicare Advantage's structure: The idea originally was that Medicare Advantage plans would be cheaper for the government than traditional Medicare. These private plans bid against the county-wide costs of traditional Medicare, then were supposed to keep the difference as a rebate, spending it on offering supplemental benefits that may or may not be used.

I finally found someone to ask about this complicated fabric, the patterns woven into its cloth, in Mark Schlesinger, a professor of public health at Yale. I had already read some of Schlesinger's work before he began to answer my questions over email, sending me a series of articles that spun my brain. (This was where I had learned of the MCCA, and its failure despite AARP's support.) He had written elsewhere that through the boosting of Medicare Advantage plans, beneficiaries have moved from "passive patients to active consumers." The freebies of these plans were popular: particularly, Schlesinger pointed out to me, the drug coverage. But "as they get older," Schlesinger told me, "beneficiaries will switch out of MA [Medicare Advantage] plans as their health needs increase and the limitations of MA plan coverage become more evident or consequential for their own health care . . . relatively few switch INTO MA plans as they age." A huge portion of Medicare Advantage plans—93 percent—offered fitness benefits, which Schlesinger noted was a 'healthy people' preference." It was unclear, he said, whether this was because younger beneficiaries were choosing Medicare Advantage plans or because these kinds of benefits "induce more favorable selection"—people with fewer health issues enrolling, thereby saving the health plan money overall.

As Medicare Advantage plans have ballooned, they have actually become *more* expensive for the government, not *less*, than traditional Medicare, in large part because of the spending on these rebates, but also because of aggressive diagnosis and billing. In 2021, for instance, Medicare Advantage plans were overpaid by $23 billion. But beyond this, there was also the issue of identification. There are almost 4,000 Medicare Advantage plans today (on average, 41 plans are available in a given person's area). There is one Medicare. This kind of fragmentation and privatization could, Schlesinger wrote, "weaken beneficiaries' collective identity," as well as their identification with the public program sitting behind their individualized Medicare Advantage plan. In an email he wrote to me later, he hypothesized three results of this lack of identification with traditional Medicare, emphasizing to me that it had not been studied.

> Hypothesis number one: By identifying with a private health plan rather than the program as a whole, beneficiaries become less supportive with Medicare policies and practices that have broad social benefits for the general public or the elderly/disabled public as a whole.
>
> Hypothesis number two: By identifying with private health plans rather than the program as a whole, public support declines in investments in Medicare's infrastructure—which reduces its capacity to monitor program performance, identify inequities (geographic and otherwise), and intervene to improve healthcare quality and equity.
>
> Hypothesis number three: By identifying with private health plans rather than the program as a whole, the public fails to take advantage of other programs that are intended to help consumers navigate the complexity of dealing with MA plans. These include the state-based SHIP programs supporting consumer choice... as well as Medicare's coverage appeals process... Beneficiaries thus become less willing to engage in these ancillary programs and less supportive of public investments improving those programs.

All hypotheses seemed to point toward less future support, socially and administratively and economically, toward the public program that was supposed to wait for us, however imperfectly, at age sixty-five, or before if you had a disability. It reminded me of the failure of the MCCA: that the future of these benefits could be determined by the precarities, and wealth, of a present-day group of older people. *Because* they had been carved out in the first place. Now, so far in the future of the MCCA, there had been more carving out, a whittling away of solidarity and connection. I thought of a triangle, the widest part being "everyone," the pointiest part being older people. But the triangle kept extending, I felt, its point becoming pointier, so that it wasn't just older people anymore; it was, somewhat suddenly, one day, going to be *one person. You. Me.*

In a sense, all this pointed toward identification, or a lack of it, with the sociopolitical entity of "senior citizenship." Were we—youngish people—going to become old, or weren't we? Could we identify with present-day older people, or not? AARP seemed to tell me that we were heading in that direction. On its website, and on its Instagram, people who looked almost startlingly young to me abounded, going about their lives as bicycle mechanics and baristas, musicians and builders of historic ship models. Many of them were in their forties, and I read there that nearly 70 percent of Gen Xers did not have a retirement strategy. Gen X's birth years stretch between 1965 and 1980. I was just eight years away from AARP's doorstep, I realized. It made sense: You could now be a member of Generation X and be nearly sixty—five or so years from receiving Social Security, and being on Medicare, if you were not already. Linear time brings us toward oldness, obviously, and I thought about Jeremy's semijoke about needing a handbook for life. Increasingly, it seemed to me that AARP was exactly this handbook, or wanted to be. It would be waiting for some of us: a source of help and guidance, and even, I understood now, of insurance for those places where the government-offered kind fell short. It would offer us choices, choices tailored to each of our tendencies and quirks, our beliefs, and our highly specific needs. This was the promise. Yet I found it harder and harder to say for certain and within such an increasingly individualized landscape, with so many different versions of reality, what Medicare even was, let alone what any shared, real vision of oldness looked like.

AARP is a behemoth, but it is not the only map through the precarious forests of aging and insurance. There are other guidebooks to being a consumer of health insurance, other ways for an individual to feel as if they understand, and can buy, the best decision for them. On a rainy Thursday evening, I started driving north, in and out of a road called Old Perry Highway. The road was named for a Revolutionary War hero who tromped around in these hills, pushing back the British. Now, it was a vestigial little path that wiggled back and forth across a bigger thoroughfare, McKnight Road, whose auto dealers and strip malls, outlet stores and discount mattress warehouses seemed to stretch forever. Two minutes on McKnight erased any sense of being in Pittsburgh; you were somewhere else, anywhere, really: My childhood in San Diego would spring to mind, and my time in Iowa, in grad school, when I went to the Coralville Mall on the occasional weekend. Perry Highway was something different. Space and time compressed there, along the old route's incredibly curved segments that pushed you up and over hills and into, suddenly, graveyards. Smokersville Tobacco&Vape, selling kratom and cigars. Charizma Hair Designs. Dental offices out of people's houses. Three Degree Road. Dairy Queen (Treat). Auto shops. The community college, my destination, was out here somewhere, tucked away and gleaming in its largeness like a dew-spangled frog.

I was going to learn. The class I had signed up for, Medicare: What You Need to Know, sat at the far end of a labyrinth of corridors within the community college. "Betcha everyone in here's over thirty-five," said one man as we settled into our expectant hush, preclass.

"Thirty-four," I said, but no one seemed to hear. It cost $75 to be here.

The teacher was an almost terrifyingly terrific steward. He was about the same age, if not slightly younger, than most of the people (not me) in the room. "Great question," he'd say after every question, and timed things just right, with the same mixture of boredom and proficiency as a seasoned flight attendant doing the preflight seat belt presentation. It was a long class, and in anyone's hands it would have been predominantly stultifying. In his, it was too—but the overarching sense was that he was guiding us through an unavoidably unpleasant task, and we trusted him. He passed out a printout of the PowerPoint, headed by a cartoon of a small, foreshortened man standing in khakis in front of a maze with seemingly no end (and, I noted, no cheese). "Welcome to Medicare ENROLL HERE," the maze's wall blazed, in the Comic Sans typeface.

We began at a gallop: We needed to know what we didn't know, the man told us, and so we started, understandably, with Medicare. What was it? It was government-run and government-created health insurance—hospital (Part A) and medical (Part B)—in which you could enroll at age sixty-five. The premium ($164.90 per month for Part B) was deducted from your Social Security check. But here was the thing, the man told us, clicking into a slide that laid out the stark balance sheet. On the YOU PAY side of things were numbers, and on the MEDICARE PAYS side of things was very little—words like "balance," and "all," which seemed dwarfed by his explanation of out-of-pocket sums we might soon be bearing. He lingered on the $400 daily copays for days 61 to 90 of a hospital stay, and the $800 per day after that, and the blank, presumably vast sum we'd be responsible for after day 100 in a skilled nursing facility. He did not mention Medicaid.

The man wasn't wrong, of course, about Medicare's expenses or its flaws. Meanwhile, the room felt suffused with a daunted feeling, an overwhelm. It was "as clear as mud," the man said, emphasizing that feeling with which he'd started the presentation: We were all standing in front of that maze, begging it to yield what we thought it might. "If you're brave enough to go with regular Medicare," he said, well, then that was that—but there was another option, or rather, two: Medigap, which he'd come back to later, and, most importantly, it seemed, Medicare Advantage.

So: "How big's your stack?" he asked us. He was referring to the mailers he knew we'd all gotten (not me), all the marketing material that he said was probably 99 percent of what we were getting in the mail: advertisements for different Medicare Advantage plans. He could get the names—our names—he told us, to personally spam us with such material, but he didn't do that. That was basically illegal, a scam, what they were doing on TV, what they were doing over the phone, calling us up and trying to sell us these plans. Put it in the trash can, he told us. And then he said: They're like Ragú. Medicare Advantage plans. Everything's in there.

He showed us a sample Medicare Advantage plan. Eighty-five percent of the folks in Western Pennsylvania had Medicare Advantage plans, he told us, and began to do a verbal comparison of this balance sheet to the previous one, regular Medicare. If you held this example Medicare Advantage plan, you only had to pay $275 per in-network hospital stay (the length of days subject to "medical necessity"). You also paid zero dollars per primary care physician visit (in network), and zero dollars for diagnostic tests and procedures (in network).

Later, through some googling, I found the example plan. It was something called Aetna Medicare Advantra Premier Plus (PPO). The premium, which the man didn't mention in his presentation, was $33 per month. The plan covered chiropractic services (for a $20 copay), diabetes supplies from a particular company, glucose monitors, home health care, preventative colonoscopies, dental exams, and much else, as long as, generally, they were in-network. It looked pretty good.

Perhaps it was overdoing it to think of Medicare Advantage as, in some way, like the fake Geek Squad on the AARP scam map—pretending to be one thing while actually being something else. After all, it wasn't called Medicare, it was called Medicare Advantage. On forums online, I read both arguments: that it covered people's medical needs just fine, and that it bilked them irreparably. Still others seemed to be making the case that Medicare Advantage was assembling a new definition of care and sickness altogether. To be *too* sick, or *too* costly, could leave you wanting different coverage—when people got sick, Medicare Advantage plans' popularity dipped. At the same time, to have a host of issues deemed both lucrative and treatable made you a perfect patient. "The government pays Medicare Advantage insurers a set amount for each person who enrolls, with higher rates for sicker patients," explained *The New York Times* in an exposé of the way some insurance companies have used Medicare Advantage to drain Medicare. "And the insurers, among the largest and most prosperous American companies, have developed elaborate systems to make their patients appear as sick as possible, often without providing additional treatment, according to the lawsuits."

Denials of care were high: Medicare Advantage plans denied 17 percent of initial claims, one study found. While more than half of these denials were later reversed, the denials most often involved Black or Hispanic patients. Another study logged a 15.7 percent denial rate for Medicare Advantage plans, compared to a broader claim denial rate of 15 percent. "Prior authorization" was the term that shadowed Medicare Advantage; before receiving a certain exam or procedure, a patient themselves very often had to apply for approval from their insurance company, which might deny the request (and did at a rate of around 7.4 percent in 2022). If you were denied this authorization, you would either have to pay for your treatment out of pocket or abandon it altogether. You could appeal, but less than 10 percent of people did so in 2022. A vast majority of doctors reported that prior authorization requests were increasing. So too was the use of AI to determine which authorizations went forward and which were denied. The surgeon general, already interested in loneliness and burnout, suggested that AI tools could help in these kinds of administrative structures. Deceptive marketing for Medicare Advantage plans often targeted "low-income beneficiaries." The State Health Insurance Assistance Program provided education on Medicare coverage, but lower-income people didn't always have easy access to such resources.

This whole thing was confusing, the man at the community college told us. He wasn't even speaking of anything I just mentioned in the previous paragraph, but he was right. There were so many plans and possibilities, he said, that the right one—the right one for us, specifically—was out there, but we just didn't know it. We needed help finding it. We could set up an appointment. He could—and did—email us, all together, so that we suddenly learned each other's contact information—something that was not necessarily illegal but felt dubious and strange. Same for the community college class as a whole, of course: It felt educational, but was, truly, one man's private advertisement for his Medicare Advantage consultation business. We got his card. To this day I receive emails nearly weekly from his Social Security counterpart, from whom I took a cousin of a class at the South Campus, and who seemed a soft and gentle man, a man who took it upon himself to point out the importance of Social Security and its history, something that the Medicare Man did not. That man didn't actually seem to like Medicare very much.

There was no real surprise here that the man was not neutral—he told us as much. He was an insurance broker, he said, after phrasing aloud the hypothetical question we must all be wondering: *So, how do you benefit from this?* Well: He didn't have an allegiance to one plan or another, or to one insurance carrier or another, as his commissions from all of them were the same. He didn't care which plan we chose, he said, as long as it was a Medicare Advantage one. Meanwhile, on the AARP website, the organization staunchly defends Medicare, arguing for its strengthening, as well as the need to offer "choices." As for its perspective on Medicare for All, AARP "has not taken a position."

There is a book I have long loved, *About a Mountain*, by the writer John D'Agata, who I studied with in graduate school. D'Agata wrote about Yucca Mountain, a contentious nuclear waste repository outside Las Vegas. The thrust of his book was investigating what it meant to the future that, in the present, people were placing nuclear waste in this mountain, under their various frameworks of knowledge and prediction and safety and truth. "I do not think that Yucca Mountain is a solution or a problem," he wrote. "I think that what I believe is that the mountain is where we are, it's what we now have come to—a place that we have studied more thoroughly at this point than any other parcel of land in the world—and yet still it remains unknown, revealing only the fragility of our capacity to know."

I do not think Medicare Advantage is a solution or a problem. I think that what I believe is that we have come to an incredibly fragmented, unreal-feeling moment, a moment in which a larger, clearer, and collective understanding of reality is needed if we are to actually believe in our own oldness, our own futures, as things to enter. But it is hard. Geek Squad can be both savior and scam, and an organization can be both a humanitarian force and an insurance broker, and a public health program can also be private.

In some earlier version of myself, I had wanted to be an artist, or a musician, making things of beauty. Now I lay in pain, often, in Pittsburgh, trying to find a specific position that would not hurt my back, and attempted to understand not just the reasons that things were turning out the way they were but why I seemed pulled by a thread, farther and farther into the labyrinthine weavings of this part of our present day. What had happened, I thought some nights to myself, was that I had descended into the strange subterranean structures of aging, almost as a way to avoid the contemporary world. It was a way to try to predict the future. I didn't know who I was, "really." I didn't know what was to come, either. My investigation, or whatever it was, was an effort to see how oldness worked—not just the corporate structures around aging but the actual, physical, emotional process of getting older. Of transitions: one reality to another. I wanted to see better the ways by which "things change," as we always find ourselves saying. How they become "real." In a sense, it was via older people, in the present, that the future was forecast.

And like I had landed in Pittsburgh, it sometimes felt as if we as a society had simply landed here, in our fragmentary moment, almost by accident. In fact, I was realizing, I came to Pittsburgh because I had googled it and streetviewed it from my bed in Central New York, lining the tree up against the telephone wire just right. Something had beckoned me here; I had liked some undistillable sense of the city that I had gotten from digitally zooming up and down its streets. Neither were AARP and Medicare Advantage accidental developments; both depended on the carving out of older Americans as a particular group, separate from everyone else. Medicare itself was the later result of earlier effort, under Harry Truman, for national health care for all (LBJ, who signed Medicare into law, called

Truman "the real daddy of Medicare"). Truman's original plan was opposed by the American Medical Association, among others. "The Cold War stigma of 'socialized medicine'" harpooned any chance of Truman's original plan, but the roots of Medicare focused on older people, already benefiting from Social Security, as a palatable pool on which to attempt something larger: a first step everyone, presumably, could agree on. The old were an increment toward the rest of us. "Medicare's architects anticipated that after covering the elderly, Medicare would soon expand to insure children, then workers, and eventually all Americans," write scholars. Over decades, a collection of forces—a turn toward private markets, the rise more generally of neoliberalism, and an interest in *reform* rather than expansion—defeated Medicare's original aspirations to blanket all of us in its patchy down. Now, instead of Medicare slowly turning toward us younger people, we younger people turned toward oldness, and whatever version of subsidized health care awaited us there.

For decades in the United States, we have also been enwrapped in debates about intergenerational equity—the idea that the "young are being deprived of opportunities for well-being because of the excessive allocation of resources to the old." It is not difficult to feel this way when you see, for instance, a report noting that Medicare funding is running out, and will be seriously on the rocks by the 2030s. Zoom out, Schlesinger told me, and you see a larger picture: proportionally fewer working-age people paying into the trust fund that supports Medicare Part A, the hospital/inpatient piece of Medicare that increasing numbers of baby boomers were starting to use. Surely, too, the higher payments to Medicare Advantage plans didn't help: According to Donald Berwick, formerly the administrator for the Centers of Medicare and Medicaid Services, Medicare Advantage and its overpayments are largely to blame.

Privatization and that chiseling-out of older people are intimately tangled together. The groups most pushing for privatization would seize on this idea of older people's separateness, pitting the young against the old, in their attack on what they called "entitlements." Americans for Generational Equity, one of the most active of such groups, was initially funded by, as scholar Jill Quadagno wrote, "banks, insurance companies, defense contractors, and health care corporations," and attempted, in her words, to undo "the socialization of the costs of such care across the generations, returning it to the private sphere." They pushed forth their message by emphasizing the "downward spiral" (in 1987!) of young Americans, publishing something called *Generational Journal*, which argued that the poor were victimized by public money flowing to older people, and by connecting to important think tanks, providing quotes in newspaper articles, publishing articles and books, holding conferences on Medicare reform, direct-mailing people about how children were imperiled by Social Security, and creating a bipartisan congressional advisory council, among other things.

It was not hard to hear echoes of this past in how we talked about older people, with terms such as "boomer remover" and others. There was a lot of anger toward older people and a sense that their needs were a drain on an already-precarious system. It was also maybe easy to imagine a kind of blurry pastel alternative—young and old, hand in hand, in perfect health. This was less what I was interested in, I realized. More than anything, I was realizing the individualizing effects of all this: how something originally pitched as public and universal became the province of the old, and how this designation, in fact, helped to begin to demolish it. In Canada, Schlesinger told me, where there had been no chiseling out—their Medicare covered everyone—"intergenerational equity" was not nearly as powerful or destructive a force. You could expect, as you aged, to be doing so under the same umbrella as everyone else.

It is extraordinarily reasonable to be afraid of the financial realities of getting older. That is an unremarkable fear, in current circumstances, as fears go. So was a fear of murk, of scams, of not knowing what is "surface" and what is real, and making a wrong choice. As ever, I mostly just wanted to stop thinking about myself—to return to the diffuse self I liked to be. To not be frustrated and bored by pain, and subjectivity. To be multiple, in the way that so many of our structures are able to be. But humans, no. There was no way *not* to think about yourself as an individual: You *had* to navigate the system ahead by yourself, and with varying outcomes depending on your financial situation, your access to information, and any number of circumstances you couldn't yet plan for. It was easiest to simply assign older age a sense of mystery and distance, ahead in linear time. To behold it like a mountain on the horizon, while Bruce Springsteen sings over the car speakers of wanting things from the darkness around you.

6

PRODUCTIVITY, THE GRAY PANTHERS, GRATERFORD/PHOENIX

When I was young, it occurs to me now, with no small amount of wryness, I would always call myself an old woman. I have since noticed this proclamation among young people when referencing something they don't feel comfortable with: drinking, flirtation, or just the vast, sweeping current of the mainstream. I didn't really want to go to dances with boys, and I didn't really want to be watched in the way that I noticed them watching girls. I ate lunch in the second-floor bathroom on the day when the boys would be asking the girls—this is how we spoke of ourselves, as boys and girls, or "guys" and girls—to the dance. It was best to be alone, I felt, for reasons I couldn't completely explain.

In keeping with my assumed identity as a spinster—such a strange word to remember myself identifying as, as a kid—I played up my aversion to the things I was uninterested in or supposedly scared of. I didn't like to be driven around by other people—boys—because I was afraid, I said, of their speed, and the way they shut off their headlights and announced they were going into "stealth mode" on the streets of Urbana, Illinois, at midnight, the old-fashioned cobblestoned streets bumping the car, lightly mocking the male attempt to rev and float through the darkness.

But I wasn't actually afraid, I knew. I was self-distancing because I was not comfortable with certain aspects of the world, the main one at that time being asked to be secondary to men. Being an old woman, I guess, if I am to extend some kind of logic to my sketchy adolescent thinking, loosed me from objectification, and from caring about what others thought. This distancing would turn to skepticism of men and what they seemed to want from me. How they wanted me to be: present, pliable, accommodating. I didn't like to be told what to do, talked over, taken for granted. Thusly self-removed, I watched as my male high school classmates stuffed porn in people's lockers, called our female vice principal a "whale," surreptitiously filmed our classmates' sexual exploits, made a game of "boxing in" a girl walking down the hallway. I felt a chafe and a gasping desire to be somewhere else, somewhere very far from them. "I'm eighty," I'd say by way of explanation, because it was strange to others that an eighteen-year-old wouldn't want to be involved in things that could be honestly and objectively fun—sneaking out or smoking cigarettes. The phase slowly faded: My first boyfriend drove me down the streets in stealth mode, the headlights of his ancient tan Volvo turned off, nothing to see but everything to feel, the corn respiring in the dark, his biceps flexing on the gearshift. We lay on the tennis courts of a public park at night, the heat from the day pushing into our bodies. I snuck out and smoked an entire pack of cigarettes one night, on the front porch. The first time I got high I couldn't believe life, and youth, could actually be easy. I'd then spend years bouncing back and forth between those two feelings: extreme acts of stricture and extreme forms of relief. I had no idea how to live in the middle—how to be a part of a larger group of people while also being myself.

Years later, in Pittsburgh, I toiled away at a high stakes–feeling article about a financial advice–giving radio host and the history of corporate radio. I no longer felt the ease of youth or the (perceived) freedom of oldness at this time in my life. Mostly I worked. The article haunted me. I worried I'd get it wrong in any number of ways, and lost an increasing number of days and nights to sleeplessness. I see it in my journal now: Every day from that time says "anxiety," "spiral," "stress," "what might happen," "tiring," "nervous." I took on another project: copyediting an editor friend's book about a nuclear remediation disaster, and I wondered how I'd fit this work into my ongoing schedule, which toggled between reading about corporate debt, interviewing people laid off from radio jobs, and walking Helgi his requisite eight miles a day, up and down the hills of the city. Then I took on yet another project: the nuclear remediation writer friend connected me with Ralph Nader, who needed an editor for a collection of essays he'd written over the course of decades, which I collected and organized according to subject: "philosophical ruminations," Covid, "environment, health, and safety," "corporate crime and corporate welfare," voting, the media, "money, banking, and class," "law and corporate power," "heroes," "Congress and civic engagement," and more. Each of these subjects was meant to contain fifteen to twenty essays from a pool of many, many more. It was my job to read them, separate the wheat from the chaff, and then organize them according to what a casual reader might most enjoy. It was a project that could have taken a year, and I had taken it on alongside several other intense demands. My life, I saw very clearly, had become my work, or maybe it was vice versa.

At that time, Nader was in his late eighties. He asked for my mailing address and sent me a flotilla of books he'd written, including *How the Rats Re-Formed the Congress: A Fable* and *Breaking Through Power: It's Easier Than We Think*. He seemed to always have extra work for me: copyediting his sister's book for tweens (on civic engagement), starting a series of "civic biographies," firing up a newspaper that would cover the workings of Congress, from DC. I found out what many others had found out before me: This man was not just tireless, he was devoted to his exertions in a way that could unnerve. He'd chosen not to pursue having a family, he said in one interview, so that he could devote his life to his work. Now he was nearly ninety, and showing me a pathway for my extreme tendencies, which were taking the form of a workaholism that kept me both inside and outside my own life.

I turned down the opportunity to start the paper on Congress and the civic biography series—actions that show me in retrospect how stretched-thin I must have felt, as I have always found it truly impossible to say no to jobs. Instead, I focused on the tasks at hand. In the evenings, when I had no choice but to take a break to make dinner, I panicked while chopping vegetables, sure I couldn't handle it all: the swirl of disgruntled radio DJs and off-the-record former employees, the relentless number of columns about things like "omnicide" and OSHA, the stories about nuclear contamination. During the day, which I was beginning to dread, I bounced from one commitment to the next, unable, it seemed, to make a dent in any. Ralph sent me hundreds of buttons that read "AXE THE MAX" and featured two swooping 737 Max airplanes on either side of a skull: his grand-niece had died in one of the crashes of that plane model, a horrible irony considering that Ralph had focused to some degree on airline safety, publishing, in 1993, a book called *Collision Course* on the topic. I became fixated on what Ralph seemed to represent to me: an old man who had spent his entire life fighting for what he believed, increasingly in some degree of solitude. It had, of course, not always been like this. Long before the 2000 election, after which he was seen by some as a spoiler, Ralph had enjoyed much broader and popular status, spurring people to write books about him with titles like *Citizen Nader*.

On one of our phone calls, Ralph mentioned he'd done some work in and around nursing homes. Of course he had: He had done, I was discovering via my indexing, work in almost every subject known to humankind. "Check out *Old Age: The Last Segregation*," he told me, and I did, buying a copy of the out-of-print book from some small corner of the internet. In it, I saw that Ralph had in 1971 financed and organized an expedition by a group of fresh high school graduates—all women—into a few nursing homes in and around DC. The women had gone undercover, and had emerged from their experiences to collectively write and edit *Old Age: The Last Segregation*, which opened with a version of Jonathan Swift's "A Modest Proposal," originally written to skewer mainstream attitudes toward the poor in the eighteenth century. "Why not cut down . . . on the increasing number of old people, who are *not* fun to have around, who merely clutter our streets, break our backs financially, are an eyesore, and a drag on our economic growth?" the girls wrote, cheekily but also somewhat horrifically. In the nursing home, "one lady, I was horrified to see, had a catheter tube in her, but without the urinal bag attached to it," Elizabeth Baldwin, one of the authors, had written. "The patients on warm days were wheeled up to the front porch where they were able to watch the cars rush by on a dirty highway," Janet Keyes, another researcher, had reported. Claire Townsend, whose name was stamped on the front cover, announced to her friends that she would commit suicide before growing old—then, interviewed later in *The New York Times*, amended her pronouncement: "Suicide isn't the thing, but I do know I'm going to age gracefully and I'm going to plan for it." She would die in her forties, of breast cancer.

"The report does not offer profundity, or any startling new information, unless you are totally unaware of how badly off old people are in a society that gears itself toward satisfying youth while neglecting the needs of the aged," summarized *The New York Times*. Indeed, so many decades later, I didn't find the report surprising or very helpful, beyond its own existence as an effort. The authors were around seventy or seventy-one now, and I tracked down as many of them as I could, interviewing them out of curiosity about their lives and this book that they had written as teenagers. The women couldn't really remember very much about it. Facing older age themselves, now, none of them planned on entering into nursing home care, though few people do plan on such a thing. They seemed relatively well-off, with structures in place for the years to come. As for Ralph, he seemed to be constantly shuttling back and forth between Connecticut and DC, and would work pretty much forever.

"Maggie Kuhn," he said one day, in some discussion of all the many interlinked topics: pensions and retirement and nursing homes and the rest. Begin to dig into the history of senior rights movements, if we might call them that, and Maggie Kuhn will be the most immediate figure to arrive, like a neighbor who sees you in distress and wants to be of help, bounding around the corner with a tire jack or a glass of water. Ralph had known her and supported her, and told me briefly about the Gray Panthers, the advocacy group she had started. From there, I began to read. Very quickly, learning about Maggie's life took precedence over all the other work I had put on my plate. In her, I recognized what I wanted for myself: to

be fiercely independent and also part of a larger community. I recognized my grandmother in her, too. And I considered the fear that seemed, increasingly, to be underpinning my drive to constantly be working. I feared a strange and complicated and frankly embarrassing thing: I feared growing old and being forgotten, not making any sort of dent, doing nothing with my life. It was this fear that propelled the manic productivities in which I increasingly found myself trapped.

Maggie Kuhn was born in 1905, the same year as Donald Trump's father, and the start of the first Russian Revolution, and the invention of novocaine. She was raised in Cleveland, Ohio, in a family whose patriarch placed ritual social importance on churchgoing. They sat in pew 72, amid Cleveland's business leaders—Maggie's father, born into a German immigrant family with very little money, had moved into a career in banking, and was the kind of man, Maggie wrote later, on whose back "corporate America blossomed." He was, furthermore, "an excellent manager, but he never fixed a faucet"—well-meaning and dictatorial both, it seems, and dependent on her mother's input, while he would never explicitly ask for it. It was his clenched hand, Maggie wrote as an (actual) "spinster"—I use that word ironically, with a nod toward my own earlier pretenses—that prevented her from dating. In her estimation, her father was an authoritarian. In college, Maggie and her female classmates—all freshly admitted to an until-recently all-male institution—were taught biology by a man who wore a visor to better avoid eye contact with them. She ached with desire for men, and also with resentment for the type of man, like her father, who did not allow women's desire to flow. Her desire, and theirs, was bottled by their male supervisors into a kind of glassy shame. The visored professor, avoiding the eyes of the young women, lectured on the "aorter." When all the young women spelled it that way—"aorter"—on the test he administered, he flunked them all, convinced they were jeering at him. So much, Maggie must have thought, for trying. Later, she mused about how, in her older age, it was finally "an age when it is appropriate to form new coalitions of the people whom society has cruelly separated"—à la AARP, but different. From the beginning, she was explicitly interested in the experiences of women, poor people, people of color, and *other* groups inside and outside oldness. For instance, Maggie wrote, "Older women have the most to gain from the women's movement."

In school, she learned more thoroughly of class structure in America, and in her sociology class, she visited Cleveland's other sides, far from pew 72 and her father. She walked through the city's jails and welfare institutions, its sweatshops, its poorer neighborhoods. She started to date, and bought a diaphragm, completely uninterested in the shame she was supposed to feel. Instead, she developed a reputation as exactly who she was. Over the next decades, Maggie Kuhn did not get married, an unusual choice for the time. She favored pleasure, and engaged in relationship after relationship. She also worked hard for the YWCA, where she focused at first on the welfare of women war workers, who slept on the ground because no housing had been constructed for them, and whose hair fell out from exposure to chemicals. When the war ended, women were laid off, en masse, and Maggie began to sink so deeply into work that she also began to disappear into health problems: chronic sinus infections that led to a course of treatment with Argyrol, a medication that seeps through the skin and contains colloidal silver. Tired of going to the doctor, she administered the Argyrol herself one night, pouring out a heavy dose. She was forty-three when her skin was made permanently gray by the overdose of colloidal silver. "To this day I have my silver lining—a souvenir of the war," she'd write. Elsewhere, she wrote that "the process of aging begins at birth." Oldness was simply one fixated-on part in a natural process. When I encountered this thinking, it felt beautifully simple, and like it was a version of what I had been approaching: Old age was both real and not-real, its boundaries forced by those with an interest in maintaining them. I became preoccupied with how she *used* her oldness.

It was in the spring that I started to read about Maggie. Spring in Pittsburgh is a time of fits and starts, when even the sallow shoots of future weeds emerging from the soil are gratefully perceived, then destroyed by another round of snow and rain. Mud dries in patches on the wood floors, creating a thin, stubborn film, and the light promises, impossibly, summer, filtering in weakly. There is one week in which ramps, harvested by an Amish man in the watery gullies outside of town, can be bought by the half pound, carefully cleaned, stripped of an outer filmy layer of root, and then turned into a spicy, bright paste. There are the weeks when you learn to watch the ends of the trees' branches, monitoring every new millimeter's growth of bud. There are the many weeks when time slides backward and all is lost again, into mud and a soft sort of snow. I read about Maggie and wondered how many hours she spent, in the long expanse of her life, working toward justice, knowing that the result would never really be known. Like the difference between winter and spring in Pittsburgh, for such a person, work and life overlap to such a degree that it's nearly impossible to extricate one from the other. Was this what I wanted when I said to myself I didn't want to be forgotten? Yes: I didn't want to reach older age and realize that my life had been passive, afraid, or in vain.

When Maggie herself became "old," not just via colloidal silver but chronologically, she began to spearhead perhaps the most overtly and clearly political movement involving fellow older people that has ever existed in the United States. They were called the Gray Panthers. They still exist today, sprinkled around the country, but in their heyday, they numbered in the many thousands, made headlines regularly, and received hefty donations to keep them afloat. In 1972, when they really started in earnest, Maggie's "message . . . was not one of senior citizen interest-group politics," writes Roger Sanjek, a historian of the movement. "Her major concern," read a *New York Times* spotlight on Maggie, "is with issues that transcend age: war, peace, poverty, hunger, racial justice." A visibly older person claiming her age, she posed herself, then, against a current in gerontology at the time that insisted there was something innate in all older people: a tendency to withdraw from the world, met by the world's tendency to withdraw from them. "Aging is an inevitable, mutual withdrawal or disengagement, resulting in decreased interaction between the aging person and others in the social system he belongs to," announced a major text, published in 1961 by Elaine Cumming and William Earl Henry, and titled *Growing Old*. To use one's oldness toward multi-issue activism—"age and youth in action!" went the GP motto—was a canny and radical act, and not something that had occurred to me as a kid, when I playacted at older age and its supposed inherent separations.

By 1984, theories of aging, at least in gerontology, or the study of older age, were changing, according to gerontologist Robert John, who argued that there were (just) "eleven theories of social gerontology that explain the experience of aging." Maggie's beliefs, which did not wait for the 1980s but were formed long before that decade, fell somewhere between two theories. The first was that of age stratification, the theory that old people, young people, and everyone in between were classified by age and our social understandings of age, and kept apart from one another along those lines. Age stratification has given rise, implicitly or explicitly, to intergenerational work and thinking—and it also underlined projects like *Old Age: The Last Segregation* by Nader and Townsend, which argued that nursing homes effectively worked to separate older people from larger society. The second was a sharp political economy theory of aging developed by Carroll Estes, a collaborator of Maggie's, who wrote that aging was "conditioned by one's location in the social structure and the economic and political factors that affect it." Later on, Estes would write that "the aged, whatever their previous background, are made dependent upon an aging enterprise and its agents." And in 2014, she would write that "public policy has created an 'aging enterprise,' which assures that the needs of older adults will be processed and treated as a commodity (e.g., medical services) and sold for a profit." It was the political and social carving out of old age as *separate* that allowed for its commodification—in other words, both theories could be true, and seemed interrelated. I thought of Medicare Advantage; the Taco Bell staging of a retirement home, with young people playing old; the trying-on of AGNES, the old-age suit. And the distance with which old age always seemed to be treated. This distance, which insisted that older age was not embedded in you already, there was a line you would someday cross, and afterward be different—it seemed, in its insistence, to betray another, oppositional possibility, which the Gray Panthers invoked.

When Maggie began her work on oldness in earnest, Medicare and Medicaid had just been passed. The youth had led the revolt of the 1960s; the rest of the 1970s were rolling in and Reagan was rumbling on the horizon. The people who had been activated by their experiences during the Great Depression, or even World War II, were on the cusp of something too—some might call it the Third Age, or retirement, or elderhood. Maggie understood the tension between the social so-called nothingness of old age and its vibrant realities, between the falseness of the many ideas attending elderhood and the ways in which they could be weaponized. She was an old woman, but she'd still be an old woman for a long time, and she could use that oldness assigned to her to create change. "Never forget we are also on a lark," Maggie would remind her colleagues. The spirit sat behind ideas like the one her colleague Janet Neuman had, to further the aim of world peace by focusing on "banks linked with war industries and colonial exploitation." The Gray Panthers could rub some of the "shine" off them, wrote Janet, thusly:

> 100 or more older people could gather at one or more branches of a bank and gum up the works by making $5 deposits. The management always solicits new accounts—and it would not look nice for them to turn away a nice respectable group of "seniors." These same people might want to withdraw their deposits—simultaneously—who knows? Just so the point is made.

As I read about Maggie, time ticked on in my own era. Workers in France protested the raising of the minimum retirement age from sixty-two to sixty-four. The raising was necessary, their president said, to keep their Social Security system afloat; critics argued that higher corporate taxes might do the trick. I was reminded of a passage in Peter G. Peterson's *Gray Dawn* in which the billionaire cofounder of the Blackstone Group argued for "reduc[ing] dependency among the elderly by encouraging longer work lives." "A vast behavioral inertia," wrote Peterson, "still surrounds the expectation of early retirement throughout the developed world." I had noticed this kind of support for working longer elsewhere, decades after 1999, when *Gray Dawn* was maybe somewhat apocalyptically published. In a sense, working longer could be an antidote to the age stratification theory: I saw this implicit rhetoric in contemporary appeals to older people "staying productive" and "keeping active."

In today's social context, it is hard to see such appeals and not connect them to the realities for younger people, not just older: Retirement feels unlikely for many members of Gen Z. Housing prices have skyrocketed, and the feeling in the air is one of uncertainty and caution, with threatened structures that have supported previous generations' abilities to retire. "If we don't secure a job with just the right package of retirement offerings, good health insurance, and adequate pay to endure outrageous housing costs, then it feels like we are at risk of setting our lives on an uncorrectable trajectory," commented a young person in a *New York Times* article about how Gen Z saw the future. Encouraging people to work longer was perhaps less about "reducing dependency" than about trimming already-fraying social safety nets. And anger toward older people—or "intergenerational equity"—also fit neatly in this picture, emphasizing their separateness as a group, instead of, maybe, the sense that their present was also, at best, our future.

In the sixties and seventies, the trend was not toward encouraging longer work lives but cutting them short; mandatory retirement was a widespread experience, with about half of all working men on track to be compulsorily retired. Maggie Kuhn argued with gusto, and lark, that retirement should *not* be mandatory: that people, if they wanted to, should keep working as long as they wanted. Of course, in the early seventies, getting older looked different than it would in 1999, or the 2020s, when I write this. In the early seventies, life expectancies were shorter. The protest movements were barely a memory at all. While Maggie and others saw it as a civil rights issue—the lifting of mandatory retirement would coincide with a startling increase in workplace age discrimination claims—people who argue for longer work lives today are often coming from a different angle, one also interested in longevity and productivity, not to mention the fact that we have far greater numbers of older people than we used to. "When people choose to keep working for eighty, ninety, or a hundred years, it will fundamentally change the way our economy works," writes Harvard scientist David A. Sinclair, in his book *Lifespan: Why We Age—and Why We Don't Have To*.

"Not having to" age was not something Maggie Kuhn was ever interested in. To her, the forced separation away from her work was discriminatory, in part because her work was so clearly her life. I related, and still relate: I have never found a greater pleasure than forgetting myself in the middle of a project, going about the day in solitude while my mind spins around the question of what the project is truly about, how to write it, what it reminds me of. "It's work, then family, then the dog, then me," an ex-boyfriend complained to me once: and presented with that bare hierarchy, I found I could not argue with it. Work has long been the reason, for me, or the excuse I have used, anyway, by which I take distance from others, and feed myself solitude. And it has alternately nourished and drained me. Every project done brings a new project, usually before the first one is over. Every project has a crisis, or many, which tempt total abandonment. Projects, as I clearly call my writing—not "essays," "articles," or "books," they are *projects*, a word that emphasizes the sense that they are always in-process, and messy, and ongoing—have melted weight off my frame and dropped hair from my head, nourished years of too-casual drinking, and mined a rich vein of anxiety that has never revealed its end. In my mind, all the projects relate to one another. Taken further, *I* am the project, the living carrier of all the interconnected works, the throughline. I have been formed from the fear of becoming unproductive, of not making a dent. I don't expect it to ever totally end, until I myself do.

Similarly, then, for Maggie, the year of her retirement didn't feel much different than the previous year. Her coworkers bought her a sewing machine for the occasion, a suggestion she never forgot, and a machine she never used. During the "work" phase of her life, Maggie had worked, and diligently, for the Presbyterian Church as the editor for their social justice journal, and on the council on church and race. Near the end of her career there, she served on the board of two "rather posh Church retirement homes," where she learned that the rest of the board had no interest in developing a resident council with voting power. "The incident taught me a powerful lesson," she wrote later. "Many rich and powerful old people—particularly men who serve on prestigious boards of directors—have trouble identifying with their less fortunate peers."

She found such deep meaning in her work that when she was suddenly expected to be gone, at age sixty-five, she was floored. "I felt dazed and suspended," she wrote. "I was hurt and then, as time passed, outraged . . . Something clicked in my mind and I saw that my problem was not mine alone. I came to feel a great kinship with my peers and to believe that something was fundamentally wrong with a system that had no use for people like us." *Use*, I thought: Is that what she was after, fitting inside a system with some kind of *role* for her and other older people? In a sense, yes. She convened a meeting to which around a hundred people came. They decided to focus their efforts on resisting the Vietnam War, and called themselves the Consultation of Older Persons. If work would not have them, they would find a use for themselves elsewhere.

In 1971, Maggie met Hobart C. Jackson, director of Philadelphia's Stephen Smith Home, the oldest African American eldercare institution in the country. Jackson called aging while Black "double jeopardy," and would be remembered, in the words of one historian, as "the father of Black gerontology." The year before, Jackson had founded the National Caucus on the Black Aged, in preparation for the White House Conference on Aging, and focused on the general lack of input taken, in gerontology and aging policy, from Black older people. "The Social Security system was based on white mortality tables and life expectancy," noted Maggie, meaning that many older Black people, particularly men, didn't live long enough to collect Social Security in the first place. The National Caucus and Center on Black Aging gathered in DC, some seven hundred in number, in order to not be "forgotten" by the White House Conference on Aging. By the end of the Black caucus, the group, Maggie included, marched to the White House with demands for the president: "guaranteed income, more extensive Medicare coverage, removal of the income ceiling for some Social Security recipients, and an end to the war in Vietnam," as a *New York Times* article summarized it, noting, too, how seventy-two-year-old Fannie Jefferson, the moderator of the conference, was arrested at the protest. "As blacks, we were born into America with one strike against us. And now that we're old and poor, we have three strikes against us," said Jefferson.

Racial and economic justice were pillars of the Gray Panthers' platform from the beginning, though membership was heavily White. In the spring of 2023, I traveled to Philadelphia, where a good deal of the Gray Panthers' archives sat, along with those of Maggie Kuhn (in two different places: Temple University and the Presbyterian Historical Society, respectively). At Temple, I read a voluminous report on the Gray Panthers from 1978, prepared by sociologist Ruth Harriet Jacobs, which noted tensions between several factions of the group: the more conservative and the more radical, the ones wanting "gray to help gray" and those more interested in intergenerational work, anti-Communists nervous about proposals for things like better public transportation, and those interested in "socialist ideology." Jacobs noted victories among the branches, or "networks," now, of Gray Panthers across the country: The chapter in Boston got $15,000 with which to pursue an "interdependent living project for isolated persons," Cincinnati Gray Panthers pushed for "normal aging course content" in schools, San Diego members (inspired by a twelve-year-old member in their midst) fought for better school cafeteria food, Oregon members successfully fought off a welfare freeze, and in DC, wrote Jacobs, members successfully stopped the District from cutting forty thousand people off Medicare. Still, wrote the sociologist, "to be widely effective, the Panthers probably must develop a wider membership base. They are deeply aware of the fact that they are too middle class, white and intellectual."

I saw in the archives, and in her autobiography, her schedules. Maggie traveled constantly, and often alone. Once, she was so used to the rigmarole of it, and so fatigued, that she got on a flight going in the wrong direction. In 1976 alone, Maggie flew more than 100,000 miles.

In 1977, when she was seventy-two, she was assaulted in her hotel room by a stranger who had followed her down the hotel corridor. He tried to rape her, then fled. Perhaps, she mused later, he recognized her from TV and worried he'd be caught.

In 1978, she spoke to audiences two hundred times. She had become a figurehead, not just because she was old, but certainly in large part because of it. "You'd be amazed," she wrote in a letter, "how responsive the elderly are to being radicalized!" Someone phoned Janet, Maggie's friend, and told her, of the Gray Panthers: "it sounds so much better than the A.A.R.P.!"

As she worked, she seemed simultaneously energized and ground down, depending on who was doing the assessing and at what point in her long "retirement" you were looking. It was possible to see her life disappearing into her work, but it was equally possible to simply see her life and work as one and the same.

Today, if the height of the Gray Panthers organization is remembered easily, it is often because of Maggie, who became their figurehead, leading a "panther roar" of crowds of supporters, sending letter after letter, and going on speaking tours where she said things like, "Old women should not be lonely but should shack up with men . . . life is a continuum from erection to resurrection . . . our movement is experimenting with sharing men since there are not enough to go around." That last statement she made in front of three hundred clergymen at the 1977 conference of the National Interfaith Coalition on Aging, where she also urged the legalization of marijuana. Three months later, she'd win the annual Peacekeeper Award from the United Presbyterian Peace Fellowship. Less forthcoming, in the public memory, are the Gray Panthers' more radical attempts and achievements. An over-sixty health clinic, free, in the Bay Area. A Media Watch program that examined cultural representations of oldness. "Bank actions" that forced certain banks to offer free checking accounts to older people without the collateral they usually demanded from them. Almost-successful lobbying for a publicly regulated hearing aid distribution system. Constant agitation for an NHS-inspired universal healthcare system and Congressman Ronald Dellums's United States Health Service Act bill, which languished, always, in legislative purgatory, despite being pushed back into discussion every two years. Something like the Medicare Catastrophic Coverage Act of 1988, which AARP had supported, wasn't enough for the Gray Panthers: They were not incrementalists. A resident bill of rights for people in nursing homes. The founding and distribution of *The Network*, a national newsletter with headlines like "Food Stamp Cut Imperils Poor and Elderly."

In the archives, I paused repeatedly on the evidence of actions the Gray Panthers, under Maggie, had taken, many of which straddled seriousness and outrageousness. But I also found myself snagging not just on her Gray Panther work but on other parts of her life: the parts that existed underneath her activism. It turned out that her life outside her work teemed with activity, love, and pain. As she cared for her mentally ill brother alone; as she stroked the backs of a succession of cats named for figures in British literature; as she had her love affairs, including one with a man fifty years her junior who, she wrote, looked, when he was naked, like a Greek god. I lightly resented myself for becoming interested in this activist's personal life—particularly her romantic life—but I couldn't seem to help it. Her lustfulness, for lack of a better word, thrilled me. In the archives, I read the proof: scraps of paper attesting to warm nights along the Charles River, in Boston, with a married man who called her Margo; and phone calls with a man who called her his *wild, lovely GG*. She had a fifteen-year affair—though his marriage was the real affair, in her mind, she'd say—with a colleague, a minister at the church, with whom she planned constantly to deepen the Presbyterian Church's commitment to social justice. They wrote to each other "every hour on the hour!" their code for how often they thought of each other, alongside *Romans!* And *Romans again!* referring, they had decided, to the biblical passage Romans 1:9–12 ("without ceasing I make mention of you always in my prayers . . . that I may be comforted together with you by the mutual faith both of you and me").

In Pittsburgh, I was beginning to wonder what the elements of my own life were outside my work, and outside my own productive resistance to aging, that lived and breathed. They didn't have to be anything important, and in fact maybe they shouldn't be. They were slim. Few people, if any, knew about them. But they were mine: the walks I took multiple times each day through the West End, the elder-law radio show I smiled upon finding on the car radio dial, the lamp Anita had given me that made my entire living room glow pinkly at dusk, the small terrors and large joys of being alone. Increasingly I felt that my self-separation tendencies were not out of fear: They were out of how *large*, in actuality, my desires were. I was reminded of one definition of loneliness: the gap between desire and reality. What, from reality, was missing that so clearly populated my desires? A road map for growing older with other people all going through their versions of the same thing at the same time, with the same tools in their pockets.

The group shared a devoted anger about the pollution of rivers, inner-city homelessness, bankruptcy on the farms, the increase in the number of children living below the poverty level, and health care for the middle income and the poor at disgracefully lower levels. In the archives, I read that "old and young people should live together—as housemates and as friends." "'Denture breath' and 'irregularity' are frequent excuses for keeping us out of job markets." "Let [retirement communities] change their White Anglo-Protestant mindset and become multipurpose, multiracial centers of a great variety of community services. They will then radiate out to serve many instead of turning inward to serve a few. They'll provide such services as legal and financial counseling, credit unions, health clinics, and rehabilitative therapy." "Aging is a natural process that is shared at every moment by all living things—from birth to death," read the Gray Panthers' organizing manual. As such, to be ageist, as was understood within this framework, was to deny commonality between humans, and the purpose of humanity, in Maggie's eyes, was to collectively work to improve the world.

As she aged, disability entered Maggie's life. And I found, in the research, the name of Maggie's last assistant, a woman named Sue Leary, who now headed the American Anti-Vivisection Society, an organization working against the use of animals in science, which had been founded in nineteenth-century Philadelphia. Speaking with me, Sue remembered her interview for the job, a chat between the two women on Maggie's back porch on an August day in Philadelphia. "Physically," Sue remembered, "she looked frail to me." Arthritis left her fingers crooked, and she was very thin. "But when she talked," said Sue, "she was very sharp, and very gentle, and very kind."

Sue couldn't remember everything Maggie had asked. "But what I really remember is that I thought that I should disclose to her that I was an animal rights person . . . not everybody's that crazy about animal rights people. I should say who I am. So I did. I said, 'You know, I've been in the animal rights movement since I was in college . . . And that's really my passion.' And she said, 'My dear, you're on the cutting edge.' And I thought, 'Okay, I love her.' Like, not only did she accept it, but she recognized that it was something that had a future."

Sue's job would span the last few years of Maggie's life. Her role was to make sure everything—speaking, traveling, life itself—went smoothly. "A lot of people wanted to get through to her," Sue told me. She wrote letters for Maggie, bounced people away from her, and watched as the woman who for the past few decades had been using her own oldness as a cudgel for justice continued toward her end. Maggie's arthritis worsened, a disc in her back disappeared and left her gasping in pain. She seemed to try to keep this part of her life private. But it occurred to me that speaking of one's disabilities as an older woman could have actually become an important piece of Maggie's Gray Panthers work. She seemed to resist this. "Mind over matter, my dear," Maggie would tell Sue. "Maggie, dear Maggie, / What can we do / To make you ease up? There is ONLY ONE YOU!" ran a poem by Janet Neuman, during one of Maggie's more workaholic, pained stretches. Of course, she clearly knew that there was nothing they *could* do for someone who worked and lived like Maggie.

As I read on, I became interested in the overlap between older-age activism and that around disability, particularly as Maggie herself became disabled. Jane Jackson, a contemporary of Maggie's in the Gray Panthers who shows up in various histories of the disability rights movement of the time, wrote to Maggie, "First: I love you. I have more respect for you than most anyone I know." Jackson was an activist—she'd sometimes detain buses unequipped for her wheelchair by sticking her foot in their door. In 1982, Jackson went on a kind of hunger strike directed at Ronald Reagan. "Monday I began an open ended water fast for life and peace on earth," she wrote in a Mailgram to the president. "As a disabled seminarian fasting for disarmament I feel it is critical that we not further erode: social services, the regulations which implement disabled people's rights or the moral fiber of our nation by continuing our present unethical, racist, sexist, immigration policies and our escalating interventionist, extravagant, immoral defense policies." In particular, she was protesting Reagan's attempted erosions of Section 504 of the Rehabilitation Act of 1973, which supported students with disabilities. Jackson's work as the chair of the National Gray Panthers' Access Task Force ruffled some feathers even among the Gray Panthers, she hinted to Maggie.

"The notion of equal access must move beyond the we's and they's syndrome of the disabled vs. the non-disabled or temporarily able bodied into the general interest arena because it *is* important to all of us. It is only that some of us comprehend because we are disabled or are just more aware, and others of us are so afraid of aging and disability that we reject all aspects of activism that get *too* personal,"

Jackson wrote to Maggie, two years before the hunger strike. The split Jackson seemed to point at, in the Gray Panthers, between those members explicitly interested in disability activism and those less so, is a topic explored today in any number of books and articles about the overlaps between aging and disability. The "positive aging" movement, and its overlap with longevity and productivity discourses, contains a resistance to disability at its core. And this drive to disconnect disability from aging fit neatly within the boom of thought, in recent years, around working longer and later into life. If your work is your worth, then the idea of retirement, already inconceivable for many of us, also becomes inexcusably "unproductive." This idea found a painful irony in Maggie herself: She never retired from her (very active) retirement.

I tried to find more information about Jane Jackson, and emailed a Canadian reverend who seemed to be her grandson. He wrote back: "I do not have any extensive recollection of Jane's comments about the Grey Panthers, other than a returning comment to the effect that they were not happy with her push against the exclusion of the differently abled. But, again, these are recollections from comments made almost in passing." Another relative told me of Jackson that she had been a proud member of the Gray Panthers until she wasn't, "after which she bad-mouthed them." "Disability rights may have had some salience," recalled this relative, but disability "was definitely not the focus." Meanwhile, Jackson had a long career beyond the Gray Panthers focused on disability rights, in particular on agitating for the passage of the Americans with Disabilities Act. "The BART elevators run better, as do the wheelchair lifts and access to buses with lifts in Oakland and DC, and I'm sure other places," one of Jackson's relatives told me. Jackson also worked on Black Panther Bobby Seale's Oakland mayoral campaign, chained herself to a federal building in argument for better-funded research into AIDS, fasted for forty-one days in protest of the war in Iraq, and was eventually given a state funeral in Cuba, where she had moved.

Today, chapters of the Gray Panthers still exist: There is one in New York, which occasionally works with the United Nations, and in San Francisco, where the group's activism builds on deep and savvy roots. In Long Beach, "the most vibrant network," according to a San Francisco member, as in Detroit, the Gray Panthers engage young interns. At a recent meeting in San Francisco, the group hosted Professor James Lance Taylor, who spoke at length about the need for reparations to Black Americans, and Chesa Boudin, the progressive San Francisco (former) district attorney who had been successfully recalled for being, opponents argued, too soft on crime. Members spoke passionately about the closing of the Laguna Honda hospital, the "last public almshouse" in the country. "I just go and run at the mouth so they know we're watching them," said the Gray Panther who used to work at Laguna Honda, describing public meetings about the city's proposed demolition of the home.

Art Persyko, the convenor of the San Francisco Gray Panthers, described to me a "survivor's guilt," as he put it, for his generation having property and pensions when younger generations do not. He didn't really want to talk, I sensed, about younger people's antipathy toward older people, the flood of antiboomerism that I imagined Maggie, if she were around today, would find both flabbergasting and sadly understandable. Persyko understood it, too, even if he was loath to address this sentiment. He used to work as a long-haul trucker, was an active member of the Teamsters, and even spoke in Mexico about the possibility of unionizing Mexican truckers as they crossed the border into the US. He compared the perception, from some young people, that "you old people have an advantage over all of us," to dominant narratives about unions that he used to encounter. "That perception of unions as selfish," he described. "That corruption that unions might have. But with old people, we don't all live in Orange County. It's a stereotype." Persyko grew up in a time, he said, when you paid $125 per quarter to go to college in the California state system. "I benefited from the peak of American prosperity and its freedom, and now, I am seeing the decline of America, and its increasing conservatism, and the results of the campaign of fifty years to take over the levers of power. It's very discouraging," he mused. While he was no longer handing out pistachio nuts to fellow activists ("Nuts to NAFTA")—he found the Gray Panthers, it seemed, to be a launching pad for serious work in the latter decades of his life. Speaking with him, I began to realize what I was seeing: Today, and maybe always, the Gray Panthers was not built, like AARP, to be a group for "senior citizens." It was more a group where people who knew about the possibilities and challenges of communal action ended up, then agitated for a future they wouldn't be a part of. "We care about the world as it is," Persyko told me. "We care about the future. We are fighting for the present, for the future. We care so deeply, maybe too deeply, because there are so many things needing repair."

In the archives, I felt my neck strain and cramp, and the faint pangs of hunger growing bigger and bigger, like a neighbor's music being turned up, to annoy. The ghosts' words swirled, impassioned, for instance, from Zelma Corning Brandt, a renowned activist and self-proclaimed heterodox, writing to Maggie in 1983 from the Connecticut nursing home that she termed her "gilded cage."

"I feel that there are a number of things wrong with this place and probably others in the same classification," Zelma wrote to Maggie. "They do not have health supervision (except the building code health) because they are privately financed." Then, Zelma continued, gingerly:

> The next thing is very personal and maybe none of my business—but I am very concerned about you, personally. You have already and are still doing a magnificent job; but I want to make sure that there was money enough to care of you or that there was family to do so. I have come to think quite differently about my will and am remaking it; and find that my concern is over and over again about older friends.

(In Maggie's notes for a response interview with Brandt, she writes that Brandt could, like her, put the Gray Panthers in her will. But in her eventual letter, meanwhile, she states, with slightly tortured directness, that she needs a travel companion for her lecture circuit: "I have diminished eyesight and some uncertainty about walking.")

I tracked down another letter from Jane Jackson, the disability activist. With a round hand, on paper from a yellow legal pad, she wrote to Maggie about incarcerated people: "What do you think of the idea of offering a proposal to the State Legislature, along with our Alternatives to Incarceration Committee's report, stating an alternative to incarcerating frail elderly and some severely disabled people? . . . Some people have been in prison so long that it is all they know—and they are surely less threat to society than taxation by the legislature to cover their ever increasing incarceration costs." Nearby, I saw the name *Graterford* on a list of active Gray Panthers chapters, and it immediately stood out: the name was not a city or a region, unlike the other chapter locations. It was something else: a prison—or, in the correct language, a state correctional institution.

Fairly recently, Graterford had been phased out and was reborn into a new prison, across the street, with the apt, I guess, name of Phoenix. Sitting outside the Philadelphia metro area not far from Maggie's old headquarters, Graterford—now Phoenix—held the life of, among many others, a man named Tom Schilk. He killed lanternflies one recent summer. We were all supposed to, Pennsylvania told us, because they threatened agricultural yields. I myself stamped them on my front steps in Pittsburgh but didn't like to, and often avoided the task. The bugs were beautiful. They had the coloring of a lamp, or a gorgeous old heirloom rug, with blush wings all freckled when closed, and when opened, a crimson flash just slightly orange: what was the color, carnelian or vermillion? Painter's colors. They were everywhere. We were all supposed to kill them, but Tom Schilk also painted them.

In the painting, it was Tom's head, bruised up, on the thorax of a crushed lanternfly. What he was able to make with prison supplies astounded me. Painting after painting, often with himself in the frame. The lanternfly-Tom—goatee and askew glasses—but then, too, an alien Tom, greenish skin, a pilgrim Tom, buckle-hatted on a blank background, a tiny little elf Tom, a totally fucked-up Tom in front of Notre Dame Cathedral, a clown Tom, a satyr Tom, a smiling jumpsuited Tom next to the words I AM HUMAN, a Frankenstein Tom, and then, I think, if I am looking at it correctly, a tiny Tom with his arms spread, as if to say either *Come and get me* or *I surrender*, behind bars, next to seventeen other men, each behind their own set of bars, one of them dead, another blind and with a cane, one raging in underwear, one munching a drumstick.

Schilk entered Graterford in 1986, serving a life sentence for the death of a man he tied up in his Philadelphia apartment and robbed of a wallet and wristwatch, and who then somehow, while Schilk was downstairs, fell out of the third-story window. Schilk fled. Now he had been in prison for almost forty years. Memory preoccupied him. He remembered the last drink he was able to make for himself, a noxious jailhouse wine made of sugar, orange juice, a potato, and "five days worth of impatience." He remembered the Catholic school he was sent to as a kid, where Schilk identified an invisible hierarchy defined by who could bully whom. He remembered the move from Graterford to Phoenix, which he says he felt acutely not for the usual reasons, maybe, but because of the people he loved who died in Graterford, who he could no longer connect with there, through that particular place.

Graterford, when it existed, had been a strange place: special, people told me, though the word seems wrong, in its particular blend of friendship and horror. It was an "old-fashioned" kind of prison, inefficient, Rutgers professor Nancy Wolff told me, describing how she spent a great deal of her career there, working with incarcerated men on meditation and creative projects meant to funnel trauma into new directions. In Graterford, the men wore street clothes and had conjugal visits. They worked in the kitchens making food. The windows of the building opened, although there was no air-conditioning. Around nine hundred people lived in a two-tiered block, and when a guard opened the door, those nine hundred men would flow out. Many of them knew each other not just from their proximity inside Graterford but also from their previous lives on the outside. It was "its own little city," Jamie Tait told me. He was released from Phoenix in 2022, after being incarcerated there—and earlier, at Graterford—since 1998. And it was a city, in large part, of the old.

Much of this had to do with Pennsylvania specifically, the state that Graterford represented, and whose laws formed and bound the prison. Until 2024, Pennsylvania was the only state with a mandatory life sentence without parole for first- and second-degree murder. A 2018 report found that the state sentenced more people to life in prison than any country in the world (besides, redundantly, the United States). "As prisoners with long sentences 'stack up' in the prison population, it is not surprising that the number of older prisoners is growing and that older prisoners are more likely to be serving longer sentences than younger prisoners," wrote Jamie Fellner for Human Rights Watch. From 1995 to 2010, Fellner noted, the total population of people in federal and state prisons grew by around 42 percent. In that same time, the number of prisoners aged fifty-five or older grew by 282 percent. Today, many of the men inside Phoenix are called "lifers," which means they're serving life without the possibility of parole. Some of them call it DBI, or Death by Incarceration. There are 5,300 such people in the Commonwealth of Pennsylvania as I write this; 99 percent of those sentences were automatically applied. Because inmate statistics are not publicly shared, one resident estimates that 683 of those—approximately 13 percent of the total—live at Phoenix State Correctional Institution.

Today, 28 percent of residents of Pennsylvania prisons are over age fifty, a number that translates as "old" in an incarcerated setting, Kevin Evans, the head of the Gray Panthers of Phoenix, told me. By 2030, a third of incarcerated adults in the US will be over fifty-five, and classified as "elderly" as early as fifty, because people age much faster in prison. Evans himself was in his early fifties: an old man, by the prison's definition. "Eldership means EVERYTHING 2 me," he wrote to me. "It's the way I was raised." His grandparents, he remembered, "told stories of our family's struggles 2 achieve what we had at that time, space, & place (the 80s), & those stories & experiences R engrained in the fibers of my soul, & make me who I am today."

It was Evans who originally told me about the switch from Graterford to Phoenix. The way he described it seemed to indicate that it was not nearly as simple an issue as building a newer facility.

"Phoenix is VERY different from Graterford," said Evans. "it's hard 2 explain. As i said, u had 2 B there. The history & spirit @ Graterford, mystically in the buildings itself, & the spirit of the men . . . IT WAS THE SAFEST FACILITY WITHIN THE [Department of Corrections.]" (This is arguable: residents in the facility reported racism and unsanitary conditions. In 1981, a group of them took thirty-five people hostage.)

One day in 1989, a group of older Graterford residents waited for Maggie Kuhn's arrival. They wanted to start a Gray Panthers network in the prison—"the first prison charter of the Gray Panthers in the world," ninety-year-old Frank Ross, incarcerated in Phoenix, remembered to me. "She started the heck out of us," he said. "The lady actually grew right before our eyes." He'd never forget it, he said. And I thought of the plaque I'd read about that the older Graterford residents dedicated to Maggie, on the grounds of the old prison, reading, in part, *According to Ms. Kuhn, even a scoundrel has the right to maintain dignity and self-respect. R.I.P. Gracious Lady.* She had encouraged the men gathered there to teach "us, the outsiders," she wrote later, about sentencing and prison reform. But Kevin Evans told me he thought the plaque was just an "urban legend." He'd heard about it too. As best as I could trace it, the plaque was announced in a Gray Panthers newsletter, in an article titled "Maggie Goes to Prison." If it existed at all, it was no longer looked at, even glanced at—for the plaque would be at Graterford, the phased-out prison, not Phoenix, and was likely overgrown by crabgrass.

The men paused when they mentioned the move from Graterford to Phoenix. It showed up reliably in their stories. They had spent years waiting for the day it would happen, and were told, they said, different things about what to expect. "I believe it was July tenth," Jamie Tait told me, that the prison got put on lockdown. That wasn't unusual, but that the administration was sending people back early from visits was atypical. Jamie ran to the phones, jumped on one, he said, because he sensed what was happening. "They locked us in for three days," he remembered. "On the third day, they began to move everybody. It was like a concentration camp"—a simile Jamie resisted using but didn't know what else to reach for instead. "They came to the cell, they put your stuff in a moving container, and they pushed you down the hallway like cattle. Searched every part of your body. There were no guards we knew." They were thrown on a bus, Jamie said. "Took you over to Phoenix and threw you in a cell."

Why would such a move matter to people who expect to spend the rest of their lives in a carceral setting? What was the difference between one prison and another? For any number of reasons, including the differences between the two facilities, the ways in which the new one took the place of the old made Graterford's memory stronger, sharper. For instance, Graterford had not had air-conditioning. Phoenix did, and because of this, its windows were not constructed to open. Many of the men who had lived in Graterford for decades were not used to the new temperature, which Jamie remembered to me as 63 degrees Fahrenheit. "Everybody was just in shock." The move, he said, "literally killed numerous individuals. The fear, the concern, the change itself . . . Some of these guys lived in eight-by-ten cells with everything they loved and had for thirty years . . . People were emotionally and mentally destroyed from that move and they still are today."

Phoenix also treated its older residents differently than Graterford had. It was rumored, and then borne out, that there would be fewer single cells at Phoenix than there had been at Graterford. Men who aged in those eight-by-ten cells had lived there often alone for much of their incarcerated lives, and the privacy and autonomy to be found in such an arrangement was rare and vital. Cell-sharing in Phoenix corresponded to new levels of assault, Jamie told me. Twenty-year-old white residents with only a few years left on their sentences would potentially be roomed with seventy-year-old Black residents who were in for the rest of their lives. "The old individual is stuck in his ways," Jamie said. "It's his house. When you move in there, it's still his house and it thus becomes very volatile. The assaults on the elderly . . . some of these guys haven't had a misconduct in forty years and now they have numerous within one year." Later, I'd read a piece of creative writing by an older resident touching on the experience.

"The most devastating source of stress for me," wrote the resident, in the voice of a character named Bruce, "was the forced double celling of lifers. Being forced to live with another prisoner in a cell the size of a parking space is killing me. I lived in a cell by myself for forty years . . . I feel like I'm being slowly crushed by the weight of time."

Saleem Mines described to me the realities of life for older residents in Phoenix. He had seen men in their seventies urinate on themselves outside, because a guard wouldn't let allow them inside to use the toilet. When Covid hit, Mines watched three years go by without a hot meal, and without a place to eat besides bed. "Prisoners in their mid- to late sixties and seventies having to double cell and climb onto top bunks," he wrote. "Older lifers suffering from dementia not bathing and being attended to unless another prisoner come to their aid; seniors wheelchair bound, mute and deaf with a diaper or urine bag not being changed and unable to wash themselves for days. One older Lifer (age 68), who had been granted commutation by the Pardon Board just a little more than a year and a half ago, was simply waiting for Governor Wolf to sign his release, when he was given a cellmate who had COVID, he caught the COVID and died. He never made it home."

Kevin Evans told me that in part because of a recent assault on an older resident—"which *NEVER* would have happened at Graterford"—he was contemplating asking for a transfer. If this happened, not only would he leave Phoenix, he would leave his post as head of the Gray Panthers. "This is how bad it is here."

The majority of the Gray Panthers inside Phoenix were lifers: people who acutely understood a certain version of their future before they were even old. They drafted cost-benefit analyses on their own lives: the price of keeping them incarcerated at age ninety, say, versus letting them out. They started a peer-to-peer hospice program. This was a different way of thinking about work. You did it—"it" meaning work you *believed in*—because you collectively needed to.

"What's to understand?" that older woman had joked to the younger one, in the personal care home in Pittsburgh I'd visited doing research for an article—her implication being that the youth were simple, that they had nothing of the complexities or realities of the old. Or maybe the joke was about the contemporary emphasis on empathy all the time, I don't know. I listened to that recording a lot, and thought about Maggie's offhand statement about society not having a "use" for older people, putting them in places she likened to "daycare centers."

I had been working so hard, forever, I think, to prove my "use" to some unnamed, invisible power, so that in the end, I would be absolved of something. Of what: probably not finding a different "use" for myself outside this transactional version of work. Not having a life, basically. I had thought, I saw now, that working so hard would one day somehow allow me to enter society with an ease I had never felt. It would grant me entry *inside* something. For as journalist Marco D'Eramo writes, "The wage relation [may be] considered a hellscape . . . True damnation consists in being banished from it." Who wants to be banished?

But people are. Historically, people deemed or rendered surplus have been prevented from social integration. Abolitionist scholars point toward both mass incarceration and institutionalization (of various kinds) dominating the lives of disabled people. Working longer, into older age: a way to avoid being made surplus. "Productivity" had long fueled this country's understandings about what disabled people were and were not: The Social Security Act, for instance, defined "disability" as an inability to "engage in substantial gainful work." The resultant legislation establishing a national minimum wage excepted disabled people. Today, work requirements are being reerected inside Medicaid—one of the systems that helped older people (though poor people more broadly) survive. In a strange irony, Maggie's push to abolish mandatory retirement is echoed again, so many years later, under the mandate that as many people as possible stay "productive."

The article about the radio host proceeded toward publication. He had a steady presence in church financial planning classes across the land, and one day, I drove to one of these church classes, in a southern suburb of Pittsburgh. There, I felt my stomach drop as, along with the rest of the class, I stared at a graphic of one man's financial planning versus another's. The PowerPoint slide showed us that we should have started investing for retirement when we were in our twenties, and that Jack, a fictional and optimal representative example, had been putting away $2,400 in mutual funds each year since age twenty-one. Jack now had $2.5 million, while his counterpart, who started at age thirty, simply "never caught up." I had never invested anything this way. Judging from the feeling in the room, that of slightly embarrassed terror, it didn't seem like many people in the room had, either. We faced our individual futures now with a sudden clanging worry. Working: We were encouraged in that room to scrounge nickels from under the couch cushions, sell extraneous belongings, and teach our children to have the requisite ethic. The night before the article was published, I decided I would not write again for a long time. Something had broken. There was no way to not-work forever, but it was possible for a week, anyway. I drove several hours to a cabin with no Wi-Fi in West Virginia, where it rained the entire time I was there, and I immediately got food poisoning from eating a Mason jar's worth of homemade dill-sausage soup. From bed I read more Maggie, and listened to the water sliding down from the trees.

Maggie did not escape what some people call the indignities of older age: the way they say your body fails you, the way they say it is inevitable. She was in private pain at the end, and I heard a story about how the intergenerational housing she fought for, and practiced, had a different edge to it: younger Gray Panther members, concerned about her, moving in maybe just as much to help Maggie as to further the intergenerational work. In the archives, I tried not to be sad, reading of the inevitable thing, and the inevitable privateness of it. The way she worked pretty much up until the end. It was admirable and exhausting to witness. I saw the end of her life in a new largeness to her looping hand, formulating an elegy for one of her cats, who died shortly before she did.

7

LIFE, SCAVENGER HUNTING, BANJOS

Summer in Pittsburgh is swampy and lightly itchy—pollen and insects and water and filaments of things in the air. Patches of irises bloom on the hillsides, next to guardrails, and turtles soak in the rivers. People rush the farmers markets for tomato plants. Goats are hired to munch on invasive plant species. Bars keep their doors open. It is so beautiful, in a watery way. I had an idea one day to walk as much of the city as possible, copying down every medically related sign or store I came across. I wanted some kind of cap for the past two years, and the idiosyncratic journey I'd taken through the shallows and depths of this river, seemingly, of oldness. *Hyperwellness and Cryotherapy. Medly Pharmacy. Novacare Rehab. Peace of Time Wellness. Fresenius Pain Management. Scrubs Outlet. Foot Pain Relief.*

Also, a version of this had once been my job.

A very long time ago, I lived near the 1 train 125th Street stop in New York City. Most mornings I traveled to the Times Square station, got off, and walked to a small office on the fourth floor of a building on West 38th Street. From there, I either sat behind a computer or was dispatched to a different neighborhood to write scavenger hunts. The scavenger hunts were usually for corporate events: team building or a celebration. I would collect pieces of visual history and public art and signage, knitting them together with puns and indirection, attempting to craft a solid two-hour loop for people who wanted a "dose of culture," and "tricky, witty questions" through which they could feel excited about the place they were exploring.

I was barely twenty-five. That time felt and continues to feel viscerally atmospheric in my mind. The summer sunlight off the Hudson River slanting through the tree leaves in Riverside Park, dancing and piercing so that you felt almost inside Seurat's famous pointillist painting *A Sunday Afternoon on the Island of La Grande Jatte*, notable for being a "stage-like vision of contemporary society that is at once restless and calm, particular to its moment and timeless," MoMA tells me. The smell of the subway stations: a weirdly sweet mixture of black olives and disinfectant. Some days I traveled elsewhere, flying to cities across the country to write hunts there. In these cities, I noted similar, undistillable impressions. Nashville's oaky parks and hot metal statues. The lushness of Portland's gardens.

In New York, where I lived, I walked everywhere, and while I did so, I called Anita, who had initially encouraged me to take this job. She was from New York. She had impressed upon me, in one way or another, that I would benefit from being in this place, being around so many other people from so many other kinds of work and life. As usual, she was fundamentally correct. On our phone calls I told her what I was passing on the street, what I was looking at, what block I was on. She would tell me what she remembered of that location, in a different time. We created something together, not present or past but a meeting of the two that extended for as long as we were talking and sometimes afterward, as I walked through a landscape that I felt I had memories of, memories that were not mine.

Now I was doing a version of my old walking and hunting in Pittsburgh, ten years later. I had lived in Pittsburgh for only two years and a few months, which was long for me. That day I wrote to myself, "I can't believe I used to do this jfc my whole body hurts." I kept the list going on my phone. I had had some plan here, some seed of a more precise idea, but it quickly dissolved in the city's humidity. I had set a route that covered as many neighborhoods as I could hope to penetrate in one day of walking. *Comfort Keepers. Medical Malpractice Lawyers: 1–800-MedMal1.*

A big part of the scavenger hunting job was checking on what had changed in a city, a neighborhood, or a museum. Scaffolding was an expected old foe, rising overnight sometimes to cover a plaque about the pope's visit to St. Patrick's Cathedral, or a small, high-up piece of street art that would give our corporate clients a frisson of satisfaction when they "discovered" it. Some changes were temporary, like the scaffolding, or a can of vegetarian haggis removed from a window display in the British shop in the West Village. Others were as permanent as a razed building.

In those years, I didn't see my grandmother more than a few times, though we talked often. I noted, upon each visit, how she too was changing. Some ailments were temporary—a torn rotator cuff that would slowly recover. Other conditions, like osteoporosis, were permanent, and seemed like they would only intensify over time. I wondered to myself if a person, and cities, had "true" selves from which these changes diverted them. There was something both seductive and repellent about the idea. The alternative, that we—our cities and our bodies—changed over time, in unexpected ways that we could, more largely, expect to happen, unnerved me, a person who preferred to stay rigidly stuck in the present.

I had, of course, changed. My own body and mind had altered since the days when I wore heeled boots on my multimile power-walks through various urban landscapes. A herniated disc right before moving to Pittsburgh had determined that I couldn't drive for more than five or so hours from my old home. (And this was, in fact, how I had chosen Pittsburgh in the first place.) I had stopped the car every hour to gingerly get out and stand, elongating my spine while trying not to think of the whole thing toppling slowly, like a Jenga tower. For the next few years, a litany of small, strange health issues arose, some of them temporary, some of them not. I could not see their shape, altogether, but I sensed I was shifting.

As I walked Pittsburgh, I thought about a scientific article I had read a few months earlier, in March. It was called "The Trouble with Vulnerability," and I had laughed to myself upon seeing the title. "That sums me up," I thought to myself. The authors used written narratives by older people in Finland in the early months of the pandemic to explore a tension: Older adults had been *biomedically and psychosocially* understood as vulnerable to the virus, they wrote, while also living under the performance paradigm of "successful aging," a cultural doctrine emphasizing resiliency, positivity, activity, and able-bodiedness in older age. Successful aging is everywhere: in the Instagram videos of boisterous actor-retirees playing pickleball, in the relentless news stories about elder dance troupes, in the Netflix shows focused on later-age daters.

In the Finnish diary entries, I read from "John":

My wife and I are [over seventy]—in the so-called risk-group but both without underlying health issues . . . The pandemic has changed the way we shop, buying food that can be used for more than one meal, and to be prepared for freezing. This hasn't been any sort of hardship. We haven't needed any help, but our daughters have on occasions delivered stuff, home-made cakes, for example. If we needed help, we would turn to our daughters in the first instance, or the health services if it was a health problem. We are not worried for ourselves, just cautious.

"John is careful to take a step back from the imagery of older people as people in need of special protection, and as people not capable of making informed rational choices. They will ask for help if they need, but the choice is their own to make," wrote the article's authors.

Then there was "Lisa":

This is my first year of retirement and little did I think it would be like this! After retiring last [autumn] I gradually built up new routines, hobbies and ways to fill my weeks. It was all going nicely until recently when I went from a rather full diary to an empty one. And it all happened so suddenly leaving me sort of in shock. So, I had to think what to do now in order to fill my days. Luckily, I am very healthy with no illnesses, and I have always been active.

"Like John," wrote the article's authors, "Lisa actively highlights her resilient ability to practise organised and careful self-management in the pandemic context."

The article's authors continued that there was a "constant, dialectic movement between different images related to older age," indicating what they called a "trouble with vulnerability." The authors seemed to argue for understanding aging through its precarities, not the ways in which it could be made positive, perfect, youthful, able. Actually, they said, you could understand all life through "dependency on others and social support." What if vulnerability was not an individual condition, they asked, but a universal one?

I had to admit, I realized as I walked, that *the* fear underlying a great deal of my explorations of growing older in this country was, in one way or another, about precarity, and about what you can't prepare for. Within this fear was a related fear about disability. As someone who didn't consider herself disabled, my fear was even more specifically about aging *into* disability without expecting to. I envisioned my own third-person narrative: *Lucy constantly highlights her ability to work as a way to avoid thinking about the worries of the future. Disability, for her, is a scary fate, one she does not know how she would handle, and would likely think of it, in the words of some scholars, as 'a tragedy to be defeated.' She is, in fact, very good at turning to scholars for help in summarizing her feelings and beliefs, because she is afraid to interrogate them on her own, or share them herself. She notes how scholars say that tropes about disability being a 'tragedy to be defeated' reinforce the idea that suffering must be overcome. That if you can't or don't overcome suffering, your fate—in poverty, social exclusion, institutionalization—becomes rationalized. To be outwardly vulnerable, she has thought for most of her life, is to be stigmatized. And so she pushes herself too far, while never really sharing with others. Her hands have become shaky, and she can see a fatigue glowing out of her cheekbones. Is there a way out, she wonders sometimes, of what her oft-cited scholars call 'the neoliberal fantasy of individual will and mastery that shapes contemporary austerity agendas'?*

I knew that I had been orbiting this thing during my entire investigation: this *trouble with vulnerability*. This discomfort with it, this chafe against it, and a general resistance to the concept. Age, I understood now, was a helpful distancing tool: older people's vulnerabilities, including those of my own grandparents, helped to distract me from my own present and future. I was tough, I had thought. If necessary, I could help *them*. I had not needed their assistance, their key—as Anita had once offered it to me, in case of emergency—under the flowerpot.

But the resilience I was supposed to have, and was used to thinking I had, had in fact almost mortally wounded me. It was still wounding me. I had not known how to get over my grandmother's unnatural death. More than that, though, I still did not know how to seal over the gaping wound of the pandemic, how to move forward, as we often say, returning as ever to the march of chronological time. Something had changed for me. In most dimensions of my life, I was rumpling like a wet paper bag.

As I walked, eyes peeled for signs, back and feet aching with a new-old fatigue, a LIFE van passed in the street, to my left side, and I sighed to myself, annoyed and relieved, because I saw these vans *everywhere* around Pittsburgh, and they always felt like cheerful omens of some kind. The vans proclaimed *Living Independence for the Elderly!* Most days, I saw them swimming around the city. Later, I learned this was likely because they had several such vans, and several centers across Pittsburgh. Joann Gago started LIFE Pittsburgh, in the late 1990s, after a career as a nurse. "When I was in the beginning stages of nursing," she told me, "it was just a little too hard for me to believe that I was going to put my grandma in a semiprivate room." She asked if I could imagine my own future this way: "You're going to be in a semiprivate room with another lady, and maybe have a nightstand and maybe have a little closet." Maybe the institutional setting would be a little nicer now, she thought, than it was when she started LIFE: a TV, perhaps. But back then, there were no home- and community-based services, Gago said. "None. Zero."

"You seem like a very bright-eyed person," Gago told me, "who clearly loved your grandmothers." She was right, I thought, but didn't know the difficulty I had had with showing that love. "Many people don't," she continued. "Yeah, they just don't. Their parents weren't exactly angelic . . . but I think we know that those people have a right to stay in their own home. And that's who I'm going after, the people who don't really have anybody. And I really like the idea in my mission that we will never let you alone. We will never leave you alone. We will stay with you till the end. And we do."

It was an "illusion," Gago told me, the trust we had in long-term institutional care. The way a child, faced with an aging parent, felt they could "make them safe" by putting them in an institution. "That's not what Mom or Dad want," said Gago, who remembered one of the first times she learned this. Early in LIFE, she sat across from a woman who "wasn't telling the truth about herself"—about what she needed, how she was feeling. She knew that Gago knew the truth, since Gago had been coming to care for her here and there, but she refused to "tell the truth," Gago said, to a doctor. "Talk to me," Gago urged the woman, asking her why she didn't share more with the doctor, who could help. "She says," Gago remembered to me, "'You tell him the truth, and the next thing you know, they're slapping your ass in the nursing home.' And she said, 'They take complete control over whether I have my mind or not, and I'm not telling them whether I do or don't have my mind. I'm not telling them anything.'"

Gago paused and wondered aloud about how much fear that woman must have had—and the toll of keeping quiet about her interior state. Gago had had a hard time marketing LIFE because of this, she said, this ubiquitous fear, and also, I understood, the institutional bias toward nursing homes as opposed to LIFE-like care: "The firemen can find this out and put me in a home. The doctor can. The police officer can. The Meals on Wheels lady can. They can all do this to me. So I'm not talking." This was a version of a trouble with vulnerability, I understood, but more than anything else, it was an accurate assessment of what might happen to you if you *admit* vulnerability.

LIFE was a PACE program, and the first PACE program, in fact, in Western Pennsylvania. PACE programs—or Programs of All-Inclusive Care for the Elderly—work via traditional Medicare and Medicaid, and provide community-based care and support for people who otherwise qualify for nursing home care. Many of their clients are "dual eligibles," as they are often called, the people who are both on Medicaid and on Medicare—like N, John's Papa. The particular PACE program's insurance becomes the older person's sole source of benefits: In other words, you receive all medical care through the PACE in which you are enrolled. PACE programs exist around the country, although seventeen states do not have such programs, the reason for which has been explained by their relatively lower population density, and the fact that establishing a PACE program, ensuring it can work with the state's Medicaid, etc., is a tall order. Some PACE programs are for-profit (and increasingly entwined with private equity); others, like LIFE, are nonprofit. They fall under the idea of "community care," which disability rights activists have ongoingly and often successfully pushed for, including in 1999's *Olmstead* decision, which ruled that the segregation of disabled people in institutions can constitute discrimination.

Even in the states where they operate, PACE programs can feel somewhat rare and anomalous. In 2019, it was estimated that nearly 70 percent of Medicaid beneficiaries who could use PACE did not have access to it, though this has improved somewhat. According to a study surveying PACE program administrators, some state officials have expressed a telling worry that people might "come out of the woodwork" to use PACE instead of not using Medicaid at all—in other words, it might be too popular an antidote to fears around institutional care. Indeed, what PACE provides to people on Medicaid is something very basic, and something ideally like the plan that the Kendal residents developed for their compatriot with Alzheimer's: an individualized care plan for every person served, "regular, high-touch care" including doctors' visits and therapy and home amendments and socialization and meals, and, crucially, independence and dignity and the ability to continue to live at home, as 95 percent of people using PACE services do.

Of course, like other services provided by Medicaid, income limits dictate, to some degree, eligibility. The long-term care benefits that Medicaid can cover, writes Jill Quadagno, are "not given as a right": You have to qualify, even prove your case. And avenues toward institutionalized care are still present in the structure of Medicaid, writes Judith Feder, among others, noting that "half the states direct more than 70 percent of their long-term spending for older people and people with physical disabilities to nursing home and other institutional services. A comparison across states showed that people at home needing long-term care were more likely to go without services—risking falls; being unable to bathe, eat, or dress; or soiling themselves—in states with more limited coverage."

PACE programs owe their existence to a group of activists in San Francisco's Chinatown in the early 1970s—that rich, strange time in the history of eldercare work, so clearly in response to the passage of Medicare, which would nourish, in one way or another, so many pieces of my two-year investigation: most obviously the Gray Panthers and AARP. The Chinatown activists developed PACE, or the first iteration of it, in response to the needs and desires for culturally appropriate care for older people who had at some point immigrated to the US. William L. Gee, a public-practicing dentist, and Marie-Louise Ansak, a social worker, created what they called On Lok, "blazing a bold path in culturally appropriate care for underserved seniors." In Chinatown, the population of older people grew, even doubling, almost, as wives joined husbands who had immigrated years earlier. How would these older people, who lived in a Chinese-speaking community, receive thorough, thoughtful care when they needed it? There was only one nursing home, said Ansak, in San Francisco in the early seventies that had Cantonese-speaking staff. Beds were limited, all across the city, and the Chinatown population found itself having to "go to San Jose and what have you, into these Anglo nursing homes where nobody could communicate with them. And the food was strange."

On Lok, then, was conceived as a center for adult day health-care services, developing programs over time to deliver meals to older people living at home, to bring them into a center for socialization and activities and health checks, to bring supportive services to them, on their terms. By 1979, On Lok had a grant from the Health Care Financing Administration to develop a Medicare-reimbursed long-term care program. The constant criticism, Ansak remembered later, was that something like On Lok, "a very unusual little project," only worked in Chinatown, in San Francisco, but that it wasn't "applicable to the rest of the world"—a phrase that reminded me of Beryl Goldman's experiences with the antirestraint work. The board members of On Lok, many of whom were themselves from Chinatown—used their own homes as collateral as the program worked to grow. By 1980, On Lok had three adult day health centers and fifty-four apartments for older people, subsidized by the Department of Housing and Urban Development. By 1987, it had established what it called PACE. And PACE, then, spread, to some degree, across the country. Perhaps it was only a "very unusual little project" in the sense that it made fundamental sense for people whose potential vulnerabilities were recognized and made room for.

Joann Gago spoke frankly and in an old Pittsburgh accent. She introduced me, over the next few months, to LIFE Pittsburgh, its different departments of operation. She spoke philosophically about what they were doing and why, and encouraged people to talk: a nun who brought the rest of the sisters in her convent to LIFE, as they were aging now with no young people joining up and able to help them with their various medical needs. Then there was the woman I will call Stephanie, who spoke to me about the trajectory of her life: She had spent her career jumping around from job to job, mostly in Ohio. She had exited an abusive marriage to a police officer, raised her son alone, and now lived in an apartment two miles away from where she had spent her childhood. "Fifty years," she mused. "A lot of things changed. I don't even know where certain things are anymore. I don't even know neighborhoods anymore. Yeah. They've all changed." Via those vans I'd seen around the city, Stephanie came to the LIFE center regularly, a few times a week, for doctors' appointments and activities: "There are all kinds of people here," Stephanie offered, "with all different kinds of things wrong with them. None of that really bothers me. Some people get, like, freaked out, because you know, maybe someone can't walk." But Stephanie had been a VISTA volunteer at a settlement house in Ohio earlier in her life. She called herself a super-social person: Her mother had told her that she would never be without a friend. She particularly loved LIFE because of its "sociability."

Stephanie had never learned anything about computers, working at a friend's grocery and butcher shop and resisting what she felt was an oncoming, relentless incursion of digital technology in her life. Now, she found herself forced to use these technologies without really knowing how. "I'm at the point right now where I have to order my groceries through my phone and I can't do it. And well, I mean, I asked the dietician if she would write down step-by-step how to do it. And she did. And then I did something wrong. And I'm stuck now and I don't know how to get out of it," she told me. She continued, and I listened later to the recording on my phone:

> *I was having a lot of trouble with them not accepting my SNAP benefits. And so it would always go into a credit card and it was like a nightmare, because then I had to scrape up the money to pay for that.*

I asked what the grocery store was, and what happened when she got stuck in this digital purgatory.

> *It's through Giant Eagle. It's really frustrating. And that customer care thing is a joke. Because when you call up for them, they just say "I don't know, we don't know."*

Stephanie struggled with this form of precarity, particularly after a lifetime of being a caregiver for others. She found the increased reliance on digital technologies to be sudden in its arrival, and it seemed to strand her in a place that felt, quite abruptly, alone.

> *I was always the person that took everybody else to the store, took my family, you know, to their jobs. And then, now, everything is like totally different. And it kind of snuck up on you like you didn't really, I didn't really think we would ever get to this point. And it's just, it's like, so irritating when you call someone and they say we have a better way for you to, or there's another way and you know, they give you www dot*

> *whatever it is dot com. And it's like, and I tell them when I finally get someone that I can speak to, I just say, you know, everyone does not have a computer, or have access to one. And they don't seem to understand that.*

As Stephanie spoke, she began to describe a situation that she often found herself in that disturbed me. Attempting to digitally order groceries, she confused herself and got lost.

> *I don't even know for sure what I did. But I just can't get back to the place where I can order groceries again. I'm just stuck in a cycle, really. And so I've just every day I put it off and I say no, I won't do it today. And then you know, I've started thinking okay, now what else? I raid my refrigerator. What else is in here? What can I eat? You know, sometimes, I have to be honest, sometimes I don't eat at all, you know. I just take a lot of medicine. And a lot of it makes you sleepy. I have adult onset epilepsy. So I have to take medicine for that. I have to take an anxiety pill for that. And then the other thing I take high blood pressure pills, I take for not osmosis, osteoporosis. I take a lot of medicine, anyway. I've had the same doctor for twenty-five years and she's always said to me, anything that makes you dizzy, or feel faint or feel, not, you know, on-kilter, take it at night, while you're sleeping.*

Stephanie was analog, too, in her assessment of loneliness. She clearly found the internet, and using it, more isolating than not. She didn't want to depend on it for the fixes that came, increasingly, over its invisible networks. "Loneliness," she mused. "All these people that think, okay, I can find an answer to loneliness through the internet, through all these programs that, you know . . ." On the recording I have of our conversation, she trails off here, then restarts. "I think it's just awful. And I don't know what the answer is, except to have places like this. A lot of people where I live say, 'Ooh, you're going back to that place again?' Yeah, it's called LIFE Pittsburgh. And I tell them what LIFE means. 'And what do you do there?' And I say, 'Well, you know, I have breakfast. I go to PT. On every other Tuesday, we have a worship service here, if you want to be a part of it. If you don't, you don't have to. There's always something in the main room called recreational therapy. There's always something, you know. Go in there.'"

"It seems like there's a pill for everything," Stephanie told me. We looked at each other in the little LIFE conference room. I tried to remember that moment later, from far away in time and space. She was clearly saying that there were things that pills—real or metaphorical or digital—couldn't fix, that there were vulnerabilities out of reach of fixability. I was reminded of Maggie Kuhn's fundamental theory of aging: that it was something we all, at every age, shared. And Stephen Katz's theories around "fragility, dependency, and impairment" being "probable for all of us throughout the life course." This stuff was so obvious, in retrospect, and what was so painful about it was that its obviousness had been made *private, personal.* I flashed to Stephanie lying in her apartment hungry at night while her grocery list sat somewhere out of reach, in the deep warrens of her phone's internet browser. And then I tethered back to her sitting right there in front of me. I met her twice, for two long conversations that stuck in my mind for a considerable amount of time afterward. I admired Stephanie for the way she spoke, in particular, about cell phones: how so much of life, now, was lived or enacted *through* them. In the years after speaking with Stephanie, both Medicaid and SNAP came under fire. The American Association of People with Disabilities noted, in their response to the proposed changes to Medicaid, exactly what

Stephanie had explained: that "many Medicaid recipients do not have a computer, smartphone, broadband internet, or reliable transportation to assist with navigating complex administrative systems."

While trying to write about old people and oldness, tracking those "actual circumstances" around aging in this country, which are bramble thickets of policy, history, inequity, and completely mind-scrabbling density, I came back often to a short essay by the writer Joseph Mitchell. Mitchell is famous for many things, and one of them is his long (thirty-year) stint of writer's block that *The New Yorker* paid him for anyway. One biography I read of him indicated that the block was actually a kind of grief about the way that the city he loved—New York—was changing. The old fish markets, the tight communities of oystermen and shad fishermen, the memories visible in the buildings that were razed in the eighties and replaced with glass.

"In the fall of 1968, without realizing what was happening to me," Mitchell writes, "I began living in the past." Almost immediately, then, he interrupts himself: "I am not entirely satisfied with the phrase 'living in the past' as a description of my way of life—it makes me sound like some kind of sad old recluse.

"And I should also say that when I say the past I mean a number of pasts, a hodgepodge of pasts, a spider's web of pasts, a jungle of pasts: my own past; my father's past; my mother's past; the pasts of my brothers and sisters," he continues, and the sentence unspools further, moving backward to North Carolina, where Mitchell was from, but also laterally, to "the pasts of a score or so of strange men and women—bohemians, visionaries, obsessives, impostors, fanatics, lost souls . . . whom I got to know and kept in touch with for years while working as a newspaper reporter and whom I thought of back then as being uniquely strange."

It was no wonder, I thought, reading this, that one day he simply became overcome with the past. That was where he lived. It was so full of things, and people, and memory, that it crowded the glassy present and its various despairs out. The future ticked on: Chronological time became a pain, haunting Mitchell, maybe, for what it showed as having supposedly vanished. He went in to work, wrote nothing, went home, did it again the next day. I found this simultaneously sad and valiant. He was attempting, in his way, to connect with a different world.

In disability studies, the term "crip time" refers to an alternative to linear time and its endings, progressions, and beginnings. "Disability and illness have the power to extract us from linear, progressive time with its normative life stages and cast us into a wormhole of backward and forward acceleration, jerky stops and starts, tedious intervals and abrupt endings," writes scholar Ellen Samuels. "Some of us contend with the impairments of old age while still young; some of us are treated like children no matter how old we get." Crip time could, in Samuels's words, be time travel, like Mitchell's pieces sometimes were. But she also writes of its difficulties: For Samuels, crip time is both something to relish for its flexibilities and something painful for its "melancholy" and brokennesses, its divorce from the pull of linear time, by which a great deal of the rest of the world operates. Linear time is how many of us think about aging, after all: You start young and healthy, you end decades later in a frizz of ailments, "naturally." There are seemingly few ways to step outside this arrangement, at least in the structures we are given.

Hyperwellness and Cryotherapy. Novacare Rehab. Peace of Time Wellness. Foot Pain Relief. All the signs I passed advertised—well, if not cures, then linear improvements to what ailed their potential customers.

If we were to think with linearity, the future of growing old did not look great: I did not feel, honestly, that great or good news sat ahead of us. It was not possible for me to imagine a solution to the level of fragmentation, pain, and dysfunction I saw in my research and around me. It was very possible to feel a deep despair about the future, and what it might look like for those of us currently in our twenties, thirties, or forties. Then again, Barbara Ehrenreich reminds us that opposition to despair does not come from, simply, working on yourself to feel better, or forgetting the pain of what has happened, like the rest of the world seems to. It can come from, as Ehrenreich puts it, a "vigilant realism." "A vigilant realism does not foreclose the pursuit of happiness, it makes it possible," she writes in *Bright-Sided*. "How can we expect to improve our situation without addressing the actual circumstances we find ourselves in?" So maybe it was less about linear thinking than it was attempting to map and catalog the real circumstances we were in, in the present moment, kind of like I had used to walk around cities, cataloging every surface I found.

But also: cataloging the past. I have learned to be resistant to easy nostalgia, but I do, like Joseph Mitchell, think that there is something large and worth holding on to from a deep connection to past, or pasts. The past of eldercare in this country has never been glorious, or even good, but while collecting information, attempting to organize it, and feeling myself shift into a different version of the person I thought I was—I sensed that it was all changing. The changes that were happening were years, even decades, in the making: the holes, for instance, built into Medicare, which have allowed private insurance companies to fill them. Or, stepping further back, the fact that Medicare was built only for older (and, later, disabled) people in the first place, and not, as originally proposed, for everyone. I saw slowly what I had been doing the whole time: making a partial city out of the past and present, through which I wandered, attempting to make sense of where we were and why.

It is often said that everyone becomes old. This isn't true. I got tired of this hackneyed phrase, which I encountered over and over again in my reading, my research, my interviews. Young people die, you know, I thought. All the time. Statistically, to get old in this country means you are a White woman. Another phrase often cropped up, too: Growing old is a privilege. This *was* true. But was also not true in many ways, at least not in this country, where the majority of older people are, in one way or possibly many, entreated to hide the elements of themselves that get called vulnerabilities.

So many times, I simply came back to Mitchell's panicked but beautiful desire to catalog, to collect, to write down everything not just of the past but, until he was no longer able to, the present in which he lived. Today, as I write, it was announced that Social Security benefits may very well be cut by 2034. The proposed, more stringent work requirements for Medicaid eligibility highlight the connection between a certain version of productivity and who is deemed worthy of receiving health insurance, or health care. As ever, many of the "changes"—very passive word—are said to have something to do with rising healthcare costs: In Medicare's case, a group of baby boomers inflating like a bouncy castle, and fewer working-age people, proportionally, working the gears of the air pump.

Then again, you can always zoom out. For instance, in many countries, healthcare costs are given a budget each year. Not in this one, where Part A of the Medicare trust fund drains.

Years after leaving Pittsburgh, I caught up with Joann Gago, of LIFE, who had since retired. If Medicaid were to get cut, for the average PACE program, Gago said, "It's going to cause a shutdown. They wouldn't be able to tolerate that kind of loss." Same for nursing homes: "Most nursing homes are pretty much on the brink" already, she said, imagining aloud a scenario in which nursing home residents were relocated upon a facility's closing. "Can you imagine going en masse, ten of you to, you know, this other county, this other state?" she asked.

As for herself, she found retirement difficult: the lack of interest her neighbors seemed to have in her previous life, and the ways in which she spent her time during the day. "It's absolutely terrible," she reported, about not working. "Retirement really isn't my jam. You can only clean so much." She couldn't determine what brought her joy, and had started doing consultations for people with older relatives. She took a look at a friend's relative, nearly ninety years old, assessing, for the family, if the woman might be able to move out of her home. "I hate to have been right, but I was right," Gago said. "She knew where everything was, how everything worked in this house, because she had lived there forever, and she now has no family except for this relative who wanted me to give an honest opinion about her ability to move out of this home. And I strongly recommended *not* to do that." The woman was out of money, it was true, and no one wanted the house to be foreclosed on, but moving, Gago observed, would be dangerous. "If you want to see her fall, move her," she advised the family. The woman nonetheless moved into a smaller apartment. And she fell. And the house was sold. Which was of no help to her, because she now wouldn't qualify for Medicaid, and also couldn't afford assisted living.

It was strange returning to Gago, who had been a large figure for me in the last few months of my time in Pennsylvania. My life had since moved again in a different direction: I had gotten a faraway job, and packed everything into one of those gigantic metal pods that traveled across the country all the way to West Texas. Coming back to everything I had done in Pittsburgh—a strange collection of late nights reading assisted living magazines and long morning dog walks and offhand conversations with strangers who changed the various directions of my daily life and research—felt, at times, like walking from an austere air-conditioned room through sliding doors into a blast of fragrant, mulchy humidity. I remembered how when I was a scavenger hunt writer, the images I encountered from my job stuck with me for years afterward. They still pop up: weird street corners I didn't realize I was even noticing however many years ago, and the treetops, and the edges of skyline. Images and memory snippets from Pittsburgh joined the repository, blooming like small, scrappy hollyhocks through concrete.

For instance: On a trip with Caroline to a fish market before I left Pittsburgh for good, the hot streets were completely slammed with cars and people, and the cars didn't want to stop for the people, and Caroline was having trouble breathing because it was so humid. She slowly pushed her walker across the street, and I attempted to do a kind of traffic control, particularly with one car impatiently edging. We got inside, where it was cool and salt-smelling, but no less trafficked. Codfish, red snapper, whitefish, and little fish I didn't know the names for. The men behind the ice-laden display cases descaled the fish with a straightforward, efficient near-violence. Caroline moved serenely around: I was the one swooping and stuttering, working overtime to hold doors open preemptively. On the way back she pointed out a few houses she had memories of, from a very long time ago.

Pittsburgh was, I remember now, one of the cities that I went to as a scavenger hunt writer. How could I have forgotten this for so long? I spent three July days there, I think, wandering alone, collecting information, a different me, who would find herself doing the exact same thing ten years later, but with everything changed. And now it is the future again. In Texas, I no longer feel dropped by a gigantic hand. I don't get the sense of watching myself from the outside. Under the mostly unceasing sun, many days I forget about myself, and forget about linear time. A new dog trots at the end of the leash. I run into fewer people on walks; there is no baseball diamond where I glance at the passive-aggressive reminder to volunteer. There are no grandparents in my life, either. But it is so funny how certain things from the past find you: a lamp, a key, a visit to a city you'd forgotten about. A 2012 essay by the Pittsburgh-born writer Mary Ruefle made its way to me one day recently: It was called "On Fear," and she had, unbelievably, made a list of many human fears, as I had once done, long ago, it felt, in my tiny house on the side of the hill in Pittsburgh. Among the fears on Ruefle's list sat death, illness, pain, suffering, being unloved, the unknown, loss of dignity, failure, oblivion, "outliving the mind." She was just as afraid as an older woman, she wrote, as she had been as a young one.

Everything remains unresolved. There is no neat narrative end to life or to my project. Fear of aging in these structures abides, but maybe there is something to the fact that a large group of people share these fears, or versions of them. I don't know what else to hold on to in the face of what can feel hopelessly individualizing. But there are moments inside that you can live, lit up and glowing, like a lamp, with hope and humor. A memory crops up, almost from out of nowhere, of how my walk that summer day ended at the Pittsburgh Banjo Club, on the north side of the city, where a group of thirty or so older people somewhat maniacally strummed their banjos in unison for a raucous audience, just like they did every week. They'd been doing it for a long time. The group played things like "Yes, We Have No Bananas" and "Cabaret" and "This Land Is Your Land," all in the same key, which they refused to ever change. Carol, one of the players, told me that members kept dying. But the group carried on, looking out for one another in various small ways: not letting one of them notice he'd left his keys somewhere really obvious when he couldn't find them, or texting someone's family to let them know he was on his way home at the end of the night. Every week was a "rehearsal": There was no "real" performance for which they were gearing up. It was just indefinite, outside time, all these people gathering together under some shared life force, waves of them leaving the group slowly, a few new ones trickling in, all to the soundtrack of this thunderous music in the same basic key. Laughter rang out and the players screwed their faces up as they practiced and one of their spouses walked around the room selling raffle tickets. Dozens of us watched from our slightly sticky tables on the floor. It was serious, Carol said, enumerating the joys and pains of participating in the group, with its occasional sexisms and tragedies, and its ongoing sense of energy. She came every week to play and sing. "Somehow I got sucked into this vortex of darkness, and I can't get out of it," she said. A banjo twanged. There is a long pause on the recording, and then we both laughed.

ACKNOWLEDGMENTS

Over many years, many people have been generous, kind, and loving to me, in such numbers that I am astounded upon beginning to compile their names. It feels like a whole world of people, which I guess it is, and they're all spread out. I will start in Iowa, with Inara Verzemnieks, whose contributions to my life and work have been positively gigantic, and whose voice I hear in my head when the going gets tough. Always. Thank you for writing "grit" so many years ago on the back of a pin, which sits in my jewelry box. Thank you to John D'Agata, whose many generosities and eye continue to steer me in ways both subtle and not: You changed my life. Emily Mester, Micah Fields, and the rest of the Nonfiction Writing Program have my heart and offer infinite reminders of good writing. My friend Matilda Bathurst: from Iowa through New Mexico to hopefully many other places. Though we didn't meet in Iowa—exactly—thank you to my friend Jason England for your reliably true thinking and bravery, which inspires me. Richard Preston, who I first met in Iowa, thank you for your specific generosities, and tree climbing, which I will never forget. Thank you to Alyse Burnside, also technically an Iowa friend, but also not, for always being there. Emily Russell, mother to Arthur, who also changed my life, offered me so much kindness across visits and phone calls to Iowa and Maine, and I am thankful to have known her.

In Colorado, thank you to Marjie Montrose, and Pam, Bonnie, Ketty, and many more. Mag Hayden and Andy Clark gave me some of the best memories and much support for a very long time. Henry Clark deserves thanks for being my red-haired cousin, among other things. Thank you to Abby McKelvy for being great, and to Kate Davis. Thank you to M.A.G.D. for teaching me how to be an artist. I think about you every day.

In New York, Daniela Gabb nourished me with a very particularly important friendship and a sense of the world that has sustained me across years and geography. I always look to you. Betsy Morais has been a terrific editor and friend at CJR for a long time now, and I often think of her voice, literal and otherwise, as I write. Thank you to Jennifer Brice and CJ Hauser at Colgate University for welcoming me, and to Jennifer again specifically for all the towpath walks (and much else). Thank you to Maggie Millner for Ottolenghi in Cherry Valley, among many other bright spots.

In California, to the Moran-O'Neil family I owe many thanks for being my oldest friends (!) and a constant support to so many people. Deep thanks to Maddie Cargas for loving all the same things I do, with me, whenever possible, and always picking up where we left off. Thanks to ShinJoung Yeo and James Jacobs. Thank you to A.L.R.S., for so, so many things. I think about you every day.

In Texas, thank you to Curtis Bauer, Idoia Elola, Jill Patterson, Katie Cortese and Robby Taylor, Marcus Burke, Mary Coates, Nathan X. Osorio, Kristi Osorio, Michael Faris, Elissa Zellinger, Zara Amdur, Michael Fausnaugh, Chris Taylor, Whitney Koo, Bon Koo, and many, many more. Thank you to Masha Perlman, and, though they predate Texas, Ray Bepko and Blue Chevigny. Zoe Kurland, thank you for being my friend, for the tireless voice memos and reassurance and Valentine.

In Sweden (this is a short one), thank you to Kim Khavar Fahlstedt for so much friendship over the years, always equal parts fun and maniacal and meaningful, and to Cissi Khavar Fahlstedt for inspiring with her fierceness of spirit and aptitude for literally everything.

I have been lucky to enjoy many "virtual friendships" over the years; I'll just list some of them here, in thanks: Lucy Little, Nick Greer, Matthew J. C. Clark, Ralph Nader, Josh Frank, Thomas McGuane. Also: Hallie Schaeffer, for majorly steering this book through, Julie Will for picking it up, and Veronica Goldstein for everything. Laury Frieber: You are the best, and one day I hope to eat herring with you.

Thank you to Bryan McGrath Bello for being my joyful companion brimming over with language, kombucha, love, and warmth. And to Eileen, Mark, and Sam for welcoming me many times over. Thank you to Maddie Foy for being a sister-friend. Thank you, Zach and Gail, for everything from train journeys to DC trips to Pittsburgh check-ins.

That leaves three people for whom I can only really say thank you in the loudest, widest, deepest way—for everything, ever, in this lifetime and the lifetimes before and after it—S.G.D., D.T.S., E.D.S.

NOTES

1: A NEW HOME, LARD SPONCON, A LIST OF FEARS

4 **around 825,00 people in the US died:** Paula Natalia Barreto Parra et al., "The Effect of the COVID-19 Pandemic on the Elderly: Population Fatality Rates, COVID Mortality Percentage, and Life Expectancy Loss," *Elder Law Journal* 30 (2022): 33–80.

5 **a CNN article:** Judith Graham and KFF Health News, "Thousands of Seniors Are Still Dying of Covid-19. Do We Not Care Anymore?" CNN, February 8, 2024, https://www.cnn.com/2024/02/08/health/aging-discrimation-kff-partner-wellness/index.html.

5 **"as the national death toll":** Martha Lincoln, "Necrosecurity, Immunosupremacy, and Survivorship in the Political Imagination of COVID-19," *Open Anthropological Research* 1, no. 1 (2021): 46–59, https://www.researchgate.net/publication/351908826_Necrosecurity_Immunosupremacy_and_Survivorship_in_the_Political_Imagination_of_COVID-19.

6 **"their names are buried":** Alicia Puglionesi, "Spiritualism's Shadows," *Yale Review* 110, no. 3 (September 1, 2022), https://yalereview.org/article/spiritualism-covid-flu-puglionesi.

9 **"diffuseness":** Sarah Chihaya, *Bibliophobia: A Memoir* (Random House, 2025), 43.

10 **"of everything that is vile":** William Ian Miller, *Losing It* (Yale University Press, 2011), 40–41.

10 **"Antiquity ploughs furrows":** Simone de Beauvoir and Patrick O'Brian, *The Coming of Age* (W. W. Norton, 1996), 122.

11 **One 1974 report:** National Council on the Aging, *Myth and Reality of Aging, 1974*, vol. 7657, Inter-University Consortium for Political & Social Research, 1979.

12 **when the life expectancy:** University of California, Berkeley, "Life Expectancy in the USA, 1900–98," 2019, https://u.demog.berkeley.edu/~andrew/1918/figure2.html.

13 **"It depends":** National Council on the Aging, *Myth and Reality of Aging, 1974.*

13 **more than 20 percent:** "Harper's Index," *Harper's Magazine*, May 2025.

13 **Speaking of that study:** Aria Bendix and Katie Mogg, "When Does 'Old Age' Begin? Public Perception May Be Skewing Later," NBC News, April 22, 2024, https://www.nbcnews.com/health/aging/how-old-is-old-age-study-rcna148619.

13 **Cynthia Ozick essay:** Cynthia Ozick, "Spells, Wishes, Goldfish, Old School Hurts," *New York Times*, January 31, 1982.

14 **"platysma prominence":** Introspective Market Research, "Anti-Aging Market Expected to Reach USD 2.29 Billion by 2032, Growing at a CAGR of 7.6 percent from 2024–2032 | Introspective Market Research," GlobeNewswire News Room, Introspective Market Research, December 12, 2024, www.globenewswire.com/news-release/2024/12/12/2996350/0/en/Anti-Aging-Market-Expected-to-Reach-USD-2–29-Billion-by-2032-Growing-at-a-CAGR-of-7–6-From-2024–2032-Introspective-Market-Research.html.

14 **Being old, someone tweeted:** @burial_grid, "This, to me, is nothing but a very public, very self-flagellating admission of being old. And when I say 'old' it has little to do with biological age and has everything to do with letting the world grow over them like a fairy ring of mushrooms over remnants of a rotted oak stump," Twitter post, May 17, 2023.

15 **Brendan O'Connor later:** Brendan O'Connor, "Beyond All Boundaries," *Baffler*, June 2, 2025, https://thebaffler.com/after-the-fact/beyond-all-boundaries-oconnor.

18 **"Only the retirement destination":** Julia Fraser, "Pittsburgh's Population Problem," *Pittsburgh Quarterly*, Spring 2023, pittsburghquarterly.com/articles/pittsburghs-population-problem.

19 **it was known:** "Turtle Island Decolonized," *Decolonial Atlas*, October 9, 2023, decolonialatlas.wordpress.com/turtle-island-decolonized.

20 **"This momentous achievement":** Rebecca Pifer, "UPMC, Highmark Ink 10-Year Contract After Years of Fighting," *Healthcare Dive*, June 25, 2019, https://www.healthcaredive.com/news/upmc-highmark-ink-10-year-contract-after-years-of-fighting/557498.

21 **"monopoly power":** KDKA News, "Congresswoman Summer Lee Says UPMC Has 'Monopoly Power,'" CBS News, January 19, 2023, https://www.cbsnews.com/pittsburgh/news/congresswoman-summer-lee-rep-sara-innamorato-upmc-monopoly-power.

21 **"man-killing jobs":** Emily Buder, "Braddock, PA: The Environmental Racism of the Steel Mill," *The Atlantic*, August 31, 2018, https://www.theatlantic.com/video/index/569023/braddock.

21 **"low, as at the bottom of an excavation":** James Parton, "Pittsburg," *The Atlantic*, January 1, 1868, https://www.theatlantic.com/magazine/archive/1868/01/pittsburg/536130.

21 **a report in *The Pittsburgh Press*:** Fred Jones, "Steel Mills Most Obvious Polluters," *Pittsburgh Press*, July 11, 1968.

22 **Fined $10 million:** Kiley Bense, "Beaver County Residents Say Shell's Ethane Cracker Plant Has Become a 'Shockingly Bad' Neighbor," *Pennsylvania Capital-Star*, May 16, 2024, https://penncapital-star.com/energy-environment/beaver-county-residents-say-shells-ethane-cracker-plant-has-become-a-shockingly-bad-neighbor.

22 **Historian Gabriel Winant:** Gabriel Winant, *The Next Shift: The Fall of Industry and the Rise of Health Care in Rust Belt America* (Harvard University Press, 2021).

22 **writes historian Andrew Simpson:** Andrew T. Simpson, *The Medical Metropolis: Health Care and Economic Transformation in Pittsburgh and Houston* (University of Pennsylvania Press, 2019).

22 **"transplant patients":** Lindsey Gruson, "Center for Transplants Aids Pittsburgh Ascent," *New York Times*, September 16, 1985, www.nytimes.com/1985/09/16/us/center-for-transplants-aids-pittsburgh-ascent.html.

23 **"poor condition":** Charlie Wolfson, "Explore Details on Each Poorly Rated Bridge in Allegheny County," *PublicSource*, February 1, 2022, www.publicsource.org/allegheny-pittsburgh-bridge-rating-infrastructure-collapse.

2: "OLD-AGE HOMES," BIG WRINKLES, A DIED-OUT CULT

35 **tweet by Palmer Luckey:** @PalmerLuckey, "If someone could do a good job of housing elderly citizens for the price of a Social Security check (~$1500/month), they could massively disrupt the existing nursing home/assisted living industry ($240B/year). Seems doable with existing and imminent tech/autonomy advances," Twitter post, August 6, 2021.

36 **Medicaid might pay:** Priya Chidambaram et al., "What Services Does Medicaid Cover in Assisted Living Facilities?" KFF, March 14, 2025, https://www.kff.org/medicaid/issue-brief/what-services-does-medicaid-cover-in-assisted-living-facilities. The story of Medicaid residents of assisted living facilities is complex; as of 2025, one in five assisted living residents has personal services paid for by Medicaid, but it is unknown how many such facilities accept residents on Medicaid. In some states, while room and board is not covered by Medicaid, it might be lowered for Medicaid residents. If a Medicaid resident is unable to pay their monthly fees at an assisted living facility, they might be moved to a different "place."

43 **"some residents were essentially turned":** James Chappel, *Golden Years: How Americans Invented and Reinvented Old Age* (Basic Books, 2024), 115–18.

43 **2019 report in *The New York Times*:** Katie Thomas, Robert Gebeloff, and Jessica Silver-Greenberg, "Phony Diagnoses Hide High Rates of Drugging at Nursing Homes," *New York Times*, September 11, 2021, https://www.nytimes.com/2021/09/11/health/nursing-homes-schizophrenia-antipsychotics.html: "The share of residents with a schizophrenia diagnosis has soared 70 percent since 2012, according to an analysis of Medicare data. That was the year the

federal government, concerned with the overuse of antipsychotic drugs, began publicly disclosing such prescriptions by individual nursing homes."

43 **Some facilities today:** "Systemic and Individual Advocacy to Reduce Restraint Use in Nursing Facilities," Justice in Aging, September 5, 2024, https://justiceinaging.org/systemic-and-individual-advocacy-to-reduce-restraint-use-in-nursing-facilities.

44 **They are "stigmatized":** Margaret Morganroth Gullette, *American Eldercide: How It Happened, How to Prevent It* (University of Chicago Press, 2024), 47.

44 **words of Alex Spanko:** Alex Spanko, "Everyone Is Right About What's Wrong with American Nursing Homes," *Skilled Nursing News*, February 24, 2021, https://skillednursingnews.com/2021/02/everyone-is-right-about-whats-wrong-with-american-nursing-homes.

46 **Nearly half of people over sixty-five:** Kim Painter, "Understanding Long-Term Care Insurance," AARP, October 13, 2021, https://www.aarp.org/caregiving/financial-legal/understanding-long-term-care-insurance.

47 **Many insurers exited:** Jordan Rau and JoNel Aleccia, "Why Long-Term Care Insurance Falls Short for So Many," *KFF Health News*, November 22, 2023, https://kffhealthnews.org/news/article/dying-broke-why-long-term-care-insurance-falls-short.

48 **median cost, nationally:** Jeff Hoyt, "Nursing Home Costs in 2025," Senior Living.org, https://www.seniorliving.org/nursing-homes/costs.

48 **"Few people dream":** Michelle Cottle, "Nobody Wants to Live in a Nursing Home. Something's Got to Give," *New York Times*, August 1, 2021, https://www.nytimes.com/2021/08/01/opinion/aging-nursing-homes.html.

50 **"immensely wealthy communist capitalists":** Karl John Richard Arndt, *George Rapp's Harmony Society, 1785–1847*, rev. ed. (Fairleigh Dickinson University Press, 1972), 603.

50 **only a few Harmonists remained:** Jeffrey Snedden, "From Economy to Ambridge: The Marvel City," *Beaver County Times*, April 26, 2016, https://www.timesonline.com/story/lifestyle/around-town/2016/04/26/from-economy-to-ambridge-marvel/18541000007.

52 **according to the county commissioner:** KDKA News, "'Help Is Here': National Guard Members Deployed to Help Fight Coronavirus Outbreak at Beaver Co. Nursing Home Where More Than 70 Residents Have Died," CBS News, May 11, 2020, https://www.cbsnews.com/pittsburgh/news/brighton-rehab-coronavirus-beaver-county.

52 **some argued:** Deb Erdley and Natasha Lindstrom, "Brighton Rehab No Stranger to Federal, State Scrutiny for Resident Care," *Pittsburgh Tribune-Review*, December 30, 2021, https://triblive.com/local/regional/brighton-rehab-no-stranger-to-federal-state-scrutiny-for-resident-care.

52 **A woman who watched:** Jamie Martines and Natasha Lindstrom, "'Covid Cannot Be Used as a Cover-Up': Brighton Rehab Residents, Families Outraged by Lax Oversight During Outbreak," *Pittsburgh Tribune-Review*, August 9,

2020, https://triblive.com/news/brighton-rehab-residents-families-outraged-by-lax-oversight-during-outbreak.

55 **would be found guilty:** Amy Stulick, "Comprehensive Healthcare Legal Saga Culminates in Acquittal of Individuals, Guilty Verdict for Corporate Defendants," *Skilled Nursing News*, December 18, 2023, https://skillednursingnews.com/2023/12/comprehensive-healthcare-legal-saga-culminates-in-acquittal-of-individuals-guilty-verdict-for-corporate-defendants.

55 **"willfully denied":** "Federal Court Awards $35.8M in Back Wages, Damages in Historic Recovery After Investigation Finds Wage Theft by Pennsylvania Healthcare Employers," news release, US Department of Labor, July 30, 2024, https://www.dol.gov/newsroom/releases/whd/whd20240730.

55 **asked the presentation:** Live Oak Project, "Boldly Advocating for How We and Where We Age: Reimagine, Redesign and Transform Long Term Services and Supports," September 27, 2021, https://www.pioneernetwork.org/live-oak-project.

55 **"functionally broken":** Live Oak Project, "Boldly Advocating for How We and Where We Age."

56 **Kadima Rehabilitation and Nursing at Harmony:** Kadima did not respond to a request for comment.

57 **a hundred residents in total:** CMS Data, Centers for Medicare & Medicaid Services, https://data.cms.gov/covid-19/covid-19-nursing-home-data/data?query=%7B%22filters%22%3A%7B%22rootConjunction%22%3A%7B%22label%22%3A%22And%22%2C%22value%22%3A%22AND%22%7D%2C%22list%22%3A%5B%5D%7D%2C%22keywords%22%3A%2216037%22%2C%22offset%22%3A110%2C%22limit%22%3A10%2C%22sort%22%3A%7B%22sortBy%22%3Anull%2C%22sortOrder%22%3Anull%7D%2C%22columns%22%3A%5B%5D%7D.

59 **attorneys for Comprehensive argued:** Paula Reed Ward, "Nursing Home Operator Says Without Sale of Some W. Pa. Facilities, They May Close," *Pittsburgh Tribune-Review*, September 27, 2023, https://triblive.com/local/regional/comprehensive-healthcare-if-sale-of-western-pa-nursing-homes-is-blocked-they-may-close.

60 **sits at one star (out of five):** "Find Healthcare Providers: Compare Care Near You | Medicare," Medicare.gov, updated September 24, 2025, https://www.medicare.gov/care-compare/details/nursing-home/395758/?city=Harmony&state=PA&zipcode=16037&measure=nursing-home-health-inspections.

60 **Academic Carroll Estes put:** Carroll Lynn Estes, *The Aging Enterprise: A Critical Examination of Social Policies and Services for the Aged* (Jossey-Bass, 1979), 107.

62 **"there is something private about aging":** James Chappel, *Golden Years: How Americans Invented and Reinvented Old Age* (Basic Books, 2024), 15.

64 **one of the reasons:** The Kendal Corporation, "Kendal Outreach Announces Virtual Elimination of Physical Restraint Use in Pennsylvania Nursing Homes," news release, June 7, 2016, https://www.kendal.org/news/parri-at-20.

64 **reduction in their use:** Per *Nursing Home Abuse Guide*: "State laws for physical restraint may vary from state to state. For example, Florida law requires that physical restraint use must be authorized in writing by a physician or another licensed practitioner who is permitted by state law and the nursing home facility. The authorization must specify an explicit amount of time during which the restraints may be used. In cases of emergency, only a licensed, qualified nurse can apply physical restraints without a physician's authorization. The incident and use of physical restraint must be noted in writing in the resident's records." "Physical Restraints on Elderly," *Nursing Home Abuse Guide*, Paul & Perkins, PA, March 26, 2014, https://nursinghomeabuseguide.com/abuse-injuries/elderly-restraints/physical/.

65 **George Alexander quoted:** George Alexander, "Untie the Elderly: The Story of a Confused Man," *On the Kendal Journey*, August 9, 2020, https://kendaljourney.com/2020/08/09/untie-the-elderly-the-story-of-a-confused-man.

66 **"sure beats being a restraint manufacturer":** "Untie the Elderly: Quality Care Without Restraints," Symposium Before the Special Committee on Aging, United States Senate, December 4, 1989, https://www.aging.senate.gov/imo/media/doc/reports/rpt589.pdf.

70 **Gullette's words:** Margaret Morganroth Gullette, *American Eldercide: How It Happened, How to Prevent It* (University of Chicago Press, 2024), 21.

70 **piles of trash:** Jatara McGee, "11 Investigates Why Trash Piled Up Inside, Outside Beaver County Rehabilitation Center," Yahoo News, June 26, 2024, https://www.yahoo.com/news/11-investigates-why-trash-piled-210145112.html.

71 **As of this writing:** "Find Healthcare Providers: Compare Care Near You | Medicare," Medicare.gov, updated September 24, 2025, https://www.medicare.gov/care-compare/details/nursing-home/395015?city=Beaver&state=PA&zipcode=15009&measure=nursing-home-health-inspections.

3: FAMILY ON DEMAND, WOODEN TEETH, MEMORIES OF A FARM

78 **"fear of losing one's independence":** Eric Klinenberg, *Going Solo: The Extraordinary Rise and Surprising Appeal of Living Alone* (Penguin, 2012), 170–84.

80 **"margins of every error":** Garielle Lutz, *Backwardness* (Hobart Pulp, 2024), 760–61.

81 **loneliness came from "human connection [being] edged out":** Vivek Murthy, *Together: Loneliness, Health & What Happens When We Find Connection* (HarperCollins, 2020).

81 **"part of the problem":** Vivek Murthy, "Work and the Loneliness Epidemic: Reducing Isolation at Work Is Good for Business," *Harvard Business Review*, September 26, 2017, https://hbr.org/2017/09/work-and-the-loneliness-epidemic.

82 **"precious compact between the generations":** Maggie Kuhn, quoted in Nancy Henkin, "Remembering Maggie," *Medium*, August 3, 2020, https://gensunited.medium.com/remembering-maggie-21ba2ff8c424.

82 **students would be "carefully selected":** "Papa FAQ," October 12, 2017, https://web.archive.org/web/20171012213830/http://www.joinpapa.com/faq.

82 **"I don't want to say that Covid":** Katie Jennings, "Digital Health's Newest Unicorn Provides Lonely People with a 'Family on Demand,'" *Forbes*, November 4, 2021, https://www.forbes.com/sites/brucejapsen/2021/11/04/digital-healths-newest-unicorn-provides-lonely-people-with-a-family-on-demand.

83 **twenty-two large companies:** Molly Kinder, Katie Bach, and Laura Stateler, "Profits and the Pandemic: As Shareholder Wealth Soared, Workers Were Left Behind," Brookings, April 21, 2022, https://www.brookings.edu/articles/profits-and-the-pandemic-as-shareholder-wealth-soared-workers-were-left-behind.

83 **"anyone that didn't believe in loneliness":** Jennings, "Digital Health's Newest Unicorn Provides Lonely People with a 'Family on Demand.'"

83 **"I call loneliness the only universal disease":** Gary Tan, "The Future of Care: How Papa Cures Loneliness Through Connection and On-Demand Assistance," *Initialized*, August 4, 2021, https://blog.initialized.com/2021/08/the-future-of-care-how-papa-cures-loneliness-through-connection-and-on-demand-assistance.

83 **read the headline of one blank page:** "Taking Action Against Loneliness," Papa, accessed July 31, 2025, https://www.papa.com/resources/news/taking-action-against-loneliness.

83 **"the traditional healthcare system is designed":** Email exchange with Papa company representatives, September 24, 2025.

84 **"Loneliness . . . is a grim fact of life for the old":** Paul Bloom, "Losing Loneliness," *New Yorker*, July 21, 2025.

85 **worries about an epidemic of loneliness have long preoccupied Americans:** Claude S. Fischer, "The Loneliness Scare," *Boston Review*, April 23, 2012, https://www.bostonreview.net/articles/fischer-loneliness-modern-culture.

86 **"a health plan starts paying for dog food":** Martha Hostetter and Sarah Klein, "CHRONIC Care Act Prompts Some Medicare Advantage Plans to Incorporate Social Services," Commonwealth Fund, January 9, 2020, https://www.commonwealthfund.org/publications/2020/jan/chronic-care-act-prompts-some-medicare-advantage-plans-incorporate-social.

89 **"No one":** "Member Benefits," Papa, accessed July 31, 2025, https://www.papa.com/members.

91 **titled this "the Medicare Gold Rush":** Richard Gilfillan and Donald M. Berwick, "Medicare Advantage, Direct Contracting, and the Medicare 'Money Machine,' Part 2: Building on the ACO Model," *Health Affairs*, September 30, 2021, https://www.healthaffairs.org/content/forefront/medicare-advantage-direct-contracting-and-medicare-money-machine-part-2-building-aco.

91 **"without seniors' full understanding":** Robert King, "House Progressives Push for CMS to End Newly Rebranded ACO REACH Model," *Fierce Healthcare*, March 17, 2022, https://www.fiercehealthcare.com/payers/house-progressive-push-cms-end-newly-rebranded-aco-reach-model.

91 **"to be opt-out vs. opt-in":** "6 Predictions for the Future of Medicare," Pearl Health, November 8, 2022, https://pearlhealth.com/blog/healthcare-insights/6-predictions-for-the-future-of-medicare.

92 **"when a health plan or employer partners":** Email exchange with Papa company representatives, September 24, 2025.

92 **"I am never lonely":** Leonora Carrington, *The Hearing Trumpet* (New York Review of Books Classics, 2021).

96 **the nuclear family has actually encouraged loneliness:** Mandy Len Catron, "What You Lose When You Gain a Spouse," *Atlantic*, July 2, 2019, https://archive.ph/SgUoj#selection-883.38–889.373; Natalia Sarkisian and Naomi Gerstel, "Does Singlehood Isolate or Integrate? Examining the Link Between Marital Status and Ties to Kin, Friends, and Neighbors," *Journal of Social and Personal Relationships* 33, no. 3 (2016): 361–84, https://doi.org/10.1177/0265407515597564.

98 **"customers by the hundreds of thousands":** "Papa Pitch Deck to Raise $18m Series-B Round," September 29, 2021, https://www.alexanderjarvis.com/papa-pitch-deck-to-raise-18m-series-b-round.

98 **partnerships with ten new insurance plans:** Simon Mainwaring, "Purpose at Work: Lessons from Papa Every Entrepreneur Must Heed," *Forbes*, December 16, 2020, https://www.forbes.com/sites/simonmainwaring/2020/12/16/purpose-at-work-lessons-from-papa-every-entrepreneur-must-heed.

98 **Gen Z, the "loneliest" group of all:** The exception to this is for younger people with disabilities, who might qualify for Medicare, and therefore Medicare Advantage, before the age of sixty-five.

98 **pattern of denying care:** Ryan Cooper, "Medicare Advantage Is a Massive Scam," *American Prospect*, April 29, 2022, https://prospect.org/health/medicare-advantage-is-a-massive-scam.

98 **article in *The American Prospect*:** Matthew Cunningham-Cook, "The Great Medicare Advantage Marketing Scam," *American Prospect*, January 12, 2024, https://prospect.org/health/2024–01–12-great-medicare-advantage-marketing-scam.

99 **"Medicare has traditionally steered clear":** Hostetter and Klein, "CHRONIC Care Act Prompts Some Medicare Advantage Plans to Incorporate Social Services."

100 **older people living in multigenerational families:** Ruggles cited in George Masnick, "Article Review: 'Patriarchy, Power, and Pay: The Transformation of American Families, 1800–2015,'" Joint Center for Housing Studies of Harvard University, January 27, 2016, https://www.jchs.harvard.edu/blog/article-review-patriarchy-power-and-pay-the-transformation-of-american-families-1800–2015.

101 **separation of daily routine:** David Hackett Fischer, *Growing Old in America*, expanded ed. (Oxford University Press, 1978), 147.

104 **"like many marketplace businesses":** Email exchange with Papa company representatives, September 24, 2025.

105 **"We take feedback seriously":** Email exchange with Papa company representatives, September 24, 2025.

111 **exposé about Papa:** Priya Anand, "Assault Allegations Plague a $1.4 Billion Home Eldercare Startup," *Bloomberg Businessweek*, May 30, 2023, https://www.bloomberg.com/news/features/2023-05-30/papa-eldercare-startup-faces-abuse-claims-by-seniors-caregivers.

111 **"we hold our community to the highest standards":** Email exchange with Papa company representatives, September 24, 2025.

112 **"the power of the loneliness meme today":** Claude S. Fischer, "An Epidemic of the 'Epidemic of Loneliness,' Part 1: There Probably Is No Epidemic and It May Not Be Loneliness," *Made in America*, September 12, 2023, https://madeinamericathebook.wordpress.com/2023/09/12/an-epidemic-of-the-epidemic-of-loneliness-part-1-there-probably-is-no-epidemic-and-it-may-not-be-loneliness.

120 **"Loneliness is grief, distended":** Jill Lepore, "The History of Loneliness," *New Yorker*, March 30, 2020, https://www.newyorker.com/magazine/2020/04/06/the-history-of-loneliness.

123 **"Fragility, dependency, and impairment":** Stephen Katz, "Precarious Life, Human Development, and the Life Course: Critical Intersections," in *Precarity and Ageing: Understanding Insecurity and Risk in Later Life*, eds. Amanda Grenier, Chris Phillipson, and Richard A. Setterston Jr. (Policy Press, 2021).

4: FEAR OF MYSELF, DEATH, ANOTHER LUCY

127 **"old age" was removed:** Kiran Rabheru et al., "How 'Old Age' Was Withdrawn as a Diagnosis from ICD-11," *Lancet Healthy Longevity* 3, no. 7 (July 2022): e457–e459.

127 **arguing for the "pathologization" of biological aging:** Josh Conway, "Debate Rages on the Inclusion of Old Age in the ICD-11," Lifespan Research Institute, January 10, 2022, https://www.lifespan.io/news/debate-rages-on-the-inclusion-of-old-age-in-the-icd-11; Evelyne Bischof et al., "Advanced Pathological Ageing Should Be Represented in the ICD," *Lancet Healthy Longevity* 3, no. 1 (January 2022): e12.

129 **"People do die":** Quoted in Martha Lincoln, "Necrosecurity, Immunosupremacy, and Survivorship in the Political Imagination of COVID-19," *Open Anthropological Research* 1, no. 1 (May 2021): 46–59.

131 **the essay was an exercise in imagination:** Stacey Patton, "Sunday Morning in MAGA Country: 'Praise Jesus and Deport Them All,'" July 6, 2025, https://drstaceypatton1865.substack.com/p/sunday-morning-in-maga-country-praise.

133 **"abdicating selfhood, dispersing myself":** Sarah Chihaya, *Bibliophobia: A Memoir* (Random House, 2025), 137.

5: A CATEGORY, A SCAM MAP, INSURANCE

145 **membership (or invitations thereof) in AARP:** AARP did not respond to a request for comment.

146 **Residents paid a lump sum:** "AARP Founder Creates Grey Gables Retirement Community," AARP, August 31, 2018, https://www.aarp.org/about-aarp/history/grey-gables-retirement-community.html.

146 **"realized that a scarce commodity sold to a captive audience":** David Devoss, "A Retirement Force," *South Florida Sun Sentinel*, July 3, 1989, https://www.sun-sentinel.com/1989/07/03/a-retirement-force.

147 **"Membership in AARP":** Dave Holmes, "I'm Gen X and I Just Got My AARP Card. This Feels Like a Mistake," *Esquire*, August 30, 2021, https://www.esquire.com/lifestyle/a37360416/50-aarp-gen-x-how-to-feel-young.

148 **why older adults were disproportionately targeted:** J. Shao et al., "Why Are Older Adults Victims of Fraud? Current Knowledge and Prospects Regarding Older Adults' Vulnerability to Fraud," *Journal of Elder Abuse & Neglect*, 31, no. 3 (2019), 225–43, https://doi.org/10.1080/08946566.2019.1625842.

149 **"he insisted he was the geek squad":** "AARP Fraud Watch Network Scam Tracking Map," AARP, https://www.aarp.org/money/scams-fraud/tracking-map.

150 **"serve as a neat foil for capital":** Hannah Zeavin, "The Victim Cloud," *Harper's Magazine*, July 2022, https://harpers.org/archive/2022/07/the-victim-cloud-gullibility-in-the-golden-age-of-scams.

150 **either financially struggling or at risk:** "Addressing the Nation's Retirement Crisis: The 80%," National Council on Aging, August 30, 2024, https://www.ncoa.org/article/addressing-the-nations-retirement-crisis-the-80-percent-financially-struggling.

151 **One report on scams:** Laura L. Carstensen quoted in Martha Deevy, Shoshana Lucich, and Michaela Beals, *Scams, Schemes & Swindles: A Review of Consumer Financial Fraud Research*, Financial Fraud Research Center, 2012.

152 **Medicare should "be strengthened and improved":** "What Does AARP Advocate for Medicare?" AARP, accessed July 31, 2025, https://help.aarp.org/s/article/medicare-advocacy.

152 **transformed into powerful "uber-citizens":** Mark Schlesinger, "The Social Transformation of American Elders," in *Medicare and Medicaid at 50: America's Entitlement Programs in the Age of Affordable Care*, ed. Alan B. Cohen et al. (Oxford University Press, 2015), 122.

153 **their members would "rally around the legislation":** Schlesinger, "The Social Transformation of American Elders."

153 **"held the promise of protection":** Debra Street, "Maintaining the Status Quo: The Impact of Old-Age Interest Groups on the Medicare Catastrophic

Coverage Act of 1988," *Social Problems* 40, no. 4 (November 1993): 431–44, https://doi.org/10.2307/3096860.

153 **"That's too bad":** Associated Press, "House Panel Leader Jeered by Elderly in Chicago," *New York Times*, August 19, 1989, https://www.nytimes.com/1989/08/19/us/house-panel-leader-jeered-by-elderly-in-chicago.html.

154 **"legislation that provided a national health insurance program":** Street, "Maintaining the Status Quo."

154 **AARP lost its status:** Schlesinger, "The Social Transformation of American Elders."

154 **AARP has received "royalties":** Fred Schulte, "AARP's Billion-Dollar Bounty," *KFF Health News*, June 6, 2022, https://kffhealthnews.org/news/article/aarp-health-marketing-partnerships-medicare-medigap.

155 **"Schiff claims that the AARP injured him":** "Full Text: Attorney's Testimony About Lawsuit Against AARP at Finance Hearing on AARP Tax and Political Status," Tax Notes, May 25, 1995, https://www.taxnotes.com/research/federal/other-documents/testimony-other-than-irs-and-treasury/full-text-attorneys-testimony-about-lawsuit-against-aarp-at-finance/131x8.

159 **Medicare Advantage plans were overpaid:** "The Overpayment Cycle: Payments to Medicare Advantage," Medicare Rights Center, accessed July 31, 2025, https://www.medicarerights.org/policy-documents/the-overpayment-cycle-payments-to-medicare-advantage.

159 **There are almost 4,000:** Ledia Tabor, Jennifer Druckman, and Pamina Mejia, *Background: Medicare Insurance Agents*, March 6, 2025, https://www.medpac.gov/wp-content/uploads/2024/08/Medicare-agents-MedPAC-03.25sec.pdf.

165 **Denials of care:** Boris Vabson et al., "Medicare Advantage Denies 17 Percent of Initial Claims; Most Denials Are Reversed, But Provider Payouts Dip 7 Percent," *Health Affairs* 44, no. 6 (June 2025): 702–6, https://doi.org/10.1377/hlthaff.2024.01485.

165 **Another study logged:** Michael J. Alkire, "Unnecessary Insurance Claim Denials Compromise Patient Care and Provider Bottom Lines," *STAT*, May 1, 2024, https://www.statnews.com/2024/05/01/insurance-claim-denials-compromise-patient-care-provider-bottom-lines.

166 **The surgeon general, already interested in loneliness:** Senator Richard Blumenthal, *Refusal of Recovery: How Medicare Advantage Insurers Have Denied Patients Access to Post-Acute Care*, US Senate Permanent Subcommittee on Investigations, October 17, 2024, https://www.hsgac.senate.gov/wp-content/uploads/2024.10.17-PSI-Majority-Staff-Report-on-Medicare-Advantage.pdf.

166 **Deceptive marketing for Medicare Advantage plans:** Melissa M. Garrido et al., "Access to Insurance Navigation Support Through the State Health Insurance Assistance Program," *Health Affairs Scholar* 2, no. 6 (June 2024): qxae072.

169 **"after covering the elderly, Medicare would soon expand":** Theodore R. Marmor and Jonathan Oberlander, "The Road Not Taken: What Happened to Medicare for All?" in Cohen et al., *Medicare and Medicaid at 50*, 58.

169 **"excessive allocation of resources to the old":** Victor W. Marshall, Fay Lomax Cook, and Joann Gard Marshall, "Conflict over Intergenerational Equity: Rhetoric and Reality in a Comparative Context," in *The Changing Contract Across Generations*, ed. Vern L. Bengston and W. Andrew Achenbaum (Routledge, 1993).

169 **According to Donald Berwick:** John Wilkerson, "A Former Medicare Official Says the Program Is in Trouble, and Medicare Advantage Is Largely to Blame," *STAT*, October 17, 2024, https://www.statnews.com/2024/10/17/donald-berwick-former-medicare-official-criticizes-ma-plans.

170 **emphasizing the "downward spiral" (in 1987!):** Jill Quadagno, "Generational Equity and the Politics of the Welfare State," *Politics & Society* 17, no. 3 (1989): 353–76, https://doi.org/10.1177/003232928901700303.

6: PRODUCTIVITY, THE GRAY PANTHERS, GRATERFORD/PHOENIX

180 **"Older women have the most to gain":** Maggie Kuhn, "Insights on Aging," *Journal of Home Economics* 70, no. 4 (1978): 18–20.

182 **"not one of senior citizen interest-group politics":** Roger Sanjek, *Gray Panthers* (University of Pennsylvania Press, 2011), 11.

182 **"issues that transcend age":** Sanjek, *Gray Panthers*.

182 **"eleven theories":** Robert John, "Prerequisites of an Adequate Theory of Aging: A Critique and Reconceptualization," *Mid-American Review of Sociology* 9, no. 2 (1984): 79–108, http://www.jstor.org/stable/23252839.

183 **"conditioned by one's location":** Carroll Estes, "The New Political Economy of Aging: Introduction and Critique," in *Critical Perspectives on Aging: The Political and Moral Economy of Growing Old*, eds. Meredith Minkler and Carroll L. Estes (Baywood Publishing, 1991), 21.

183 **"made dependent upon an aging enterprise":** Estes cited in John, "Prerequisites of an Adequate Theory of Aging."

183 **"needs of older adults will be processed and treated as a commodity":** Carroll L. Estes, "The Future of Aging Services in a Neoliberal Political Economy," *Generations* 38, no. 2 (Summer 2014): 94.

184 **"Never forget we are also on a lark":** Ruth Harriet Jacobs, "Gray Panthers Prowl Washington and America," Temple University Archives.

184 **rub some of the "shine" off them:** Letter from Janet Neuman to the National Peace Action Coalition, June 26, 1972, Temple University Archives.

184 **"A vast behavioral inertia":** Peter G. Peterson, *Gray Dawn: How the Coming Age Wave Will Transform America—and the World* (Three Rivers Press, 2000).

185 **"If we don't secure a job":** Jessica Grose, "No Home, No Retirement, No Kids: How Gen-Z-ers See Their Future," *New York Times*, June 6, 2025.

185 **half of all working men on track:** Till von Wachter, *The End of Mandatory Retirement in the US: Effects on Retirement and Implicit Contracts*, Center for Labor Economics, University of California, Berkeley, March 2002, http://cle.berkeley.edu/wp/wp49.pdf.

185 **"eighty, ninety, or a hundred years":** David A. Sinclair with Matthew D. LaPlante, *Lifespan: Why We Age—and Why We Don't Have To* (Atria Books, 2019), 255.

187 **"trouble identifying with their less fortunate peers":** Maggie Kuhn et al., *No Stone Unturned: The Life and Times of Maggie Kuhn* (Ballantine Books, 1991), 128.

187 **"I felt dazed and suspended":** Kuhn et al., *No Stone Unturned*, 129.

187 **aging while Black "double jeopardy":** Rose Dobrof, *Ethnicity and Gerontological Social Work* (Routledge, 1987).

187 **"based on white mortality tables":** Kuhn et al., *No Stone Unturned*, 135.

188 **"three strikes against us":** "Elderly Negroes Present Demands," *New York Times*, November 14, 1971, https://www.nytimes.com/1971/11/14/archives/elderly-negroes-present-demands-meeting-seeks-recognition-at-white.html.

189 **"too middle class, white and intellectual":** Jacobs, "Gray Panthers Prowl Washington and America."

189 **"sounds so much better than the A.A.R.P.!":** Letter from Janet Neuman to Maggie Kuhn, Presbyterian Historical Society.

190 **"erection to resurrection":** Jacobs, "Gray Panthers Prowl Washington and America."

191 **"every hour on the hour!":** Letters between Maggie Kuhn and Clifford Earle, Presbyterian Historical Society.

192 **disgracefully lower levels:** Jacobs, "Gray Panthers on the Prowl: Instructions for the Use of the Gray Book."

192 **"old and young people should live together":** Maggie Kuhn, "Why Old and Young Should Live Together," *50 Plus* (October 1978): 19–20.

192 **"'Denture breath' and 'irregularity'":** Maggie Kuhn, "Liberation from 'Ageism,'" *Inquiry* (September–November 1971), published by the United Presbyterian Church.

192 **"White Anglo-Protestant mindset":** Maggie Kuhn, *A New Life at Eighty-Two*, Presbyterian Historical Archives.

193 **"ONLY ONE YOU!":** Undated poem by Janet Neuman to Maggie Kuhn, Temple University Archives.

194 **"open ended water fast":** Letter from Jane Jackson to Ronald Reagan, 1982, Temple University Archives.

194 **"equal access must move beyond":** Letter from Jane Jackson to Maggie Kuhn, 1980, Temple University Archives.

195 **contains a resistance to disability:** Amanda Grenier, Meridith Griffin, and Colleen McGrath, "Aging and Disability: The Paradoxical Positions of

the Chronological Life Course," in *The Aging–Disability Nexus*, ed. Katie Aubrecht, Christine Kelly, and Carla Rice (UBC Press, 2020), 23.

198 **"very personal and maybe none of my business":** Letter from Zelma C. Brandt to Maggie Kuhn, 1983, Special Collections Research Center, Temple University Libraries.

198 **slightly tortured directness:** Letter from Maggie Kuhn to Zelma C. Brandt, 1984, Special Collections Research Center, Temple University Libraries.

198 **"Some people have been in prison so long":** Letter from Jane Jackson to Maggie Kuhn, April 6, 1980, Special Collections Research Center, Temple University Libraries.

199 **Schilk entered Graterford:** Aaron Moselle, "New Bill Could Free 1,000 People Sentenced to Life in Pa. Prisons," WHYY, September 16, 2019, https://whyy.org/articles/a-chance-of-freedom-new-bill-could-release-1000-people-sentenced-to-life-in-pa-prisons.

201 **besides, redundantly, the United States:** An-Li Herring, "Pennsylvania Leads World in Imposing Life Sentences," WHYY, September 18, 2018, https://whyy.org/articles/pennsylvania-leads-world-in-imposing-life-sentences.

201 **"number of older prisoners is growing":** Jamie Fellner, "Old Behind Bars," Human Rights Watch, January 27, 2012, https://www.hrw.org/report/2012/01/28/old-behind-bars/aging-prison-population-united-states.

201 **people age much faster in prison:** "Incarcerated Older Adults," Grantmakers in Aging, http://www.giaaging.org.

206 **"True damnation":** Marco D'Eramo, "The Biopolitics of Nursing Homes," *New Left Review*, February 12, 2021, https://newleftreview.org/sidecar/posts/the-biopolitics-of-nursing-homes.

206 **Abolitionist scholars point:** Keith Rosenthal, "Carceral Histories of Disability," *Spectre Journal*, August 23, 2021, https://spectrejournal.com/carceral-histories-of-disability-an-abolitionist-analysis.

206 **excepted disabled people:** Keith Rosenthal, "Pioneers in the Fight for Disability Rights: The League of the Physically Handicapped," *International Socialist Review* 90 (July 2013), https://isreview.org/issue/90/pioneers-fight-disability-rights/index.html.

7: LIFE, SCAVENGER HUNTING, BANJOS

217 **increasingly entwined with private equity:** Michael Fenne, "New Research on PE's Expansion into PACE Programs," *Private Equity Stakeholder Project PESP*, April 21, 2025, https://pestakeholder.org/news/new-research-on-pes-expansion-into-pace-programs.

217 **who could use PACE did not have access to it:** Neva Kaye, "Five States' Progress Toward Expanding Access to PACE Services," National Academy for State Health Policy, May 3, 2022, https://nashp.org/five-states-progress-toward-expanding-access-to-pace-services.

218 **"come out of the woodwork":** Diane L. Gross et al., "The Growing Pains of

Integrated Health Care for the Elderly: Lessons from the Expansion of PACE," *Milbank Quarterly* 82, no. 2 (June 2004): 257–82.

218 **as 95 percent of people:** "Understanding the PACE Model of Care," National PACE Association, accessed July 31, 2025, https://www.npaonline.org/starting-expanding-a-pace-program/understanding-the-pace-model-of-care.

218 **"not given as a right":** Jill Quadagno, "The Transformation of Medicaid," in *Medicare and Medicaid at 50: America's Entitlement Programs in the Age of Affordable Care*, ed. Alan B. Cohen et al. (Oxford University Press, 2015).

218 **"more likely to go without services":** Judith Feder, "The Missing Piece," in Cohen et al., *Medicare and Medicaid at 50*.

219 **"Anglo nursing homes":** Marie-Louise Ansak, "Founding and Directing On Lok Senior Health Services, 1971–1996," interview by Leah McGarrigle, University of California, Berkeley, 2004, https://digitalassets.lib.berkeley.edu/roho/ucb/text/ansak_marie-louise.pdf.

219 **"a very unusual little project":** Ansak, "Founding and Directing On Lok Senior Health Services."

219 **subsidized by the Department of Housing and Urban Development:** Amanda J. Lehning and Michael J. Austin, "On Lok: A Pioneering Long-Term Care Organization for the Elderly (1971–2008)," *Journal of Evidence-Based Social Work* 8, no. 1–2 (2011): 218–34.

224 **"do not have a computer":** Jess Davidson, "AAPD Strongly Condemns Senate Proposal That Slashes Medicaid and Threatens Disabled Lives," news release, June 25, 2025, AAPD, https://www.aapd.com/senate-medicaid-proposal-statement.

224 **"And I should also say":** Joseph Mitchell, "A Place of Pasts," *New Yorker*, February 9, 2015, https://www.newyorker.com/magazine/2015/02/16/place-pasts.

225 **"treated like children no matter how old we get":** Ellen Samuels, "Six Ways of Looking at Crip Time," *Disability Studies Quarterly* 37, no. 3 (August 2017), https://doi.org/10.18061/dsq.v37i3.5824.

226 **"vigilant realism":** Barbara Ehrenreich, *Bright-Sided: How Positive Thinking Is Undermining America* (Picador, 2010).

INDEX

ABOUT THE AUTHOR

Lucy Schiller is a nonfiction writer whose work has been published in *Columbia Journalism Review*, *The New Yorker*, *The Iowa Review*, *West Branch*, *Speculative Nonfiction*, *DIAGRAM*, and elsewhere. She received her MFA from the University of Iowa's Nonfiction Writing Program, where she was an Iowa Arts fellow.